Careers for Dreamers & Doers:
A Guide to Management Careers
in the Nonprofit Sector

by

Lilly Cohen and
Dennis R. Young

The Foundation Center

Library of Congress Cataloging-in-Publication Data

Careers for dreamers and doers : a guide to management careers in the
nonprofit sector / [edited by] Lilly Cohen, Dennis R. Young.
    p. cm.
  ISBN 0–87954–294–2
  1. Corporations, Nonprofit—United States—Management—Vocational
guidance. 2. Corporations, Nonprofit—United States—Management—
History. I. Cohen, Lilly. II. Young, Dennis R., 1943–0000.
HD62.6.C37 1989
658'.0023'73—dc20

89-38376
CIP

To our sons and daughters,
Susan and Alan Cohen, and
Seth, Barry, Cheryl, and
Mark Young.

CONTENTS

FOREWORD

At a recent meeting of the board of the United Way of Central Indiana, I asked how many of those present, staff members as well as board members, had ever taken a formal college-level course in philanthropy. One hand was raised. I said that a generation from now a forest of hands would go up in response to such a question.

My optimism is based on the emergence of a national movement to make the study of philanthropy—the study of voluntarism, nonprofit organization and management, of the "third sector"—a part of the general education of all Americans and a requirement of the professional education of those pursuing careers in this ill-defined field.

The "third sector" is sharply defined in one way, of course: it means being employed by organizations qualified as tax exempt under Internal Revenue Code 501(c)(3). There are more people employed full-time in the third sector than are employed in the federal and state governments combined. More than seven million jobs means that there is strong reason for formal professional education in what is distinctive about life within 501(c)(3) organizations.

This book sets out to do that systematically, helping readers understand what "the third sector" is and how it works, explaining what kinds of careers there are, and describing the kind of work that must be done.

The development of philanthropic studies will not be so rapid that entry into careers in philanthropy will soon be limited to those with certain educational credentials. What will happen is that those who now embark upon careers will find pressures later in life that will be difficult to bear if they are not better prepared. Philanthropy has always been complicated; it becomes more so as life becomes more complicated and as philanthropic activity, and society as a whole, expand in scale. Tax laws governing financial contributions become more complex every year. However, as in every other management field, decisions cannot simply be turned over to lawyers, or accountants, or social workers, or marketing executives. For those planning to pursue careers in philanthropy, early preparation will be increasingly necessary and continuing professional education will become essential to professional survival.

The professional education of managers of nonprofit organizations requires a blend of liberal and technical education, an understanding of nonmaterial as well as material values, and a grasp of humane as well as scientific studies. This book shows the diverse backgrounds of the successful professionals who have pursued careers in philanthropy. For example, Barry Gaberman's background in political science and in third world development in East Asia is relevant to his professional career at the Ford Foundation. His background helps him understand the organizational culture of the foundation he works for and of those organizations he works with in making grants.

Co-editor Dennis Young is one of the most perceptive students of the less-than-obvious aspects of the nonprofit field. The title/question of his book, *If Not For Profit, For What?* remains one of the most probing questions that aspiring career professionals can ask themselves. Additionally, my own thoughts about working in philanthropy have been stimulated by Donald Schon's book, *The Reflective Practitioner*, which explores ways to learn from practice, especially under the guidance of a more experienced and reflective practitioner.

This book is not a tour through an altruistic candy store. It is not simply a matter of picking and choosing among things that may strike your fancy. The notion that the authors put forward—that you should choose, plan, and prepare for a nonprofit career—still requires a strong dose of self-assessment. There are tasks to be performed, and each different task carries different rewards. The sector has many examples of people whose dedication to a cause carried them to a level of responsibility that exceeded their ability. The sector has examples of romanticized good works—of people who overestimated their commitment. Of course, the sector also has its share of people whose ego-needs are more important to them than the work at hand. The successful careers you will read about have their failed counterparts—some of whom you will meet very early in your career.

Additionally, you will also be a paid professional in an essentially voluntary field. The nonprofit society is caught in a tension between admiration of the volunteer, who sacrifices time and money for no material reward, and recognition of the need for expert knowledge and training and full-time commitment. As professionals have long stated, volunteers are usually amateurs as well.

Professionals have the advantage—or are supposed to have the advantage—of mastery of a body of knowledge that the volunteer does not possess. In certain fields the expertise required is specialized and extensive, leaving little room for nonspecialist volunteers. In other cases, the problem is one of professional arrogance and impatience in working with volunteers. These professionals think volunteers are supposed to give money and moral support and then keep out of the way. However, as becomes painfully clear, the loss of volunteer participation and commitment is often a sign an organization has lost its way—the voluntary nonprofit impulse has been swept aside by self-interest.

Why do we have a third sector? Why do we have tax exemption? Professor Harvey Dale of New York University recently said the only rationale for tax exemption may prove to be that we have it; it exists. Otherwise, he implied, we might not have it.

If we lost the rationale for the third sector, what would we have deleted? What is the value of the sector? Why should nonprofit organizations not simply be marginal extensions or subcontractors of government agencies? Why shouldn't people have to pay for the things they want?

The aspiring professional accepts certain obligations of competence and expertise, as well as certain ethical standards in representing the interests of others. The aspiring professional in the nonprofit sector also takes on explicit claims to serve the public good.

Readers should assess themselves in the light of these aspirations. You may not pursue a career in the nonprofit field; even so, reading this book will help you be a better volunteer. Failing that, by reading this book you will learn a lot about the third sector. And this will help you become a better citizen.

Robert L. Payton
Director, Center on Philanthropy
Professor of Philanthropic Studies
Indiana University–Purdue University at Indianapolis

PREFACE

Why We Wrote This Book

As part of our work at the State University of New York at Stony Brook, Case Western Reserve University, and the New School for Social Research, we have spent many hours interviewing, counseling, advising, and teaching students and prospective students of nonprofit management. Some of these men and women already work in the nonprofit sector—others hope to.

In recent years, we have both observed and participated in the growth of information about the nonprofit sector. However, in talking with students, academics, and others with experience in our sector, as well as professionals unfamiliar with it, we discovered that there is no general awareness of the nonprofit sector as a source of jobs and careers. This gap is especially striking in the career counseling community and in occupational guidance literature. Despite the fact that the nonprofit sector is a large and growing part of the economy, and one that offers many promising careers and job opportunities, comprehensive career guidance information about the sector is not readily available. Therefore, we decided to compile and edit this guide to fill a gap in current occupational literature.

Professional jobs in the nonprofit sector fall into two broad categories:

- **Program jobs**—those positions filled by people directly charged with carrying out an organization's mission, i.e., the program, service, or cause that is the organization's reason for being. This includes, for example, social workers, physical therapists, dancers, and public interest lawyers.

- **Management jobs**—those positions filled by people responsible for the administration, development, and survival of the organization. This includes executive directors, public affairs officers, directors of development, and others.

The exclusive focus of this book is on management jobs, because more needs to be known about managerial work in our sector, and because program jobs are already described in existing literature. There is some overlap between program and management jobs. Some program jobs include management responsibilities or may offer promotion into management. Indeed, program experience is often a prerequisite for management jobs. Nevertheless, significant differences do exist between program and management positions.

We hope this volume will serve as a source of inspiration and reference to a wide variety of people. This includes students deciding on a field of study, college and university graduates looking for their first job, career changers, volunteers in transition to paid employment, retirees searching for new roles, and those already in the sector who need career advancement strategies. We also hope this book will become a resource for career counseling intermediaries—all the helpful professionals who work in high schools, academic institutions, counseling centers, and libraries who are called on for advice, information, and referral.

This book will be of particular interest to people who are neither motivated by business and the profit motive, nor inspired by government service with its inherent promise of security. These people may be idealists, dreamers, planners, artists, entrepreneurs, or public welfare activists. They may be people who, after long years of employment in business or government, want a different challenge or work setting. These "cause people" may not fully appreciate that there are others like them. They may not conceive that there is another employment area, a third sector of the economy to which they can make a commitment and from which they can obtain support. Until recently the most likely way to get into this type of work was by accident. Now it is possible to plan a career in nonprofit management.

What the Sector Is

Confusion about the sector is widespread. To begin with, it has at least five names: third sector, voluntary sector, not-for-profit or nonprofit sector, philanthropic sector, and independent sector. Each name conveys an aspect believed to be essential, but none of these names describes the whole.

- **Third Sector** means that it encompasses all the organizations in the economy that are neither business nor government, the first and second sectors. While this name is roughly accurate, it only says what the sector is not, not what it is.

- **Voluntary Sector** emphasizes that organizations in this sector depend on volunteer labor and contributions for their governance, operation, and support. In fact, voluntary contributions are not generally the primary source of support for organizations in this sector, although the sector does garner voluntary contributions much more extensively than the others.

- **Not-for-Profit Sector** points to the fact that organizations within the sector cannot distribute their financial surpluses. This name is perhaps misleading because governmental organizations are also not-for-profit.

- **Philanthropic Sector** refers to the fact that organizations in the sector receive donated funds and carry out work of a charitable or public service nature. However, not all organizations in the sector perform charitable or public service work or receive contributions, though most do.

- **Independent Sector** connotes that organizations in this sector are autonomous and free from the influences of politics or the market place, hence able to carry out public services or to advocate for the public good as they see fit. While this is mostly true, many organizations in the sector are highly dependent on government funding and/or the sales of their services.

Despite the inadequacy of names, the sector is a critical and potent force in the economy. It harnesses volunteer, market-based, and public-sector resources to carry out society's most essential functions—health care, social services, education, arts and culture, recreation, religion, and economic development, to name a few.

Contributors to the Book

We hope readers will benefit from the diverse points of view brought to this project by co-authors Lilly Cohen and Dennis Young, contributors Robert L. Payton, Henry Goldstein, and Anne Preston, and by the 25 managers who were interviewed and profiled.

Lilly Cohen is Director of Development of the Port Washington Public Library and an Adjunct Professor of Nonprofit Management at the Harriman School of Management and Policy Studies, State University of New York at Stony Brook. An adult educator, career counselor, and consultant to nonprofit organizations, she formerly managed several academic programs, including the Fund Raising/Nonprofit Management Program of the New School's Graduate School of Management and Urban Professions. Her publications include: *Funding in Aging: Public, Private and Voluntary* and several regional career guides.

Dennis R. Young is Mandel Professor of Nonprofit Management and Director of the Mandel Center for Nonprofit Organizations, Case Western Reserve University. He was formerly Professor of Policy Analysis and Public Management and Founding Director of Nonprofit Studies at the Harriman School of Management and Policy Studies, State University of New York at Stony Brook. His publications include: *If Not for Profit for What?: A Behavioral Theory of the Nonprofit Sector Based on Entrepreneurship, Casebook of Management for Nonprofit Organizations,* and *Educating Managers of Nonprofit Organizations.*

Robert L. Payton is Director of the Center on Philanthropy at Indiana University and the country's first professor of philanthropic studies. A scholar and writer, he was president of the Exxon Education Foundation, President of Hofstra University, and President of Long Island University.

Henry Goldstein is President of The Oram Group, a fundraising, public relations, and management consulting firm. He is a founder and Adjunct Professor of the New School's Nonprofit Management Program in the Graduate School of Management and Urban Professions. A former chairman and president of the National Society of Fund Raising Executives, he was chosen Fund Raising Executive of the Year in 1986. He is co-author of *Dear Friend: Mastering the Art of Direct Mail Fund Raising.*

Anne Preston is Assistant Professor of Economics at the Harriman School of Management and Policy Studies, State University of New York at Stony Brook. A specialist in the labor market, she has written numerous articles and papers on nonprofit compensation.

Content and Organization of the Book

This book combines resource information and research data with profiles, experiences, and insights of professionals in the field. The material has been organized into eleven sections.

Section 1—"The Private Nonprofit Economy: A Sector of Opportunity" describes and defines the sector and its subsectors and constituent organizations in legal, economic, historical, theoretical, and statistical terms.

Section 2—"Myths, Realities, Rewards, and Frustrations of Working in the Nonprofit Sector" offers a critical perspective on the work life of managers in nonprofit organizations from the vantage point of a seasoned practitioner.

Section 3—"Compensation Patterns in the Sector" examines and analyzes current research, compares compensation between sectors, and describes differences in nonprofit compensation by subsectors, fields, geographic areas, and by gender.

Section 4—"Educating and Training Managers for the Sector" reviews the dynamic education and training enterprises that are evolving in response to a need for professionalization. Program types, levels, providers, and issues are identified.

Sections 5–9—"Career Profiles" presents 25 case histories of real managers with diverse responsibilities, talking about who they are, what they do, how they got there, and why their work matters.

Section 10—"The Sector's Best Kept Secret: Associations as Employers and Professional Development Resources" describes associations as major providers of job opportunities and identifies specific associations that offer career advancement and career development opportunities for nonprofit managers.

Section 11—"Getting A Job in the Sector" briefly reviews effective job-search strategies for those seeking employment, with an emphasis on what nonprofit employers look for. Helpful resources are identified.

In Conclusion

Managers in the nonprofit sector tend to express more satisfaction with their work than their counterparts in the business and government sectors. They tend to be more inspired by public service, as well as by the humanitarian and other "noble" values espoused by the organizations they work for.

Despite the sector's diversity, there is a consensus about what characteristics nonprofit organizations value in their managers: education, a commitment to professional development, "hard" management skills, and the ability to communicate. Volunteer experience is a must, and the ability to lead and manage people, frequently in nonauthoritarian environments, is prized. Organizations that espouse these values and create work environments that embody them are magnets for certain types of people: people who are idealistic, visionary, creative, entrepreneurial, and motivated by causes—and at the same time pragmatic, organized, and productive. We call them "dreamers and doers."

Acknowledgments

We are indebted to many people who helped make this book a reality. Foremost among them is Charles A. Johnson, Vice-President for Development of the Lilly Endowment, without whose genuine interest, and moral and financial support the project that led to this book could not have happened.

At an earlier stage of the project's development we received encouragement from several knowledgeable people. Thomas R. Buckman, President of the Foundation Center, was the first to read the proposal and to endorse the idea. Others who expressed strong interest in the very beginning include: Russy Sumariwalla, Vice-President of United Way of America; Sandra Gray, Vice-President of Independent Sector; John Simon, Chairman, Program on Non-Profit Organizations, Yale University; Henry Goldstein, President of The Oram Group; and Betty Schlein of Betty Schlein Associates.

Gerrit Wolf, Dean of the Harriman School of Management and Policy Studies of the State University of New York at Stony Brook, deserves special thanks for his unflagging support of the project.

We are very grateful to other advisors who were generous with their time and ideas, among them: John J. Schwartz, former President of the American Association of Fund-Raising Counsel, Inc.; James W. Keene, Director of the Career Development Office at the State University of New York at Stony Brook; Don Bates, Administrator of the Foundation for Public Relations Research and Education; Edward H. Van Ness, Vice President, National Health Council, Inc.; and the late J. Richard Wilson, President of the National Society of Fund Raising Executives.

Two fellow academics who were generous with their time are Mark E. Keane, Director of the Master's Degree Program in Association Management, George Washington University, and Michael O'Neill, Director of the Institute for Nonprofit Management, University of San Francisco. For their valued suggestions, we also thank Anne Blouin of the American Society of Association Executives; Susan Padgett of United Way of America and Patricia Oertel, Center for Nonprofit Management; Barbara Bryan of the New York Regional Association of Grant-makers; and Michael Seltzer, a consultant and writer.

Elizabeth Wadsworth edited the manuscript both for content and style and deserves credit for her incisive review of the material, her constructive suggestions, and for pulling together diverse pieces into an integrated whole.

Claire Hartford, research assistant to the project, and a graduate student at the Harriman School, is responsible for identifying and gathering information about associations, education and training programs, and bibliographic references. She contributed to the writing. Her diligent efforts have enriched this guide.

Christine Kraus, Wanda Mocarski, Toni Mercadante, and Michelle McTernan are responsible for the transcription, typing, administrative support, and meticulous attention to detail required by this undertaking. Their devoted efforts often went beyond the call of duty.

Patricia Read, former Director of Publications at the Foundation Center, offered initial editorial and production support. After her departure Rick Schoff managed the entire project with grace and wisdom. It has been a pleasure to work with them.

We are indebted to Godwyn Morris, President of Grant Management Group, Inc., for suggesting the need for this book and to literary agent Susan Cohen for titling the book.

Our thanks go to everyone who helped us, including: the authors who contributed to this volume, the managers who were willing to describe their professional histories to us, and to anyone we may have inadvertently overlooked.

Lilly Cohen
Director of Development
Port Washingtion Public Library
Port Washington, New York

Adjunct Professor of Nonprofit Management
Harriman School of Management and Policy Studies
State University of New York, Stony Brook

Dennis Young
Director and Mandel Professor
Mandel Center for Nonprofit Organizations
Case Western Reserve University
Cleveland, Ohio

PART ONE

The Nonprofit Sector:
A Review of Employment
Opportunities

1

The Private
Nonprofit Economy
Dennis R. Young

A Sector of Opportunity

If asked what are the principal types of institutions making up their society, most Americans would probably respond "business and government." After all, most Americans work for a business and satisfy their material needs through purchases from businesses. These same citizens pay substantial proportions of their incomes in taxes to government, which in turn provides them with basic services such as police and fire protection, traffic control, and public school education.

However, a third kind of organization touches the typical citizen just as fundamentally, satisfying their needs and enriching their lives in important ways. In large measure, nonprofit organizations, which are neither in business to make a profit nor part of government, provide for the social, spiritual, physical, mental, educational, and cultural needs and wants of most Americans. Hospitals, churches, museums, orchestras, social service agencies, social clubs, professional and trade associations, and universities are the kinds of organizations in which we regularly participate—and from which we receive services and benefits that make our lives more tolerable and satisfying.

As Nielsen (1983) pointed out, in America there is a nonprofit organization for almost any interest or need. Indeed, one can follow Americans through their life stages by tracking involvement in nonprofit organizations: from birth in a nonprofit hospital, to christening in a church, to nurture and early training in a day care center or preschool, to youthful recreation and character-building in a YMCA, Girl Scout Troop, or Little League, to confirmation and later marriage in a church, to advanced education in a university, to involvement in social movements to make the world a better place, to membership in civic associations and charities as a responsible citizen, to participation in an industry trade association, professional association, or labor union as part of one's working career, to participation in a pension fund on retirement, and ultimately to burial in a nonprofit cemetery!

Yet, this scenario only partially portrays the role of the nonprofit sector in American life, for it leaves out two important considerations. First, the nonprofit sector is not separated from the other two sectors of our society—business and government. Rather, it is intertwined with them. For instance, nonprofit organizations often advocate for and demonstrate the efficacy of social programs or new laws before they are adopted by government. Once government undertakes a program, it often does so by contracting to, or otherwise collaborating with, nonprofit organizations for service delivery.

Similarly, nonprofit associations facilitate the work of the business sector. They provide a vehicle through which corporations can articulate the public policy concerns of their industry, and they can address an industry's collective needs, whether for a better public image or improvement of the communities in which they do business.

Second, the life-cycle scenario does not dramatize the sector's employment potential. Nonprofits are conventionally viewed and appreciated as informal, volunteer-based organizations—not in the same league as business or government when it comes to economic significance and opportunities for paid work.

In fact, the nonprofit sector is a major employer of paid workers. Large numbers of Americans look to this sector not only for consumer services, satisfactions, and assistance, but also for their livelihoods. As Anne Preston points out in her chapter, the nonprofit sector is a special place to be employed, where the pay may be modest but where the motivations and conditions of work are often satisfying, exciting, and challenging.

History

The recent growth of the nonprofit sector is the culmination of a long history of development, and probably the prologue to continued and increased significance in the economic and social life of our country. The American nonprofit sector goes back to the beginning of colonial times, derived in part from English tradition. Ylvisaker (1987) points out that foundations were given legal definition in the English Statute of Charitable Uses of 1601 and were common in colonial America. Certainly nonprofits are among the oldest and most venerable institutions in the land—the origins of Harvard and Yale Universities actually predate the American Revolution. Alexis de Tocqueville's observation of the prominent role of associations in the early days of the Republic is a familiar one.

Nonetheless, as Peter Dobkin Hall (1987) notes, the nonprofit sector occupied a minor and uncertain position in the country's early days, due in part to the ambivalence of the states to privately held power via the establishment of private corporations and charitable trusts. Historically, even existing nonprofit corporations were ambiguous in the nature of their control; e.g., Harvard University was governed by a coalition of both private and public interests.

By the 1840s private charitable corporations were firmly established under federal law, though still limited in certain states. After the Civil War, private charitable corporations developed rapidly to perform a variety of functions, including higher education, hospital care, libraries, volunteer fire companies, labor unions, and ministering to the needs of the poor, sick, and disabled.

The early 1900s witnessed another surge of nonprofit activity as industrial fortunes were used to establish private foundations. Also in this era, waves of immigration from Europe led to the establishment of settlement houses and ethnic charities, and this was the period of the establishment of federated community fundraising appeals, such as Community Chest and United Funds.

Giving to charity was initially independent of tax considerations. In 1917 the deduction for charitable contributions was included in the income tax code, and in 1936 the deduction for corporate giving was added. Since tax rates were very low in these early years, the immediate impact of these laws was small, but after World War II tax avoidance and new-found prosperity motivated a major growth period for foundations. The welfare programs of the New Deal in the 1930s and the War on Poverty of the 1960s had a direct impact on the growth of the nonprofit sector. Rather than replacing the charitable and public service work of nonprofits, these programs stimulated their development as vehicles for the delivery of government financed services.

By the 1960s and '70s the nonprofit sector had become a prominent part of the U.S. economic landscape. For the first time, the sector was identified, through the work of the Commission on Private Philanthropy and Public Needs (1977), commonly known as the Filer Commission. At this time the sector sought its own identity and representation via a national umbrella organization called Independent Sector. Beginning with Yale, universities began to establish new research institutes to study the sector and to create new programs of professional graduate education that both recognized the sector as a significant part of the economy and sought to educate its leadership.

A Special Place to Work

The nonprofit sector is special because it performs so many functions essential to the proper functioning of the other sectors, business and government, and to the well-being and satisfaction of people directly. Moreover, organizations in this sector are structured to allow their participants a level of self-determination that is often impossible elsewhere. Many nonprofits are democratically or collegially administered. Most are governed by boards of trustees, comprised of important members of the community and entrusted to steer the organization on a responsible course in pursuit of a public mission. These governance and management structures allow levels of flexibility that are difficult to match in more tightly structured businesses or bureaucratically controlled government agencies.

Nonprofit organizations are uniquely situated to address societal needs as their governors and managers see fit—constrained by extant economic and political conditions, but also free to define their own performance criteria. In essence, nonprofit organizations must decide for themselves what it is they are in business to do, and how to judge success or failure. Neither the profit motive nor political popularity are appropriate yardsticks for these organizations. Rather, nonprofits must formulate service objectives for themselves and maximize the achievement of these objectives within the framework of available resources. Not only does this framework offer an exciting environment for work, but it also presents special challenges and satisfactions to those who choose management careers in the nonprofit sector.

Managing a nonprofit is neither identical to managing a business nor to administering a governmental agency, but it is a unique blend with elements of each. Nonprofits are like businesses in that they must break even, i.e., they must generate at least as much revenue as they spend—otherwise they fail and must dissolve. Contrary to popular interpretation of their designation, nonprofits may actually make a "profit" in the sense of generating more revenues than they spend in a given year. However, such "surpluses" may not be distributed to those who control the organization, as is done in business. Rather, these surpluses must ultimately be used to foster the purposes for which the nonprofit was established.

Nonprofits are also like government in that they address the needs and purposes of a collective, public nature, though on a voluntary basis without the power of taxation to support themselves. Because nonprofits need not be completely driven by the marketplace nor by the imperatives of government or mass politics, they are in the unique position to define public goods, causes, and collective needs as they see them, and to pursue these missions unimpeded, so long as they can break even and operate lawfully.

There are, of course, other constraints accompanying the special tax privileges that nonprofits receive. However, the essence of the sector is that it is uniquely positioned to enable those who work in it to pursue collective needs and public service goals, according to a variety of conceptions and within a flexible organizational framework.

Types of Nonprofit Organizations

All nonprofit organizations share the two defining characteristics previously noted. First, they are privately controlled and not a formal part of the government, although they may be financed by government or have government officials on their boards of directors. Second, nonprofits observe the "nondistribution constraint" under which they cannot distribute financial surpluses to those in control. While these characteristics distinguish nonprofits from government and business, they nevertheless allow a wide variety of organizational types.

The broadest distinction among nonprofits is between "mutual benefit" organizations, producing services for their own members, and "charitable" or "philanthropic" organizations that produce services for a segment of the public at large. Nonprofits can also be distinguished on other important dimensions. For example, certain nonprofits advocate for a cause while others provide direct services, and some solicit and utilize economic resources to produce services while others raise and distribute resources for other organizations.

Precise classification of the universe of nonprofit organizations is tricky, for the variety of nonprofits is almost endless. A good place to start is with the Federal Tax Code, which divides nonprofit organizations into different groups for tax purposes. John Simon (1987) envisions this universe as a set of four concentric circles. The outer circle encloses virtually all nonprofit organizations. These organizations share the nondistribution constraint, as noted above, and are classified under Section 501 of the Federal Tax Code. With few exceptions, these nonprofit organizations are all exempt from corporate income tax, i.e., from tax on the difference between operating revenues and expenditures.

Simon's first circle includes the class of nonprofits labeled "mutual benefit" organizations, i.e., those organizations designed primarily to serve their own members rather than the public.

Examples include professional and industry trade associations, social and fraternal clubs, mutual insurance companies, and labor unions. Mutual benefit organizations cannot receive tax-deductible contributions, but they are generally exempt from corporate tax on their financial surpluses.

Moving inward to the next circle we reach the largest and most prominent group of nonprofit organizations—the "charitable" or "philanthropic" nonprofit organizations classified under Section 501(c)(3) of the IRS Code. The distinguishing characteristic of this group is that their purposes are defined in terms of benefit to a public constituency outside the people who belong to the organization itself. For example, hospitals are intended to serve the sick, universities to serve students, orchestras to serve music lovers, and environmental organizations to preserve the environment for present and future generations. Organizations in the 501(c)(3) category are permitted to receive charitable contributions from individuals and corporate sources, and these contributions may then be deducted from personal or corporate income taxes.

Categories of 501(c)(3)

Within the 501(c)(3) ring of nonprofit organizations there are three subcategories. The largest group of organizations in this class consists of "public charities." These include hospitals, colleges and universities, research institutes, social agencies, museums, orchestras, and religious institutions familiar to casual observers of the nonprofit sector. These organizations are characterized by two facts. Their work is intended to benefit the public at large, or some segment of it. Also, these organizations are supported by public sources such as grants, gifts, and charitable contributions from a variety of individual, governmental, and corporate givers. Such public support distinguishes public charities from "private foundations," which constitute the two innermost circles of the charitable nonprofit universe.

Private foundations are established by some exclusive source of wealth (for example, a private individual's fortune or a corporation) and they are intended to carry out work for the public good. However, given the more private character of their support and control, tax laws treat private foundations less favorably than public charities.

According to Simon's four-ring model, there are two classes (inner rings) of private foundations—operating foundations and grantmaking foundations. Rather than giving money away, operating foundations use their funds primarily to carry out a direct service or research agenda. For example, the Russell Sage Foundation, established by the widow of industrialist Russell Sage, supports its own staff to execute a public policy research program. To the contrary, grantmaking foundations, such as the Ford Foundation, generally restrict their activities to the disbursement of grants to other organizations or individuals, which then undertake projects and programs consistent with the grantmaking foundation's stated purposes and guidelines.

Special 501s

The classification of certain individual varieties of nonprofits is not immediately clear. For example, certain nonprofit organizations, which are private and observe the nondistribution constraint, are nonetheless governed by other parts of the Tax Code than Section 501, and thus fall outside Simon's rings. These include political parties, pension plans, and consumer and farmer cooperatives.

Moreover, within the 501 universe, there are a few important types of organization whose classification is not obvious. For example, organizations with a public purpose but whose principal activity is political advocacy are classified under section 501(c)(4) and are not eligible to receive deductible contributions. Fundraising charities such as United Way organizations or the American Cancer Society, which raise money through charitable solicitation and then allocate those funds to other charitable organizations, are considered public charities within the 501(c)(3) category.

Community foundations, such as the New York Community Trust or the Cleveland Foundation, administer a portfolio of gifts, bequests, and endowments received from members of their communities and sometimes designated for particular purposes. Community foundations then allocate these funds for projects and programs intended to benefit their own areas. Since community foundations are deemed to be supported by a broad-based public, they are also classified as public charities under section 501(c)(3), rather than as private foundations. There are some 300 community foundations in the United States.

Corporate foundations, such as the AT&T Foundation or the Exxon Education Foundation, are supported by funds from the parent corporation, and are classified as private, grantmaking foundations.

Finally, an important feature of the nonprofit sector may be missed by merely examining nonprofit classifications. In particular, nonprofit organizations are often highly entwined in the life and operations of business or government. Corporate foundations, for example, carry out a social agenda defined by and consistent with the interests of the funding corporation. Other "hybrid" nonprofits, as Weisbrod (1988) calls them, are also prominent. These include: nonprofit organizations that own for-profit subsidiary corporations; economic or urban development corporations that engage business and government in joint ventures under a nonprofit umbrella; and nonprofits established by government to carry out a service agenda through contractual arrangements. For example, the Rand Corporation is a nonprofit "think tank" originally established by the federal government to carry out studies of military problems.

What Do Nonprofit Organizations Do?

The classification of nonprofit organizations by tax treatment category provides a general sense of the functions that nonprofit organizations perform in our society. Figure 1.1 shows a set of categories that encompass the activities represented by tax-exempt organizations. However, a closer examination shows that such a classification leaves many questions about nonprofit organizations unanswered. Burton Weisbrod (1988), using the tax treatment classification as a springboard, sorts nonprofit services into three further categories—"commercial," "collective," and "trust." These categories help answer the question, "Why nonprofit instead of for-profit or government?"

Some nonprofits in Simon's outer circle perform "commercial" services to enhance the economic or professional interests of the organization's own members, or the industries or professions of which they are a part. Examples include industry trade associations such as the

FIGURE 1.1. CATEGORIZING TAX EXEMPT ORGANIZATIONS

Abstracted from "National Taxonomy of Exempt Entities," developed by the National Center for Charitable Statistics, a program of INDEPENDENT SECTOR. Washington, DC: 1987:

A   Arts, Culture, Humanities
B   Education/Instruction and Related—Formal and Nonformal
C   Environmental Quality, Protection and Beautification
D   Animal Related
E   Health—General & Rehabilitation
F   Health—Mental Health, Crisis Intervention
G   Health—Mental Retardation/Developmentally Disabled
H   Consumer Protection, Legal Aid
I   Crime and Delinquency Prevention—Public Protection
J   Employment/Jobs
K   Food, Nutrition, Agriculture
L   Housing/Shelter
M   Public Safety, Emergency Preparedness and Relief
N   Recreation, Leisure, Sports, Athletics
O   Youth Development
P   Human Service, Other Including Multipurpose (also, Social Services—Individual and Family)
Q   International/Foreign
R   Civil Rights, Social Action, Advocacy
S   Community Improvement
T   Grantmaking/Foundations
U   Research, Planning, Science, Technology, Technical Assistance
V   Voluntarism, Philanthropy and Charity
W   Religion Related/Spiritual Development
X   Reserved for New Major Group (Future)
Y   Reserved for Special Information Needs of Regulatory Bodies—Mutual/Membership Benefit (specific) and Other

National Association of Manufacturers, professional organizations such as the American Medical Association, and labor unions such as the United Auto Workers. Garden clubs, mutual insurance companies, and chambers of commerce are additional examples of nonprofits set up essentially to advance the interests of their own members.

"Collective" and "Trust"

Within the charitable 501(c)(3) part of the nonprofit world, Weisbrod (1988) distinguishes "collective" and "trust" goods, which help us understand further the value contributed by, and attributed to, nonprofit work.

"Collective" goods are those that provide substantial benefits to individuals who do not pay for them, or only pay token amounts through direct fees or charges. Such goods include medical research, assistance to the poor, public safety programs, free museums, and environmental protection programs. While government usually provides such goods, nonprofit organizations often supplement government provision, where it is insufficient, or nonprofits carry out service provision with government funding. Nonprofits may thus function as initiators, decentralized deliverers, or demonstrator-advocates of such services, enhancing the flexibility, responsiveness, or efficiency of government.

With the concept of "trust" goods, Weisbrod builds on the ideas of Henry Hansmann (1987) to explain some of the subtleties of the nonprofit world and its perceived value in our society. These subleties are widely experienced but rarely thought about. Trust goods, Weisbrod says, are those that the individual consumer pays for but has trouble evaluating. For instance, are you getting fair value in a day care center for children, or from medical care, education, or a donation to send food or medical supplies to a remote area? Nonprofits play an important role in delivering such services because, although they can be fallible like any human enterprise, they do not have the kinds of incentives to profiteer by cheating or compromising on quality that profitmaking businesses may have. Moreover, in comparison to government, nonprofits are often more flexible and responsive to needs and market demands in these service areas.

We can now examine the particular service areas, or fields of interest, in which nonprofits concentrate their activities. Gabriel Rudney (1987) demonstrates that the philanthropic sector constitutes over 90 percent of the overall nonprofit sector, as measured by factors such as employment, expenditures, or the value of services produced. This philanthropic sector is comprised of Simon's three inner rings of 501(c)(3) organizations. Within the philanthropic sector, as shown by Hodgkinson and Weitzman (1986), over 90 percent of activity—as measured by operating expenditures, wages and salaries, or employment—is concentrated in four service areas: health care, education and research, social services, and religion. Other major activities in this part of the sector are arts and culture, foundations, and legal services. These subsectors offer important and attractive employment opportunities for those interested in managing in the public interest. Assessing just how significant these opportunities are requires that we first examine the size and distribution of the sector itself, in the context of the overall economy of the United States.

Size and Distribution of the U.S. Nonprofit Sector

There are almost 900,000 nonprofit organizations in the United States, counting only those formally registered with the Internal Revenue Service (IRS). Of these, about 40 percent are 501(c)(3) organizations. These numbers compare with roughly 18 million profit-making corporations and 400,000 governmental agencies. Thus, nonprofits constitute approximately 5 percent of all organizations. Nonprofits, excluding religious institutions, own some $250 billion worth of assets, just under 2 percent of the nation's total assets and equivalent to almost half of the assets owned by the federal government. Over 4 percent of the national income originates in nonprofit organizations. Annual funds of more than $250 billion dollars flow to nonprofit organizations, not counting another $80 billion worth of volunteer time. In all, gross receipts by the sector represent almost 10 percent of the Gross National Product (GNP).

The nonprofit sector employs more than 6.5 million full-time equivalent (FTE) paid workers, and over 11 million FTE workers overall if volunteers are included. This represents almost 10 percent of the total U.S. labor force. While volunteers in the sector far outnumber paid workers, the total labor time of paid workers outweighs that of volunteers.

Nonprofits represent a significant share of the service-producing part of the U.S. economy, and this service sector is by far the fastest growing part of the economy, easily outpacing the goods-producing sector. Also, the nonprofit sector has recently been the fastest growing component of the overall service sector. In terms of employment, the nonprofit share of the service economy is roughly 14 percent, according to Rudney (1987). As a reflection of this strategic positioning, the nonprofit sector accounted for 13 percent of all new jobs created in the U.S., between 1972 and 1982.

Nonprofit organizations are concentrated in the service industries, but they are prominent in these industries to different degrees. In terms of beds, for example, Weisbrod (1988) indicates that nonprofit hospitals have 65 percent of all hospital beds, while nonprofit nursing homes have only 22 percent of nursing home beds. Nonprofit day care serves 40 percent of the children in day care, while nonprofit health insurance companies serve 43 percent of persons served by that industry. In terms of expenses, nonprofits represent 15 percent of post-secondary education, 27 percent of the performing arts, and 95 percent of libraries. With respect to employment, according to Rudney (1987), nonprofits constitute about 70 percent of the private (nongovernmental) sector in health care, over 90 percent in education, over 80 percent in social services, but less than 25 percent in arts and culture. However, in terms of employment growth in the nonprofit sector, social service agencies led over the 1972–82 period, followed by health, arts, and educational organizations.

Nonprofit organizations are distributed unevenly throughout the economy in other ways. For example, nonprofits vary widely in size and have different size distributions in different industries. As documented by Weisbrod (1988) for a selection of eight major cities in 1976, between 30 percent and 48 percent of local health care organizations had gross annual receipts of under $10,000 while only 2 to 7 percent had receipts over $1 million. Corresponding figures for educational institutions were 26 percent to 56 percent for the small organizations and 3 percent to 10 percent for the large ones. In contrast to these two industries, which feature major institutions such as hospitals and universities, nonprofit organizations in the environmental protection field were generally smaller, with 36 percent to 100 percent of local organizations having receipts under $10,000 and 0 percent to 5 percent having receipts over $1 million.

Nonprofits are unevenly scattered among regions of the country. Figures compiled by Salamon (1983) and cited by Weisbrod (1988) show that in the nonprofit-rich Northeast there are 58.2 nonprofits per 100,000 population and $522 in nonprofit expenditures per capita. This compares with 36.8 nonprofits per 100,000 population and $208 in nonprofit expenditures per capita in the South, where nonprofits are least common. The North Central and Western regions of the country fall into second and third places, respectively, in their concentrations of nonprofit organizations.

Consistent with these regional patterns, Paul Ylvisaker (1987) points out that more than half of the assets of major foundations in this country are owned by foundations in the Mid-Atlantic and East North Central regions. Twenty percent of foundation assets are based in New York City alone! Nonetheless, many of these foundations have nationally focused rather than regional agendas. Moreover, the fastest growing foundations are now found outside the regions of the country where these grantmakers have traditionally been concentrated.

Changes and Opportunities

As nonprofits are unevenly scattered about the U.S. economy, opportunities for employment are also selective. But generally, the nonprofit sector is more and more becoming the place to look for exciting new opportunities. In particular, growth of employment and wages in this sector is generally outpacing the rest of the economy.

For example, although the average wage in the philanthropic part of the sector, according to Rudney (1987), is only 75 percent of wages for all non-farm workers, the payroll in this sector tripled and the average wage doubled in the 1972–82 decade, and the average wage rose from 68 to 75 percent of that for all non-farm workers in that period. Over this same decade, the nonprofit sector accounted for 13 percent of all new jobs. The number of paid nonprofit employees increased more than 20 percent from 1977 to 1987.

These figures point to the nonprofit sector as the fastest growing of all sectors in the decade preceding 1982, although the trend was reversed temporarily in 1982–84 and has since rebounded (see Hodgkinson and Weitzman, 1988). In the seven-year period from 1977 to 1984, the nonprofit sector increased its overall shares of national income, total earnings from work, and total employment. Nonprofit employment grew at an annual rate of more than 3 percent over the period.

That the nonprofit sector has achieved such prominence recently in the United States, and promises to continue to grow in importance, can be explained in part by the increasing complexity of our society. As Paul Ylvisaker (1987) stated:

> The larger the society has become, the more predictably and compulsively Americans have created a plethora of devices enabling them to gain some leverage in the system without having to go through the wearying process of winning total control or consensus. . . .
> This miniaturization and spreading out of decision making are essential aspects of the logic of an ever-enlarging democracy—a logic manifested in the growth of foundations and the proliferation of nonprofit agencies in general. As that logic would predict, by far the greatest numbers of these institutions have been established within the past generation.

It's an exciting time to consider working for a nonprofit organization.

2

Myths and Realities, Rewards and Frustrations of Working in the Nonprofit Sector

Henry Goldstein

The last 35 years have seen tremendous growth in the number of men and women employed professionally by nonprofit organizations. In good times and bad, war and peace, high hemlines and low, the sector has continued to expand. With this growth has come increased professionalization, improvement in salaries and benefits, and new or enhanced opportunities for women and minorities.

On the plus side of employment in the nonprofit sector is the immense satisfaction many people find in bringing to reality their innermost ideals and aspirations in the arts, sciences, intellectual enquiry, and service to others.

What are some of the myths and realities, some of the rewards and frustrations of working in the not-for-profit field? My observations date from 1956, and, though my experiences as a nonprofit employee and then consultant embrace a wide spectrum, my remarks are necessarily subjective and anecdotal.

Most of Us Wind Up Where We Are by Accident

By the time we reach the junior or senior year of high school, career or work choices begin to crystallize for many of us. By the time we reach college, we set ourselves on the path we have selected. Some of us follow the road through college to graduate school, and a very few of us—clutching the terminal degree—go on to a happy life in whatever field we elected.

However, the majority of us wind up where we are by accident. This applies wherever we work, irrespective of our academic preparation, and it is common in all fields and at all professional levels. Once at work, our progression has little to do with narrow skills.

Physicians who run hospitals practice little or no medicine, though they may attempt to keep their hands in. A curator promoted to a museum directorship has little time to use his academic training. Both the physician/executive and the curator/executive are enmeshed in planning, fundraising, budgeting, personnel problems, new buildings, public relations, and—

trickiest of all—they are trying to satisfy a lay board of trustees. The most able board members are generally too busy to pay close attention, the most faithful are not always the wealthiest or the wisest, and all of them require constant care and feeding.

In observing employment hierarchies in government, private business, and the nonprofit sector, it is apparent that positions that continue to use specific training or technical skills start just above the entry level and pretty much stop at middle management.

Probably the hardest thing for a young person, in this time of over-specialization, is to become a generalist. But make no mistake: it's the generalists who run things. As noted in Figure 2.1, the higher one advances in nonprofit, the less one is likely to use the specific skills or disciplines that brought initial employment and that were often acquired at high cost in time and money.

Administrative and managerial positions are really not very skill specific; experience and leadership qualities are highly transferable and highly prized. Everyone intuitively responds to leadership, but leadership itself eludes definition. Ultimately, most positions are defined by their incumbents.

FIGURE 2.1 SPECIALISTS AND GENERALISTS—MANAGEMENT LEVELS

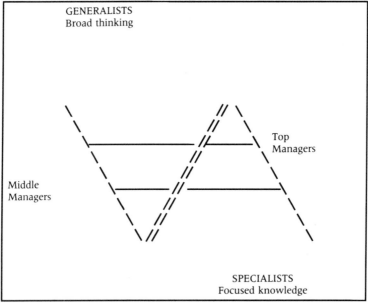

Successful and Unsuccessful Transfers

The former chief executive officer (CEO) of a profitable business sold it out of boredom, bounced around for awhile, and then found a job in a nonprofit that was clearly a mismatch. He left and was hired by another nonprofit, one of my clients. In his first sprint out of the chocks, he successfully managed a capital/endowment fundraising campaign that closed out at over $350 million—$50 million over goal, six months ahead of plan!

This gentleman freely admits that he knew little about fundraising, except as an occasional volunteer. He succeeded by applying solid business experience and well-honed management skills. He knew how to delegate authority to people who had specialties he lacked, and he understood numbers. The man is a walking spreadsheet, but he recognizes that casting spreadsheets can be safely entrusted to subordinates. His time is far too valuable for that.

Another man was recruited by our search division some years ago. His career is particularly interesting because it illustrates the path many academics follow. A Ph.D. from the midwest, he is a scholar of Middle English and on slight provocation is given to reciting *Beowulf* in the original. Except at certain kinds of parties, this is not much in demand. An alternative career choice led to the Young Presidents Organization, the Boy Scouts, and then to his present post.

In some cases, the transition from one occupation to another is more or less logical. For 30 years the former general manager of an opera company was a record company artists-and-repertory man, specializing in—what else?—opera. His knowledge of operatic voices, the singers' repertoires, and their future availability is said to have been unequaled by any impresario.

Another of our client agencies is a world-renowned science museum. Its new director was formerly chairman of the electrical engineering department at a western university—a logical transfer.

Of course, the transfers do not always take because the for-profit and nonprofit cultures are fundamentally different; this is often poorly understood. Without question, the ability to understand the professional environment and language of the organization one manages is essential and, one would think, self-evident. However, I constantly encounter successful men and women who fail to grasp this. A non-educator is hard put to manage a college, as one gentleman, who exchanged the chairmanship of a manufacturing company for an Ivy League college presidency, learned a few years ago.

A woman acquaintance of mine, Meg, was a banker. She was everything an executive should be—mature, assertive, a good delegator, and accustomed to command. She was proud of the fact that her "line" at the bank was $50 million—the amount she could lend on her signature. Meg had done well, but she saw that both her gender and the competitive pool blocked her further advancement. The choice was either another bank or another career. She elected the latter and became executive director of a small community service agency.

She lasted less than a year before she returned to what she calls "the real world." What did Meg in was the process of decision-making as it works in many nonprofits. Although a staff hierarchy exists on paper, much of the decision-making is consensual and accountability is unclear—my friend was totally unaccustomed to this.

Meg also found that the hiring/firing responsibility, which was so precisely hers in the job description, was really expected to be exercised in consultation with various board members, especially the president. She felt her authority as chief executive was compromised, yet the board members felt they were only trying to assist her. Meg told me the board interfered too much in the day-to-day management of the agency, which—unhappily—is all too common. Having to deal with a board was, she told me, the ultimate frustration, and she is not alone. Working with a board of volunteers—who are the legal owners of a nonprofit—is the greatest challenge a transferee from the business world faces.

Motivations

One of the most enduring myths you will encounter relates to the career motivations of people who work in the nonprofit sector, for there is nothing inherently noble, or ennobling, in working for a nonprofit agency. Fortunately, the best people are usually strongly motivated—until or unless they burn out. These people are often the programmatically oriented who, committed to an idea, a cause, or a movement, spark an organization. For them, personal gain is secondary. In many instances, administrative and managerial skills are lacking and of little interest. They generally abhor the constant, grinding necessity of money-raising because it pulls them away from their program interests and because they find it humiliating.

The problem is that not everyone who is well-intentioned is competent, even marginally. There are also many people with no pronounced goals or drives who find a home in a nonprofit. Additionally, there are young people with specific skills applicable anywhere. For example, a young acquaintance of mine majored in accounting and worked for a large insurance company. He hated the work, the robotic nature of the company, and living in a large city, but the one thing he liked was the good salary.

After a few years, he became chief financial officer of a small rural health agency. He loves the freedom, the benefits, the generous vacation, and he likes the environment. However, he is now starting a land survey business because as he said, "I have the skills and I want to work for myself."

A large subset of workers in the nonprofit sector are mid-life or mid-career entries who fall mainly into two categories. The first is composed of those who have been employed in government or private industry.

My friend, John, left a *Fortune* 100 company to become controller of a nonprofit with a $5-million annual budget. I asked him what the major differences were. "The work itself," he said, "is pretty much the same. A controller is a controller. But there are two major changes. The numbers are much smaller, so the consequences of each dollar's use are substantially greater. And I can't go any faster than the slowest board member. Many of them just don't understand the numbers. This doesn't happen in business."

In some cases, the people in this group, like John, are forced into early retirement as government agencies and companies "down-size," the new phrase for mass firings. Their principal motivation is to find work. Most are middle- or upper-level managers whose skills are universal. They may or may not be sincerely affected by a desire "to do good," which often arises through previous volunteer experience with various nonprofits. John, for instance, knew his nonprofit well and liked it, though he had never served as a board member or volunteer.

The second group appears more complex and largely motivated by various mid-life crises. A divorce, loss of a spouse, or another cataclysmic event often contributes to the idea of changing fields as part of a personal reorganization. Women, particularly those who surrendered careers to raise children and run a household, often attempt mid-life entry into nonprofit work.

In fact, many who have served as volunteers are top-notch managers and would make good employees. Most employers' reluctance to credit volunteer service as valid employment experience is a serious waste of human resources.

Additionally, I have frequently encountered organizations that have assimilated to their staff a man or woman who was formerly a board member. My general advice is for both the nonprofit and the person to tread carefully. More often than not, the arrangement comes to grief. When board members join the staff they usually continue to act like board members. This dynamic defies brief description. A better outcome is for the board member to convert that volunteer experience to employment elsewhere.

The Work Force

Linda F. Broessel, the head of our firm's executive search division, asserts that the nonprofit work force can be divided into four categories:

A very talented five percent. These are creative, entrepreneurial, or founder types seized by an idea or a cause, and able to realize it. A very few are superb executives.

Another achieving ten percent. These people are very good and fill the upper echelons of many of our best nonprofits, large and small. They fall short of greatness, though they are often superb number twos.

"I think of one man," Linda notes, "who has been second in command of a prominent nonprofit through two administrations over nearly 20 years. He is exactly placed. Too good to be in the ranks, but he lacks fire in the belly. Not a number one." Figure 2.2 illustrates the distribution of talent throughout the workforce.

The demographic bulge. Sixty-five percent of the work force, not outstanding enough to promote and certainly not bad enough to fire. Most in time are promoted simply because there are so many positions to fill. Turnover in the field being what it is, anyone commands a minimum of 20 percent more salary at the next station. In the main, this is a vast army of decent people who enjoy working for nonprofits.

The curse. A fifth of the people in nonprofit work simply do not belong there. They are distributed at all levels but cluster toward the lower end because, lacking strong administrative skills and secure self-identity, they are willing or forced to accept pay scales at the lower levels.

Rewards

Anne Preston addresses the technical aspects of compensation in her section, "Compensation Patterns in the Sector." However, I should like to offer some general observations. The last decade or two have witnessed considerable, continuing changes in compensation patterns.

FIGURE 2.2 THE NONPROFIT WORK FORCE

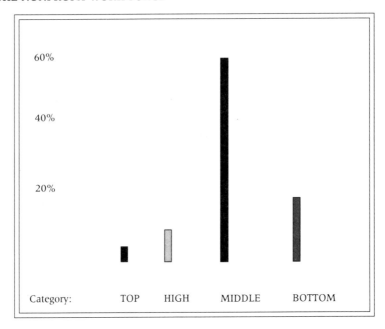

Employees of nonprofits no longer subsidize their organizations' budgets by accepting substandard wages and benefits. A nonprofit is inherently a service organization. This includes museums, colleges, scouts, hospitals, dance companies, social action groups, libraries, and civic betterment leagues. All nonprofits share one characteristic: fulfillment of a mission, rather than the manufacturing of a product.

Accordingly, the major budgetary item is labor: 65–80 percent of most operating costs is comprised of wages and benefits. Major change in a nonprofit budget can be effected only through an impact on labor costs, whichever the direction. Unionization of rank-and-file workers, particularly in the fields of higher education and health care, and collective action by employees in other nonprofits have profoundly and rather suddenly restructured the operating budgets of many groups.

Increased labor costs at the bottom have also caused an increase in the compensation of middle and top managers. If you seek employment in a nonprofit, look to join the administrative echelon rather than the programmatic. You will command a higher salary sooner, for compensation schedules are established by managers. As in business, managers take care of themselves first!

Nonprofit organizations are increasingly dominated by specialization and professionalization. As stated earlier, people who make it to the top tend to be generalists, while the lower and middle ranks are dominated by specialists and professionals. The growth of the nonprofit sector and the increasing complexities of constructing budgets from a mix of contributed income, government grants or subsidies, income on endowment, fees for service, and sale of products has, expectably, resulted in a large and still expanding mass of administrators.

Administrative functions offer a broad array of career possibilities. These include accounting, personnel, purchasing, public relations, fundraising, general management, as well as the supervisory and managerial roles related to programmatic functions.

Yet many nonprofits are still thin at the top. The layer of management just below the CEO is adequate to guide the organization, but the departure of the CEO usually triggers the appointment of a search committee. More often than not, the top position is filled externally. This happens in business too, of course, but at least as many companies select CEOs from within as without. Apparently in business there is a greater willingness to groom people for top slots. The financial constraints on the typical nonprofit simply do not permit the grooming of three or four top executives-in-waiting.

Besides, the second layer of vice-presidents or associate executive directors are generally too specialized for the search committee, and they often lack the programmatic credentials most nonprofits will (rightly or wrongly) insist upon. As a result, many top nonprofit people are forced to stay in place or look elsewhere.

Performance-Based Compensation. Aside from increasing base salaries, the major change occurring now in all areas of nonprofit employment is the move toward performance-based compensation, long a staple of the private sector. Because a private business is, by definition, profit-driven, the concept of profit-sharing is inherent. Originally, profit was shared only with the investors and shareholders, but management came to realize that output rose if employees were also given performance incentives.

The concept of performance-based compensation has always been stoutly resisted in the nonprofit sector for many reasons:

By definition, a nonprofit has no beneficial owners—except, in a larger and more philosophical sense, the people it serves. Its employees are expected to embrace a higher ideal than the staffs of dry cleaning stores or butcher shops.

A nonprofit renders a service which often cannot be provided efficiently. A four-bed burn center or a high-risk neonatal intensive care unit in a community hospital may be called upon infrequently. But if either unit is the only one in a 100-mile area, few would argue for elimination. Either unit is effective in use yet will never be efficient.

There are inherent difficulties in quantifying much of the work performed by nonprofits; how can an equitable scheme for linking performance to salary be established? For example, a story is told of management consultants called in by a symphony orchestra. After watching and listening to a rendition of Beethoven's *Eroica* symphony, the consultants offered a few suggestions for improved efficiency:

- Eliminate the second violin section; they did pretty much the same thing as the first.

- Cut out the repetition: play everything just once.

- Give the fellow waving the wand around something to do with his feet.

Donors would rebel, it is argued, because they embrace the myth that nonprofit employees truly wish to work for as close to nothing as possible because their hearts are pure.

There is merit to these arguments, and a nonprofit would do well to weigh them against the potential benefits to be derived from performance incentives, especially given the difficulty of establishing objective standards.

Preparing for Management

What is the message to a young person or a mid-career entry? First, if possible, try to figure out if you wish to be a manager, for many otherwise competent people stumble as administrators. If you are an excellent social worker, computer expert, physician, or lawyer (yes, many lawyers are entering nonprofit work and leaving law), there is nothing wrong in doing well what you do well.

Second, graduate school is time enough to specialize. I urge any young person to obtain the broadest possible education, and, above all else, read widely and learn to write simply and clearly.

Third, decide if an MBA is useful to you. On the plus side, an MBA offers flexibility, for in theory you are possessed of a transferable degree. A teaching degree, a Masters in Social Work, and the dreaded Ph.D. are of quite limited application outside the nonprofit sector. On the minus side, MBA curricula are customarily oriented to large systems, essentially public companies. The emphasis has been primarily on number-crunching, a skill that is of evident use to the management of a profit-making enterprise. The culture of a large company is different from that of a small business. It also differs from that of the typical nonprofit, which far more resembles a small business than it does a large corporation.

The budgets of the largest private nonprofits peak at $500 to $600 million, and these are indeed large businesses by any measure. But, as in the for-profit sector, 90 percent of nonprofits have annual budgets of less than $5 million.

The MBAs who fare well are generally those with the large companies, employed principally in financial or investment concerns. They will also be found in strategic planning or as chief operating officers. Because they lack programmatic expertise, nonprofits rarely employ them in CEO positions.

An emerging phenomenon is the score of universities now offering degrees in nonprofit management. Although the quality of each program must be judged carefully—all are under ten years old—their appearance is welcome. These programs occupy a significant niche, for graduate schools of business have generally shunned nonprofit management curricula as unworthy of their attention. While much graduate business course content may be adaptable to the nonprofit setting, this is not the intent.

On the other hand, the public administration programs offered by most universities are generally oriented to the public sector. Thus, the nonprofit programs fulfill a real need. (Readers are advised to look closely at Section 4, Lilly Cohen's "Educating and Training Managers for the Sector.")

Additionally, whether specialist or generalist, you should be computer literate. Most non-profits are finding ways to derive benefit from the computerization of a few of their activities. Because time is a manager's most precious commodity, the trick with the computer, as with any other allocation problem, is to figure out what you absolutely have to do yourself, and fob off everything else.

Finally, as an adjunct professor in the Graduate School of Management at the New School for Social Research in New York, I have known students pursuing Master's or Doctoral degrees in public administration. These are usually quite good students, but the orientation of the public administration curriculum is geared to government service, rather than the nonprofit sector.

Women and minorities are increasingly well represented in upper management but are still rare in the CEO's suite. Among the few real functions performed by nonprofit boards of trustees is the selection of the chief executive. Although there have been considerable advances, women and minorities are still rare in the chief executive's office. This must be laid at the trustees' doorstep, for they make the final selection.

Most boards are composed predominantly of white males high up the business ladder. While many are enlightened, others are not. Reflecting society itself, the boardroom has been slow to change, and the assimilation of women and minorities has required considerable education in most circumstances. As women, blacks, Hispanics, and other minorities reach higher levels of management, the number of applicants for the very top positions will increase. However, white male applicants currently far outnumber anyone else, save specific positions that require a woman or a minority person.

Happily, the situation is rapidly improving at the second tier. The absence of women and minorities in the CEO suite has perversely contributed to a greater distribution of women at the second levels, as CEOs seek balanced staffs and work forces.

Nonprofits are increasingly competing with the private sector and with government for professional personnel and for market share. Both compensation practices and recruiting methods are changing quickly; this is partly about money and partly about survival in a crowded, inefficient marketplace. It remains a truism that working for a nonprofit organization is not a great way to get rich, even though salaries in excess of $100,000 a year are increasingly common among senior and top managers. However, most people—even with long service—earn far less. As noted earlier, most nonprofits are small businesses. If you compare a business doing $500,000 a year with a nonprofit operating at $500,000 a year, you will find that the salaries of managers of both enterprises are comparable. The owner of a successful small business will likely reward himself better than a nonprofit board will reward its executive director, but otherwise, wages and benefits are similar.

A larger enterprise—profit-making or nonprofit—pays middle, upper, and top managers more than small enterprises because it can generally afford to and is therefore able to bid for more proven talent.

Though you may be a passionate defender of wildlife, an advocate of women's rights, or a devotee of dance, if your desire to get rich outweighs your desire to serve, go to Wall Street, start your own business, or develop shopping centers. The personal risks are much higher but the monetary rewards are exponentially greater than in the nonprofit sector. You can make a lot of money and donate generously to nonprofit causes, and you will not be the first to do so.

On the other hand, if your "cause component" is reasonably high, and if money is not your all-consuming motivation, it is possible to live a good and satisfying life in the nonprofit sector. Donald Trump or Lee Iacocca might not be happy working for a nonprofit, but not everyone wants to be a Trump or an Iacocca.

To attract competent people, nonprofits have raised salaries and enhanced benefits—so much so that, in many instances, the benefits are better than those offered in private industry. Partly, this compensates for salary differentials. Partly, the absence of the profit motive demarcates a different culture and outlook, often the envy of better-paid and more harassed colleagues in the business sector.

However, do not think for a moment that nonprofit work is stress-free. Turnover is very high in all echelons, particularly at the top. Because most nonprofits are small businesses, they often lack the resources to operate efficiently, though they may be highly effective. Moreover, board members may lack the interest, information, or experience to govern attentively. In private industry board members are usually beneficial owners, but for nonprofits they hold the assets in trust, and they may watch their personal assets a lot more carefully than those of the charities they direct.

Nonprofits are often poorly run because the CEOs are not trained managers. Size has little to do with it, for in one institution, where the annual budget exceeded $200 million annually, the CEO, a physician, said he could not read, much less understand, a balance sheet. Lack of resources and poor management exact a fearsome toll. People burn out because stress is combustible. On the positive side, high turnover also pushes up salaries. Accordingly, there is more aggressive recruiting in the middle, upper, and top ranks. As nonprofit boards and executives seek greater professionalism in their managers, they are forced to compete for the people they want and to compensate for the high risks they expect them to take.

Raiding other nonprofits is common, in part because NFPs are increasingly using executive search firms to help fill upper-middle to top management positions. Search firms fill slots by raiding, because there is no other way. As nonprofits are sometimes squeamish about raiding each other, the search firm is the buffer.

In one search the Oram Group recently completed, the "package" included an outside, windowed office, a car, club dues, and relocation expense. Though this may seem cushy, the candidate accepted a high-pressure, do-or-die fundraising job. If she fails or burns out, she will not descend to earth in a golden parachute she folded herself. More likely, she will be tossed out with a few months severance pay, no stock options—and instructions to return the car! As turnover among fundraisers is particularly high, if she stays in place three or four years, both she and the employer will be satisfied.

Competition. Nonprofits are in a battle for survival in an increasingly competitive marketplace. First, they compete with other nonprofits, as many services are duplicated elsewhere.

One of my prospective clients was a good community hospital in a New England college town. Mainly at the insistence of their public relations officer, they overhauled their maternity and new-born wing. Medically, there was not a thing wrong with what they had, but it was not "user friendly." Mothers and fathers-to-be out hospital-shopping passed by this fine hospital and went 50, even 100 miles away for what they wanted—essentially hotel services.

Second, many services are duplicated in the same community. Third, nonprofits compete against government in virtually every service category including health, education, welfare, social action, and recreation. Fourth, they compete against private business, offering the same or similar services. Though nonprofits may sometimes loosely describe these entrepreneurial activities as "fundraising," they sell travel packages, books, computers, jewelry, radio and television programs, even condoms, to name just a few items.

Myth and Reality

The nonprofit sector is truly peculiar. It has evolved within a social and economic system that is neither purely capitalistic nor purely socialistic. Both government and private business stop short of a natural compact with each of us—business because it cannot, and government because it will not.

In the breach there exists an economic system all its own, the dimensions of which are still not fully defined but probably approximate 5 percent or more of our gross national product. Over 7 million people (Hodgkinson, 1986) have accepted employment in the sector. Some are noble, some are base—some are overpaid, but most are not. For many, working for a nonprofit does their heart good. For those lucky enough to have their lives in balance, work in the nonprofit sector is a satisfying blend of good intention, reasonable compensation, and a job they look forward to on Monday—and leave with relief on Friday.

3

Compensation Patterns in the Sector

Anne Preston

Compensation in the nonprofit sector has historically been lower than compensation in the private for-profit sector and in the public sector. While this salary gap continues to exist, there is a lot of variation in nonprofit salaries. In many industries and occupations, nonprofit salaries are high and rising, while in others nonprofit salaries remain low, given the education and skill levels of the employees.

Most nonprofit executives interviewed for this book are aware of the problems that arise from a low salary distribution. In particular, organizations cannot attract and retain qualified workers if they are competing against private for-profit business firms that pay significantly higher salaries. Therefore, many people in the sector hope that nonprofit salaries will begin to increase toward competitive levels. This chapter reviews some facts and figures about nonprofit salaries and outlines national, regional, and industry-specific patterns of salary distribution.

Nonprofit Salaries

National studies generally conclude that, for workers of similar skill levels, nonprofit salaries are on average 5–20 percent lower than private for-profit salaries (Preston, 1989a), and 11 percent lower than public sector salaries (Preston, 1988a). However, these salary differences are not uniform across occupations, fields, or gender, so we will look at the specifics behind the averages.

Compared to Private For-Profit Salaries. The difference in salaries earned by nonprofit and private for-profit employees tends to increase with occupational level. Blue-collar workers and clerical staff of nonprofit firms earn wage and salaries comparable to their for-profit counterparts. However, professionals and managers of nonprofit firms experience the largest wage losses relative to their earning power in the for-profit sector, roughly a loss of 20 percent in wages (Preston, 1989).

Historically, scholars and practitioners in the sector felt that the reason this differential persisted was the high degree of psychic reward associated with work in the sector. Nonprofit employees feel satisfaction in doing work that is socially worthwhile, or they feel that nonprofit organizations allow employees more responsibility and independence. They are willing to trade off wages for these non-pecuniary benefits. However, some practitioners are beginning to question the value of such rewards. According to Liz Sode, President of the Beatrice Foundation, "If we're counting on people to be attracted to the sector because of non-salary benefits, we'd better make sure those rewards are there. I am not sure they are. Work is becoming a sacrifice." (Liz Sode is profiled in this book in Section 6, Philanthropic Career Profiles.)

As illustrated in Figure 3.1, gender differences also exist in the nonprofit/for-profit salary picture, with an interesting twist: Men who choose to work in the nonprofit sector experience a loss in wages as high as 47 percent, while women experience a loss in wages of only 0 to 5 percent (Preston, 1989b). The ratio of male to female employees in the nonprofit and for-profit work forces may give a clue to this pattern.

The white-collar nonprofit workforce, which comprises the majority of nonprofit jobs, is roughly 75 percent female. Even though the percentage of male employees increases with occupational status, women make up the majority of employees in almost every occupational classification. On the other hand, while the white-collar for-profit work force is roughly 50 percent female, the number of females in top-level management positions remains small.

Historically, occupational and wage discrimination in the private for-profit sector has resulted in women being overrepresented in lower level jobs and earning roughly 30 percent lower pay than equally qualified men. Because men have better opportunities than women

FIGURE 3.1. HOURLY WAGE DIFFERENTIALS BETWEEN FOR-PROFIT AND NONPROFIT WORKERS BY GENDER.

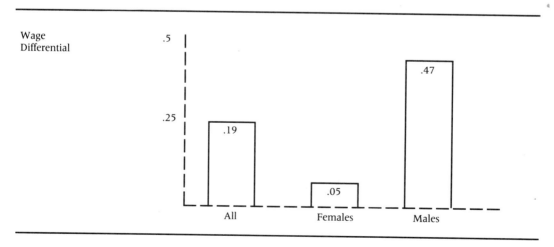

Source: "Women in the White Collar Nonprofit Sector," using data from *The Survey of Job Characteristics, 1980.*

for high wages and good upward job mobility in the for-profit sector, those men who choose work in the nonprofit sector are making a greater sacrifice. As women's opportunities for high-paying for-profit jobs increase, so will their proportionate loss in taking nonprofit jobs.

The average differential between nonprofit and for-profit salaries also differs by field. Statistics based on data from a 1977 survey of day-care workers revealed that nonprofit salaries of care givers were comparable to, and in some instances slightly above, for-profit salaries (Preston, 1988b). Also, a 1974 study of employees of nursing homes showed no significant differences between nonprofit and for-profit salaries (Borjas, 1983, pp. 231–46). However, Weisbrod's study of lawyers' salaries in 1974 revealed that private for-profit lawyers earned 20 percent higher salaries than public interest lawyers (Weisbrod, 1983, p.p. 246–63).

In fact, one can divide the nonprofit sector into three distinct types of field, each with a different salary pattern. First, there are the fields in which nonprofits and for-profits directly compete both in service provision and in staffing of similar jobs. In these fields, such as day care, hospitals, and nursing homes, the salaries of the nonprofits and for-profits are comparable.

Second, there are the fields, such as television, radio, and law, in which nonprofit and for-profit firms fill different niches. Public interest law firms serve the poor and underprivileged, while corporate firms serve businesses; similarly, public television is a different animal from network or cable television. The jobs involved in nonprofit law and nonprofit television tend to have either a high educational or social welfare component not incorporated in the for-profit jobs. Therefore, these nonprofit firms may be attracting a different type of employee: one who is willing to sacrifice wages for the opportunity to further a cause. As a result, nonprofit and for-profit salaries may be very different.

Finally, there are the nonprofit fields, like philanthropy and religion, which have no private sector counterpart. Because of the lack of private sector competition, nonprofit firms in these fields generally pay low salaries, relative to the salaries that employees with comparable skills could command in for-profit industries.

Compared to Public Salaries. The average difference in salaries between comparable nonprofit and public sector workers is, as mentioned above, 11 percent. This average difference is subject to many of the same gender and occupation variations as the average differences between salaries of nonprofit and for-profit organizations. Men choosing to work in the nonprofit rather than the public sector experience a more severe wage loss (24 percent) than women (5 percent). In addition, as Preston (1988a) notes, managers and professionals who choose to work in the nonprofit sector rather than the public sector experience a more severe wage loss (13 percent) than clerical workers (7 percent).

The difference in salaries between the two sectors seems surprising, since government agencies and nonprofit organizations provide many of the same services—social welfare, child care, education, and health services. From the preceding arguments concerning competition between nonprofit and for-profit firms, one would expect similar salaries between the two sectors. However, it is important to realize that the public sector also includes the administration of local, state, and federal governments.

If one separates government employees into administration and service providers, whether local, state, or federal, the picture is very different. Comparing workers of similar education and skills, nonprofit employees earn on average 28 percent lower salaries than public sector administrators. However, as illustrated in Figure 3.2, the average nonprofit employee earns only a 4 percent lower salary than a comparable public sector service provider. This 4 percent salary differential may be due in part to the fact that more service workers are unionized in the public than in the nonprofit sector.

Furthermore, while the service workers in the nonprofit and public sectors may be providing services in direct competition with each other, the jobs themselves may be very different. Public sector services operate in a large bureaucracy where rigid job descriptions and wage scales may limit the autonomy and scope of responsibility of a single employee. In contrast, the relatively small, independent nonprofit firm gives the employee more freedom to challenge the boundaries of the job and to introduce initiative and change into the service provision process. As John Garrison, Chief Executive Officer of the National Easter Seal Society, says, "What I like about nonprofit work as opposed to government is there is more opportunity for experimenting, more flexibility and change." (John Garrison is profiled in this book in Section 5, "General Management Career Profiles.")

Effects of Institutional and Worker Characteristics

Regional salary studies of nonprofit firms have documented nonprofit salary patterns throughout the country. The results of 1986–1987 surveys conducted in San Francisco, Colorado, New Jersey, and Long Island are outlined below. Although their data and methods of analysis

FIGURE 3.2. HOURLY WAGE DIFFERENTIALS BETWEEN GOVERNMENT AND NONPROFIT WORKERS BY TYPE OF GOVERNMENT JOB.

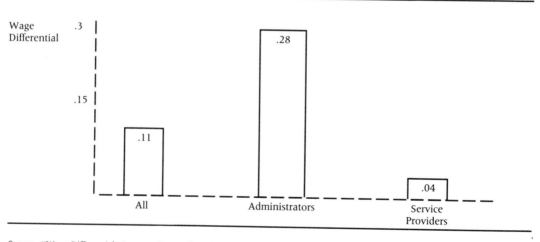

Source: "Wage Differentials Between Nonprofit and Public Sector Employees," using data from *The Current Population* Surveys, 1974, 1977, and 1979.

differ in ways that make results not directly comparable, they do suggest some dominant patterns on which those entering the field can base expectations about earnings.

From the surveys, variables with major influence on salaries appear to be size of organization, category or field of the organization, similarity of job content and requirements to positions in the private or government sectors, and, to varying degrees, gender. Other influential factors may be population served by the organization and work-relevant experience and tenure.

SAN FRANCISCO. As reported by Haroniau and Shilling (1986), a total of 297 nonprofit agencies in the San Francisco Bay area participated in a survey to determine nonprofit salaries as of January 1, 1986. The agencies had 7,360 employees, of whom 37 percent were part-time and 80 percent were women. (Part-time employees decreased as size of budget increased. Percent of women in job category decreased with increased responsibility of the job. Only 52 percent of executive directors were women.)

For the survey, jobs were classified in four supervisory (management) categories and five non-supervisory categories; professional positions topped the non-supervisory positions. Within the categories, jobs covered 42 functions, which were classified as office, administration, arts, service, or "other."

Salaries. Monthly salaries were calculated based on a 40-hour work week; any part-time worker's monthly salary was adjusted to full-time equivalent at the same hourly rate. Average monthly salaries varied from $3,161 for highest level management positions to $904 for the lowest level clerical positions.

Organization Field. The highest paid supervisory employees worked in medical, computer, legal, fundraising, and research positions; the lowest paid supervisors were in preschool education, food services, animal care, child care, and transportation. For non-supervisory personnel, the highest paid employees worked in medical, physical therapy, research, personnel, and computer functions, and the lowest paid employees worked in child care, residential care, transportation, food services, and recreation functions.

Budget Size. Salaries for all supervisory positions increased according to budget size, but the largest differences occurred for executive directors. Agencies with budgets between $20,000 and $150,000 paid executive directors on average $2,292 per month, while agencies with budgets over $2 million paid executive directors average monthly salaries of $5,099. Except for the highest level of non-supervisory job (high-level professional service providers), where salaries increased with budget size, there was no clear relationship between budget size and salary for non-supervisory jobs.

Gender. Men earned more than women for all supervisory positions, and the differential increased with responsibility level. As illustrated in Figure 3.3, in the two lowest management positions, men earned salaries 17 percent higher than women, while in the two highest management level positions, men earned salaries 30 percent higher than women's salaries. There was no significant difference in salaries for men and women in either the professional or clerical positions.

Experience/Education. Salaries increased with years of job-related experience in the field as well as with years of education.

FIGURE 3.3. MALE–FEMALE WAGE DIFFERENTIALS BY RESPONSIBILITY LEVEL IN SUPERVISORY NONPROFIT JOBS.

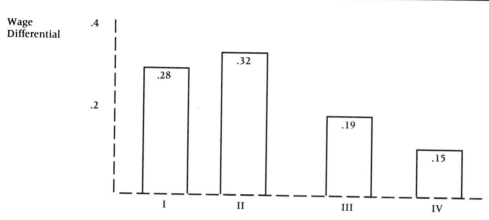

Wage
Differential

I — Top Paid Manager
II — Manager of a Major Division of the Agency
III — Manager of a Department of Agency Services or Administration
IV — Coordinator or Leader of a team or Work Unit

Source: *1986 Wage and Benefit Survey of and for San Francisco Bay Area Tax-Exempt Nonprofit Organizations*

Benefits. Information on benefit packages was also reported in the survey, and, as with wages, the larger the budget, the higher the value of the benefits given to employees. Health and dental insurance programs were the most frequent benefits: 90 percent of all responding agencies contributed to health and 65 percent contributed to dental programs. Only 35 percent and 32 percent of reporting firms contributed to life and retirement insurance programs, respectively.

COLORADO. The Technical Assistance Center of Denver reported in 1987 on a survey administered that year to 1,000 nonprofit organizations in the state of Colorado. One hundred and six firms responded, employing 11,423 paid employees, of which 32 percent were employed part-time. Salary data were collected for 13 positions commonly found in nonprofit organizations. These positions included categories for high-level management, controllers, fundraisers, professionals, clerical workers, and maintenance workers. Salaries were reported on a yearly basis, and there was no effort to adjust part-time salaries to full-time levels. However, many of the patterns that emerged in the San Francisco survey were also displayed in the Colorado survey.

Salaries and Budget Size. Yearly salaries ranged from an average of $36,874 for executive directors to an average of $8,738 for maintenance workers. As shown in Figure 3.4, in all white-collar jobs there was a strong positive relationship between size of budget and salary, and the relationship strengthened as the responsibility level of the job increased. Executive

FIGURE 3.4. AVERAGE SALARIES OF EXECUTIVE DIRECTORS BY SIZE OF ORGANIZATION.

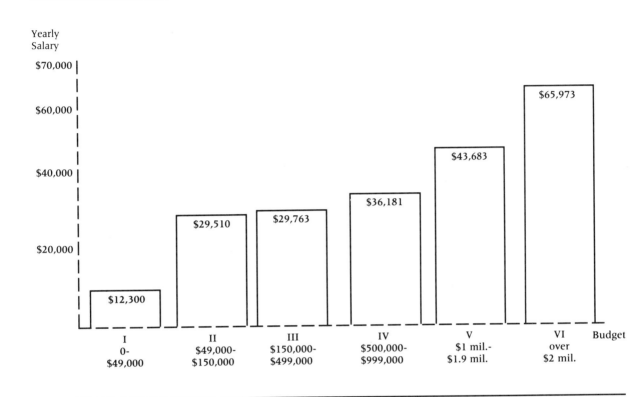

Source: *1987 Colorado Wage and Benefits Survey.*

directors in agencies with a budget greater than $2 million earned salaries that were on average 124 percent higher than salaries of executive directors in agencies with budgets between $50,000 and $149,999. The survey made no distinction between salary levels for jobs held by men and women, so no gender-based salaries were reported.

Population served. The survey suggests a salary determinant not observed in the San Francisco survey. Firms were classified according to population served: local, multi-county, state, or national. Firms serving a national population tended to have the highest average salary levels in most job classifications, and they were also more likely to have larger budgets than the agencies serving smaller populations. Agencies serving a multi-county population paid the lowest average salaries.

NEW JERSEY. A salary study of 196 nonprofits, located in New Jersey in 1987 documents similar patterns, as reported by the Center for Non-Profit Corporations in Trenton. As in the other studies, salary calculations are presented by job descriptions that range from executive director to secretary.

Salaries and Budget Size. The average salary of an executive director was $35,381, with a maximum of $86,000, while the average salary of a secretary was $13,557 with a maximum of $29,220. Again, the study documents a strong relationship between the salary in each of the job categories and the size of the organization, whether it is measured by budget size or number of employees.

Experience. Unlike the San Francisco study, the New Jersey data display no obvious relation between years of work experience and wages of employees. Additionally, tenure at the job has a positive effect on salaries for male executive directors only.

Gender. Similar to the San Francisco study, female employees outnumbered male employees in the nonprofit sector. In addition, nonprofit male employees in New Jersey generally earned higher salaries than females, and the differential increased for more prestigious jobs. Male executive directors earned 30 percent higher salaries than female executive directors, but male administrators earned salaries only 9 percent higher than females in comparable positions. The male–female differentials calculated in the 1987 survey were slightly smaller than those calculated in a similar 1986 survey. (The 1987 version of the San Francisco survey also calculated slightly smaller male–female differentials than were calculated in the 1986 survey. However, more sophisticated statistical analysis would have to be done to determine if there was a real trend toward the narrowing of the gender gap in wages.)

LONG ISLAND. The survey conducted on Long Island offers insight into the forces behind some of the salary differentials, including those documented in the other geographical regions (Preston, 1987). Salary and employment data were received from 124 non-religious nonprofit organizations. Employment data revealed that 80 percent of the work force were female, 38 percent were professional workers (rather than managerial, clerical, or blue collar workers), and 40 percent were part-time workers.

Organization Fields. The organizations were classified into categories of health, education, social services, and culture. Health care organizations, which included both regional chapters of national voluntary health organizations and direct service providers, stood out from the rest of the nonprofit organizations. They tended to be much larger than the others both in budget and number of employees.

Benefits. Health care organizations also gave the best benefit packages: 73 percent of the organizations contributed to health care and life insurance plans for full-time employees; 62 percent contributed to retirement plans; and 45 percent contributed to dental plans. Social service organizations gave comparable medical benefits (health and dental plans), but only 53 percent and 29 percent of these organizations contributed, respectively, to life insurance and retirement plans. Cultural and educational organizations had the least desirable fringe benefit plans: Only 40 percent contributed to health care and 20 percent to each of the other types of benefits.

Salaries. Based on hourly wages, a comparison of workers with similar education and labor force experience revealed that health was the highest paying sector, followed by education, and then social services and culture. Specifically, health organizations paid 21 percent higher wages than educational organizations, which, in turn, paid 13 percent higher wages than social service and cultural organizations.

Competition. These differing salary levels may result from the amount of competition that organizations in the different sectors face. This is illustrated in Figure 3.5. Health organizations face competition for employees from both private for-profit and government firms. To attract good employees, health organizations must keep salaries comparable to those earned in the other two sectors. Educational organizations also face labor market competition, from public schools and universities. However, because there is less government and business competition in culture and social services, nonprofits in these areas are insulated from competitive pressures to raise salaries to levels commensurate with the skill levels of employees.

Gender. As in the other regional studies, average wages of men in the nonprofit sector tended to be higher than average wages of women, but in this case there was no evidence that the differential increased with the prestige of the job. The male–female wage differential was 26 percent for executive directors and 34 percent for non-executive directors. However, in this study comparisons were then drawn between men and women who held the same levels of education, tenure on the job, and experience, and who were working in firms with

FIGURE 3.5. AVERAGE WAGES OF NONPROFIT EMPLOYEES BY MISSION OF ORGANIZATION.

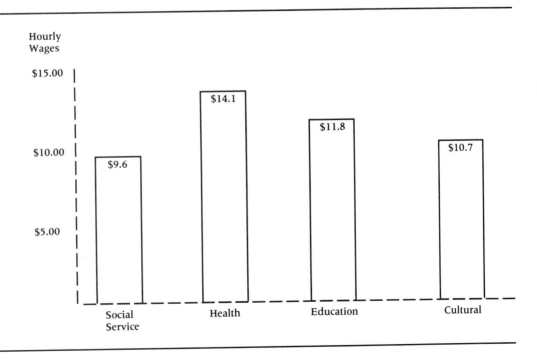

Source: "Compensation Patterns in the Nonprofit Sector: A Case Study of Long Island."

the same budget and mission. Using comparisons that control for these characteristics, there was no difference in male and female salaries.

The data did reveal that men and women in the sector have different personal characteristics and that they work for different types of organizations. Men tended to have slightly higher levels of education than women, more years of labor market experience, and higher tenure with the firm. Both education and tenure are significant determinants of wages. Even more important, men were more likely to work in organizations with large budgets. The average size of the budget of a male employee's organization was $1,110,587, while the average size of a budget of a female employee's organization was $557,566. This contrast was even more severe when comparing budget size controlled by male executive directors and by female executive directors. As in the other studies, wages increased dramatically with budget size.

Within the sector and regarding identical jobs, it appears that there is no salary discrimination against females in the form of lower pay. However, there is a selection process of men into larger organizations and women into smaller organizations, which results in gender-based salary differences. Without further study, one cannot be sure what accounts for these differences. There may be discriminatory hiring practices in the larger nonprofit firms, or there may be fewer women in the pool of applicants to the larger national organizations. Women seeking employment in the nonprofit sector may have family obligations that force them to seek work close to home in local community service organizations.

CONCLUSION. The findings of the surveys emphasize a few dominant employment and compensation patterns in the nonprofit sector. First, the nonprofit labor force has a disproportionately large number of female and part-time workers. Second, there are male–female salary differentials in the sector that may be as large as 30 percent for management positions. Third, salaries increase with budget size, especially for high-level management and professional positions. Finally, there are systematic differences in salaries by function or mission of the firm. Specifically, employees in health, computers, and research earn relatively high salaries, while employees in social services earn low salaries. Mission-specific salary differentials will be further explored in the following section.

Salaries in Some Nonprofit Fields

The previous regional studies show that nonprofit salaries vary a great deal by the type of field in which the nonprofit firm operates. These differences reflect to a large extent the marketability of the skills that the employee in the particular industry has developed. If those skills are attractive to for-profit business employers, then the employee's salary will be relatively high, as the nonprofit must compete with for-profits for skilled employees. If those skills are not marketable in the private for-profit sector, the employee is more likely to face low salaries in the nonprofit sector.

Further, if an employee invests in skills that are not transferable to the for-profit sector, the transition from nonprofit employment to for-profit employment will be very difficult. Therefore, as Jonathan Cook, Executive Director of the Support Centers of America, says, the decision by employees to "go into the nonpofit sector . . . is probably going to hurt them financially for the rest of their lives." (Mr. Cook is profiled in this book in Section 9, "Service Providers.")

The following gives representative salaries for employees in a few nonprofit fields. It points out some high-paying opportunities in the sector as well as relatively low-paying jobs. The aim is to inform readers contemplating a career in the nonprofit sector about the monetary sacrifices such a career may require. The goal is not to discourage, but to make readers aware of the price that nonprofit employees may pay for the satisfaction of working in an organization that contributes to the common good.

Art Museums. Except in the top-level positions in the largest museums, managers in art museums tend to be low paid, given their education and skills. The Association of Art Museum Directors issued a 1987 Salary Survey of active and associate member museums, which included museums with budgets in excess of $1 million or museums with university affiliations. According to the survey, the average salary for a director was $65,000; however, this average varied from $48,500 for the smallest museums (operating budget between $400,000 and $1,000,000) to $95,600 for the largest museums (operating budget over $7,500,000). The pattern in which salaries varied according to size of museum was observed for all managerial positions surveyed.

Average salaries for museum administrators and development officers was $40,000, and public relations officers earned an average yearly salary of $25,500. Chief curators earned average yearly salaries of $37,597, while exhibition curators earned only $29,000 per year.

Medical and life insurance benefits tended to be well provided, with roughly two thirds of all museums surveyed giving full coverage and the rest providing these benefits in a system where payments are split with the employee. Roughly one half of the museums surveyed paid for full coverage of disability insurance, dental insurance, and pension plans. In addition virtually all museums gave a paid vacation.

Associations. The American Society of Association Executives reported, in a 1987 survey of 6,600 associations, that compensation of association executives is average. A chief paid executive earns an average salary of $70,800, a deputy chief paid executive earns $49,700, and directors of advertising, communication, education , human resources, and public relations earn salaries in the high thirty thousands. However, salaries of all positions vary by size of organization and by geographical scope. For example, executive directors of associations with a budget of less than $200,000 earn salaries in the high thirty thousands while their counterparts in associations with budgets over $10 million earn average salaries well above $125,000.

Associations serving a national clientele pay chief executive officers average salaries of approximately $80,000, while associations serving state and local clienteles pay their CEOs salaries in the mid and low fifty thousand dollar range, respectively. Trade associations, those with company membership, pay higher salaries to chief paid executives and deputy chief paid executives than do professional associations that have individual membership. However, this pattern does not extend to all positions.

Personnel practices of associations are flexible. Only 27 percent of associations have established salary grades for management personnel and only 40 percent have established salary ranges. Only 33 percent of chief paid executives have formal employment contracts, and in 63 percent of these, there is a clause allowing the association to terminate the chief paid executive's employment before termination of the contract. Salary increases for management personnel tend to be merit-based, with 79 percent of associations giving merit raises. Cost of living increases, general across the board increases, and length of service increases are used by 35 percent, 30 percent, and 12 percent of the responding associations, respectively. Finally, bonus systems have been established for chief paid executives, deputy chief paid executives, and department heads in only 22 percent, 13 percent, and 14 percent of the associations, respectively.

Foundations. Foundation work can pay well. However, as in other nonprofits, salaries vary by size of the organization, and salaries are highest in the foundations with the largest financial resources. The Council on Foundations' 1982 Compensation and Benefits Survey showed that male CEOs in foundations with assets over $100 million earned average salaries of $100,809, equivalent to $114,513 in 1986 dollars (reported in Odendahl, Boris, and Daniels, 1985).

Male CEOs in foundations with assets under $10 million earned salaries of $35,147, equivalent to $39,925 in 1986 dollars.

Program officers earned salaries that ranged from the low forty thousands in the largest foundations (equivalent to the high forty thousands in 1986 dollars) to the low twenty thousands in the smallest foundations (equivalent to the mid twenty thousands in 1986 dollars). In most salary positions, women earned salaries between 60 and 90 percent of those of men in similar positions and in similar foundations. In addition, the type of degree earned by the employee had an important effect on salary. Employees with PhDs, JDs, or MDs received higher salaries than comparable employees with master's degrees who, in turn, received higher salaries than employees who had earned only bachelor's degrees.

Fundraising. While fundraising can be a lucrative field, salary levels depend heavily on the type of organization for which the fundraiser works. A 1985 survey administered by the National Society of Fundraising Executives collected information on salaries of 3,005 fundraisers. Although average salaries were not calculated, the information on numbers of responses within certain salary scales suggests certain patterns. First, consultants earned the highest salaries, with 61 percent earning over $40,000 per year and 15 percent earning over $75,000 per year. Development specialists at hospitals were close behind, with 58 percent earning over $40,000 and 5 percent over $75,000. Fundraisers in local community agencies, retirement communities, and environmental organizations earned the lowest salaries. Less than 23 percent of these employees earned over $40,000.

As in other nonprofit fields, male fundraisers earned higher salaries than female fundraisers. Less than one third of the men but two thirds of the women earned less than $30,000 annually. In addition, the 6 percent highest paid women earned above $50,000 while the 6 percent highest paid men earned above $75,000.

Health Care. Because of stiff competition among nonprofit, for-profit, and government hospitals, this industry pays relatively high salaries to its managers. According to the 1987 Management Compensation Study commissioned by the American Society for Health Care Human Resources Administration and conducted by Management Compensation Services, Inc., salaries are more and more being determined, at least in part, by performance of the employee. Unlike other nonprofit industries, there is a move to improve employee productivity by tying compensation to productivity.

The survey, based on 296 health care organizations, which include 34 multi-health care firms, reveals that multi-service health care firms pay significantly higher salaries than single acute care facilities for all positions. A president of a single acute care facility received an average salary of $132,300, while his counterpart in a multi-care facility received $185,200. The chief financial officer earned on average $69,100 in a single acute care and $86,500 in a multi-care facility, and a human resources officer earned $50,100 and $63,800, in an acute care and multi-care facility, respectively.

In addition, as in other nonprofit industries, pay is positively related to the size of the hospital when measured by number of employees. The top administrator in a hospital with fewer than 600 employees earned a yearly salary of $73,800 while his counterpart in a hospital with over 2,200 employees earned $132,800. This pattern extended for all positions surveyed. For example, the head of marketing in the smallest set of hospitals earned a yearly salary of $39,000, while the same position was paid a salary of $58,600 in the largest hospitals.

Bonuses are becoming a more prevalent form of compensation for hospitals. In 1987, 21 percent of the organizations offered short-term incentive plans for high-level management—an increase of 5 percent over 1986. This type of compensation plan may enable organizations to focus management behavior on high-priority goals in a highly competitive environment.

Independent Schools. A 1986 survey conducted by the National Association of Independent Schools confirms the accepted wisdom that private school education is a low-paying field. However, there is considerable variation in salaries between administrators and teachers and across different types and sizes of schools. While the median salary of school heads was $53,000, day schools tended to pay slightly higher salaries ($53,000) than boarding schools ($48,500), and boys' schools paid higher salaries ($57,250) than girls' schools ($50,575). In addition, as enrollment rose, school head salaries rose as well.

Median salaries of other administrators were significantly below school head salaries, with the assistant head, the upper, middle, and lower school heads, the business officers, and development officers all earning salaries in the low to middle thirty thousands. Teachers' salaries, which do not include any summer compensation, were significantly below administrative salaries, with median salaries ranging from $17,000 to $21,500. Similar to the pattern observed with salaries of school heads, salaries for other administrators and teachers were higher in day schools than in boarding schools and higher in boys' schools than in girls' schools.

National Voluntary Organizations. National voluntary organizations pay salaries on the high end of the scale for nonprofit firms. In 1987, the National Council, Inc., and the

National Assembly of National Voluntary Health and Social Welfare Organizations released their Management Compensation Report. This salary study of voluntary health and human service organizations reported an average total cash compensation for top executive officers of $93,000. The range of salary values reported for this position extended from $40,000 to $175,000.

In addition, while the United Way did not respond to this survey, other sources reveal that United Way pays its executive officers salaries that may even exceed these figures. As reported in the February 1988, *Nonprofit Times,* salaries for executive directors of nine large regional offices exceeded $100,000 in 1987, and the salary of the president of the United Way of America exceeded $200,000.

Other high-paying positions in these voluntary organizations included top positions in medical services ($70,800) and development ($59,100). Employees in less prestigious positions, such as public relations, program staff, or art directors, earned average salaries in the low to mid thirty thousands.

For top-level positions, salaries were higher in organizations with higher budgets and in organizations with a larger number of employees. Health service organizations paid higher salaries than youth service organizations, which in turn paid higher salaries than social service organizations. While these same relationships appeared in the lower level positions, they were less distinct.

Public Broadcasting. A career in public broadcasting is relatively low-paying, with the exception of high-level positions in the largest public television stations. A Corporation for Public Broadcasting Survey of 177 public television stations in 1987 revealed that the CEO of a public TV station earned an average annual salary of $59,111. However, this salary figure varied greatly by budget size. The CEO in charge of a station with a budget of less than $1 million earned on average $38,889, while a CEO in charge of a budget in excess of $10 million earned an average annual salary of $98,610—over 2.5 times the top salary in the smaller station.

In addition, salaries tended to vary by the type of license of the station. Those organizations with a community license, given to independently created nonprofit corporations, tended to pay the highest salaries. Public television stations with local licenses paid the second highest salaries, and stations with university licenses or state-authorized licenses paid the lowest salaries.

Other high-paid officials included vice-presidents for programming, whose salaries tended to fall right below those of the CEOs, and vice-presidents for finance, who earned salaries that average in the low fifty thousands. Development directors in public television earned average salaries of $36,740, which is relatively low within the development profession. The average business manager earned $29,301. Managers in the industry, including positions such as director of programming development, director of personnel, and director of public relations, earned average salaries in the low thirty thousands. Again, all salaries increased with budget size of the station and varied by license type.

Religion. There are very few managerial positions within religious organizations. As a result, a career path is not well defined. The top-level managerial position tends to be a church or temple business administrator, with other non-professional support staff including clerical workers, bookkeepers, and administrative assistants. Salary levels for all positions are relatively low.

According to a 1986–1987 salary survey administered by the National Association of Temple Administrators Serving Reform Congregations in the U.S. and Canada, temple administrators tended to earn salaries on the high end of the scale of church business administrator salaries. Average gross earnings for a temple administrator, which include base salary, expense allowance, car allowance, housing allowance, and annual bonus, was $41,873. Average earnings differed by gender, with male administrators earning an average of $50,779 and female administrators earning an average of $32,374. Earnings increased with the size of the temple, and male administrators were more likely than females to work in the larger temples.

Benefits to temple administrators were good; 58 percent of temples contributed at least 15 percent of salary to a pension plan. However, these figures were much higher for temples employing a male administrator than for temples employing a female administrator. Regarding insurance, 82 percent of the temples contributed 100 percent of the premiums for health care, and 72 percent covered 100 percent of the premiums for disability. Ninety-five percent of the temples offered three weeks or more of paid vacation, while 75 percent offered a four-week paid vacation to their administrators.

A 1986 Church Staff Salary Survey administered by the Ministers Financial Service Association and the National Association of Church Business Administration reveals that the compensation of church business administrators was on average $39,223. Compensation was measured by the sum of base salary, housing utilities, and auto expenses. Salaries tended to increase with the size of worship attendance and size of the budget. In addition, salaries differed by denomination, but the data showed regional variations so that national patterns of difference are unclear. However, for all regions the Roman Catholic church tended to pay salaries on the low end of the scale for all positions. This pattern was most distinct for priests, who are paid with the assurance that they will not need to support a family.

Entry-level positions, which include secretaries, administrative assistants, and bookkeepers, are low paid. Administrative assistants earned an average of $24,424 per year; bookkeepers earned $17,637 per year; and secretaries earned $13,521 per year.

4

Educating and Training Managers for the Sector

Lilly Cohen

GROWTH OF THE SECTOR

Significant growth of the nonprofit sector, in numbers and size of organizations as well as in numbers of employees, began in the mid-1960s. As Congress appropriated the funds required to support President Johnson's Great Society programs, a steady stream of new funds began to flow to the states and local communities. The creation of thousands of new nonprofit agencies and the enlargement of existing ones was the logical response to an unprecedented opportunity to develop a broad array of human service programs—in education, health, social welfare, arts and culture, civic affairs, and community services. Illustrative of this growth is the fact that philanthropic nonprofit employment grew 43 percent between 1972 and 1982 (Rudney and Weitzman, 1983).

The economic recession and funding cutbacks that followed in the mid-1970s and into the 1980s, during the Nixon, Ford, and Reagan administrations, resulted in financial difficulties for many nonprofits that had become dependent on federal funds, particularly the newer grassroots community organizations. The organizations that survived the cutbacks learned that it was not enough to concentrate their efforts on the design, content, and quality of their particular program, service, or cause. They discovered that a high degree of management competence and fundraising skill was essential to assure financially healthy organizations that could survive in a competitive environment with scarce resources. Government and private funders began to evaluate the management of applicant organizations, preferring to invest in those that were well managed. A bold idea, a noble cause, a new solution had to be supported by a demonstrable capacity to handle the practical aspects of the undertaking. Infusing professional skill into all aspects of management and fundraising became the new priority for nonprofits.

In this climate of high interest in improving the management of nonprofit organizations, many groups began to develop a variety of education and training programs. Among these were academic institutions, associations, consulting firms, nonprofit technical assistance centers, private schools, and some of the larger nonprofits themselves. Institutes, conferences, seminars, workshops, and credit courses proliferated. New graduate programs, academic concentrations, certificate programs, and individual courses were designed, some using or adapting existing business and public management curricula. A growing body of research generated new information and theories about effective management of the sector and its subsectors. Also, a new literature of practical and theoretical texts and journals evolved.

Throughout the country a number of different graduate program models were developed and tested at universities in schools of public administration, business, and social welfare and through newly established nonprofit study centers. There is no agreement about whether nonprofit management can be defined as a generic field of professional study, like public management or business management, or whether its uniqueness can be captured by a cluster of courses that cover the most significant nonprofit management subjects, which are then incorporated under existing graduate programs.

A leadership conference at the University of San Francisco in 1986 explored this and other critical issues from multiple perspectives. One result of the conference was *Educating Managers of Nonprofit Organizations* (O'Neill and Young, 1988), a collection of thoughtful essays reflecting the current thinking in this developing field of study. There is a consensus that managers of nonprofit organizations need to be educated—but no agreement on how this can best be accomplished.

Independent Sector (IS), the national organization established in 1980 to represent the broad interests of the sector, has organized an active forum to discuss educational issues and research agendas. IS also publishes periodic research and nonprofit management education directories, thereby contributing to an orderly development of this emerging field. At its May 1988 Academic Focus Group meeting on Educating Leaders and Managers of Nonprofit Organizations, IS reported the existence of 21 academic centers dedicated to the sector (Figure 4.1) and 300 college and university programs with offerings in nonprofit management.

FIGURE 4.1. ACADEMIC CENTERS AND PROGRAMS DEDICATED TO THE NONPROFIT SECTOR

Office of Executive Education
Baruch College
The City University of New York
17 Lexington Avenue
New York, NY 10016
(212) 725-3225

Boston College
Social Welfare Research Institute
515 McGuinn Hall
Room 516
Chestnut Hill, MA 02167
(617) 552-4071

Case Western Reserve University
Mandel Center for Nonprofit Organizations
2035 Abington Road
Cleveland, OH 44106
(216) 368-2275

City University of New York
Center for the Study of Philanthropy
Graduate School and University Center
33 West 42nd Street
Room 1512
New York, NY 10036
(212) 642-1600

Columbia University
School of Business
Institute for Nonprofit Management
218 Uris Hall
New York, NY 10027
(212) 280-2211

Duke University
Center for the Study of Philanthropy and
Volunteerism
4875 Duke Station
Durham, NC 27706
(919) 684-2672

Indiana University
Center on Philanthropy
241 Conference Center
850 West Michigan Street
Indianapolis, IN 46223
(317) 274-4200

The Johns Hopkins University
Institute for Policy Studies
Shriver Hall
Baltimore, MD 21218
(301) 338-7174

New School for Social Research
Graduate School of Management and Urban
Professions
Nonprofit Management Program
66 Fifth Avenue
New York, NY 10011
(212) 741-7910

New York University
Program on Philanthropy and the Law
40 Washington Square South
New York, NY 10012
(212) 998-6161

Roosevelt University
Public Administration Program
430 South Michigan Avenue
Chicago, IL 60605
(312) 341-3744

State University of New York at Stony Brook
W. Averell Harriman School of Management
and Policy
Stony Brook, NY 11794
(516) 632-7175

Tufts University
Center for Public Service
97 Talbot Avenue
Medford, MA 02155
(617) 381-3394

The Union for Experimenting Colleges and
Universities
Institute for Public Policy and Administration
1400 20th Street, NW
Suite 118
Washington, DC 20036
(202) 463-1961

University of Minnesota
Hubert H. Humphrey Institute of Public Affairs
300 Humphrey Center
301 19th Avenue South
Minneapolis, MN 55455
(612) 625-0669

University of Missouri-Kansas City
L. P. Cookingham Institute of Public Affairs
5100 Rockhill Road
Kansas City, MO 64110
(816) 276-2338

Virginia Cooperative Extension Service of VPI
and State University
Center for Volunteer Development
207 West Roanoke Street
Blacksburg, VA 24061
(703) 961-7966

Virginia Polytechnic Institute and State
University
Community, Leadership and Nonprofit
Management
2990 Telestar Court
Falls Church, VA 22042
(703) 698-6093

University of Colorado
Center for Public-Private Sector Cooperation
Graduate School of Public Affairs
100 14th Street
Campus Box 142
Denver, CO 80208
(303) 556-2825

University of San Francisco
Institute for Nonprofit Organization
Management
College of Professional Studies
Ignatian Heights
San Francisco, CA 94117-1080
(415) 666-6867

Yale University
Institution for Social and Policy Studies
Program on Nonprofit Organizations
PO Box 154 Yale Station
88 Trumbull Street
New Haven, CT 06520-7382
(203) 432-2124

Source: Adapted from INDEPENDENT SECTOR, May 1988 Academic Focus Group on Educating Leaders and Managers of Nonprofit Organizations.

The following pages are meant to assist readers in identifying the kinds of education and training programs that will suit their needs at different stages in their careers. The nonprofit sector needs educated workers, given its high concentration in service activities. A comparative study of the three sectors (Mirvis and Hackett, 1983), based on data from a 1977 Quality of Employment Survey, revealed that the nonprofit sector employed many more workers with college and graduate degrees (42.5 percent) as compared to the public sector (39.5 percent) and the private sector (11.6 percent). Furthermore, continuing professional development and learning are necessities in a sector that values and needs professionals with multiple skills. For the managers profiled in this volume, professional development appears to be a constantly high priority in their lives, suggesting that nonprofit managers can ill afford complacency and stagnation.

THE NEED FOR FORMAL AND CONTINUING EDUCATION

Job mobility and job turnover affect the sector much as they affect the business world. Many people are no longer satisfied to stay in one role or with one organization during their entire work life, and so they choose to move on. Others are forced to make such changes for economic and technological reasons not in their control. Estimates suggest that the average person can anticipate five job or career changes during his or her work life. A growing market for experienced nonprofit managers encourages movement as well. Making the most of this kind of mobility has to mean adding knowledge and skills—and that includes skills that can be learned or enhanced by short-term training or serious scholarship.

Nonprofit organization employees tend to complain that their employers either have no career ladders or short career ladders, and this forces them to seek advancement elsewhere. This is more true of agencies with less than 100 employees, as opposed to large organizations like hospitals, universities, or of multi-site organizations like United Way, Scouts, the Salvation Army, and the American Red Cross. Typical career paths in the nonprofit sector are:

- from professional or clinical role to management
- from support staff role to management
- lateral move from small local organization to larger state, regional, or national organization
- from small to medium-size to large organization

- from one side of the fence to the other—e.g., from grant-receiving organization to grant-dispensing organization, or from client organization to consultant organization.

Adapting to such career paths, or following your own particular path in one of the developing nonprofit fields, requires a generalist outlook as well as multiple skills and flexibility that often cannot be met just by on-the-job learning. In fact, "job mobility" and "career paths" are really two perspectives on the same shifts and changes. The realities of adaptation to these movements put a premium on carefully selected degree-based and continuing education.

SAMPLE PROGRAMS

Education and training programs for nonprofit management come in so many formats and from so many sources that the variety can be bewildering. Remember, there is no single best path, nor are all options available in all regions. Instead, there are many different pathways to personal and professional development. The following section presents an illustrative sample of the range of programs and credentials available.

Undergraduate Programs

In 1986, a first step toward educating college students about philanthropy and the history of the voluntary enterprise in this country was taken with the start of the Program on Studying Philanthropy. This project was initiated by the American Association of Fund Raising Counsel Trust for Philanthropy, in cooperation with the American Association of Colleges. Fifteen colleges received grants, awarded competitively, to develop and teach pilot courses for a three-year period. The purpose of the project is to create awareness and to stimulate interest in the sector. The hope is that by exposing college students to this material, some of them will be inspired to plan careers in the sector and to understand the importance of volunteer roles at an earlier age. (Figure 4.2 lists the colleges and courses.) A related effort is the Internship Initiative in the Independent Sector, sponsored by the Washington Center, which brings 25 college students to Washington, D.C., for a semester. (See Section 11 for further information on this program.)

FIGURE 4.2. ASSOCIATION OF AMERICAN COLLEGES, PROGRAM ON STUDYING PHILAN-THROPY—PILOT COURSES IN PHILANTHROPY AND VOLUNTARISM.

SCHOOL	COURSE AND DEPARTMENT
Babson College Wellesley, MA	Individualism and Philanthropy in American Life Liberal Arts Department
Baruch College City University of NY New York, NY	"And Charity for All . . .": The American Experience in Philanthropy; School of Liberal Arts and Sciences and School of Business and Public Administration
Chapman College Orange, CA	A Life of Service; Philosophy Department

George Washington University Washington, D.C.	Philanthropy, Voluntarism and Public Policy; Government Department
Illinois State University Normal, IL	Philanthropic Organizations and Global Development; Political Science Department
Northwestern University Evanston, IL	Private Interest and the Public Good: Philanthropy in America; American Culture Department
Randolph-Macon Woman's College Lynchburg, VA	Public Good and Public Service: Philanthropy and Volunteer Service in America; Religion Department
Regis College Weston, MA	Perspectives on American Philanthropy; Interdepartmental
Seton Hall University South Orange, NJ	American Philanthropy: Historical and Political Perspectives; Political Science Department
Southern University at New Orleans, LA	Philanthropy in American Life; School of Social Work
Temple University Philadelphia, PA	Philanthropy and Voluntarism; Sociology
Tufts University Medford, MA	America's Philanthropic Spirit: Philanthropy, Voluntary Action and Community; American Studies, Sociology, Center for Public Services
University of Louisville Louisville, KY	Voluntary Behavior and the City; Sociology Department
University of Southern California Los Angeles, CA	The Voluntary Sector and the Urban Interest; School of Public Administration
Western Maryland College Westminster, MD	From Charity to Voluntarism: Philanthropy in America; History, American Studies, Communications

Source: American Association of Colleges, 1988.

Many colleges offer field-specific professional preparation at the undergraduate level that leads to employment or graduate programs in clinical areas like nursing and social work. These curricula generally do not include management courses. One exception is the Human Services Management Program at the University of Tennessee at Chattanooga, which prepares students for entry-level supervisory positions. Undergraduate business programs do offer management education, but they are primarily aimed at preparing students for business employment.

Students with majors like political science and sociology, which foster interest in and understanding of social and political issues, can apply their background to many public service and cause organizations when they graduate. Students of English, languages, drama, art, dance, and music can offer these programs as credentials for entry-level jobs in arts and culture organizations. Some students plan to be practitioners or program specialists in their fields— for example, dancers, writers, artists, and musicians—and later achieve that goal. Others learn to adapt their creative backgrounds to other roles as they become support staff or managers. Ironically, successful practitioners are frequently promoted up to management positions because of their program expertise and despite their lack of management know-how!

For those students who have not identified a particular interest or direction, perhaps the majority of students, a college education that fosters self-confidence, creativity, critical thinking, and the ability to write can provide enough of a background with which to start a flourishing nonprofit career. For some college graduates, a liberal arts background and a work setting that brings out latent talents is enough to set them on a promising career path. Four of the career profiles in this book, those of Heidi Weber, Michael Seltzer, Gwinne Scott, and Jim Clark, are good illustrations of this phenomenon.

Youth Agency Leadership and Administration is an established undergraduate career program that leads directly to entry-level management jobs in agencies that serve youth. It is offered by 15 colleges in partnership with American Humanics, a coordinating agency established in 1949. Graduates of the program are recruited by 11 major organizations that serve 25 million youth, jointly filling 1,800 to 2,500 full-time staff positions. They are:

American National Red Cross
Boy Scouts of America
Camp Fire, Inc.
Girl Scouts of the U.S.A.
Junior Achievement
Big Brothers/Big Sisters of America
Boys Clubs of America
4-H Council, National
Girls Clubs of America
Young Men's Christian Association
Young Women's Christian Association

For information about these programs and graduate programs in Youth Agency Administration at Texas A & M University, The University of the Pacific, and Georgia State University, contact: American Humanics, 4601 Madison Avenue, Suite B, Kansas City, Missouri 64112. For a list of participating colleges see Figure 4.3.

Another undergraduate degree program that leads to entry-level management positions is the Health Services Administration Program offered by 100 universities. The Association of University Programs in Health Administration (AUPHA) has a list of 32 of these programs

FIGURE 4.3. AMERICAN HUMANICS BACCALAUREATE PROGRAMS IN YOUTH AGENCY LEADERSHIP AND ADMINISTRATION—CAMPUS AFFILIATIONS.

Arizona State University, Tempe, AZ
California State University, Los Angeles, CA
Colorado State University, Fort Collins, CO
Georgia State University, Atlanta, GA
High Point College, High Point, NC
Indiana Central University, Indianapolis, IN
Murray State University, Murray, KY
Pace University, New York and White Plains, NY
Pan American University, Edinburg, TX
Pepperdine University, Malibu, CA
Rockhurst College, Kansas City, MO
Salem College, Salem, WV
Texas A & M University, College Station, TX
University of the Pacific, Stockton, CA

Source: American Humanics.

that have been accredited by their association. For information, contact: AUPHA, 1911 North Fort Myer Drive, Arlington, Virginia 22209.

Master's Degree Programs

Master's degree programs have increasingly experimented with nonprofit management curricula. Concentrations and courses can be found in four general categories: generic management programs, public administration programs, field-specific programs, and nonprofit management programs. Each of these program designs has merit. The differences among the programs can be attributed to the differences in the original academic disciplines around which they were conceptualized and to the individual university's level of interest in a distinctive nonprofit curriculum.

Students who want the security of a conventional degree may opt for the Master of Business Administration (MBA), the Master of Science (MS) in management, the Master of Public Administration (MPA), the Master of Social Work (MSW), or the Master of Health Care Administration degrees. Students who are committed to the independent sector and who want programs specially designed for nonprofits—or who may be interested in the flexibility of moving among various kinds of nonprofits—may be drawn to the newer programs in nonprofit management.

Programs in Schools of Management. Generic management programs leading either to the MBA or MS degree in management are focused almost exclusively on training managers for business. They emphasize the development of basic management competencies through core courses such as organizational behavior, operations management, finance, economics, quantitative analysis, accounting, marketing, and business strategy. They are extremely popular as a general training ground for managers. The MBA degree, in particular, offers a credential for many kinds of professional employment, including nonprofit management. Because of the major role of the health care industry in the economy and the strong need for health care managers, many generic management programs include health care concentrations in their curricula.

Some business management programs claim that management education for all three sectors can be incorporated into one program, at least to the extent of acknowledging that there are three sectors. They realize that some of their students may work in or with nonprofit or public organizations, or assume significant leadership roles in voluntary organizations. The Harriman School of Management and Policy at the State University of New York at Stony Brook offers students of public, private, and nonprofit management a core curriculum in management. Nonprofit management students then take a concentration of courses relating to the situation, theory, and management of nonprofit organizations.

Yale University, La Salle University in Philadelphia, and the College of St. Thomas in St. Paul are among other institutions working with new multi-purpose management programs. Northwestern University's J. L. Kellogg Graduate School of Management offers a program in Public and Nonprofit Management. La Salle University's graduate program in Nonprofit Management is a concentration within the Organization and Management Degree, offered through its Nonprofit Management Development and Business Program.

Public Administration and Public Affairs Programs. Graduate schools of public affairs and public administration have an interest in the study of nonprofit management, because the country's public and nonprofit activities are so intertwined. Both sectors exist to serve the public interest, and both are deeply interested in public policy formulation, with many nonprofit advocacy organizations existing solely to influence changes in public policy. The interactive public/nonprofit relationship is expected to continue, as is the interest of public administration programs in preparing students who can manage these relationships.

Consequently, The National Association of Schools of Public Affairs and Administration (NASPAA) has taken a serious look at emerging curriculum issues. The report of its Ad Hoc Committee on Nonprofit Management (Young et al., 1987) recommends:

> New programs developed explicitly for nonprofit managers should feature a core of stand-alone courses devoted to managerial subject matter that is distinctive for nonprofits. These areas include the character of the nonprofit sector, basics of nonprofit management, human resources management and resource development.

Human resources management in nonprofits has a special dimension because managers have to be able to work effectively with three groups: the volunteers (board and committee members, direct service volunteers), professionals (who often enjoy substantial autonomy and whose first allegiance may be to their profession rather than their organization), and management and support staff. Resource development, which encompasses fundraising, membership development, and profit-making ventures for nonprofits, has no exact equivalent in the public or private sector.

Relatively few Master of Public Administration (MPA) programs incorporate substantial nonprofit management content, but those that do take a variety of approaches. Some university catalogs emphasize that their graduates are employed by nonprofit organizations. Others offer a single course such as marketing for nonprofits or nonprofit accounting. Other universities offer concentrations in a specific aspect of nonprofit management such as health care administration, human services administration, or arts administration. Others enlarge the scope of an existing public management course to include the nonprofit perspective, e.g., public and nonprofit budgeting or financial management of public and nonprofit organizations.

A number of universities offer concentrations in nonprofit management within their schools of public affairs. These include:

Baruch College, City University of New York
Carnegie-Mellon University, School of Urban and Public Affairs
Golden Gate University, Graduate School of Public Administration
New York University, Program in Public Administration
Roosevelt University, Public Administration Program
Sangamon State University, School of Public Affairs
Tufts University, Center for Public Services
University of Colorado at Denver, Graduate School of Public Affairs
University of Minnesota, Hubert H. Humphrey Institute of Public Affairs

Field-Specific Master's Programs. Since information about traditional programs in social work, health services, and educational administration is readily available, we will describe some of the less well-known specialized management programs.

Arts Administration. These programs are located in a variety of academic divisions. American University offers a Master of Arts (MA) in Arts Administration through its Department of Performing Arts. Southern Methodist University offers a joint degree program through its Meadows School of the Arts and its Edwin L. Cox School of Business, with the program leading to both an MBA and MA degree. The University of Wisconsin, Madison, also offers a joint degree program through its School of Business and its Center for Arts Administration. The Graduate School of Public Affairs of the University of Washington offers an option in Arts Management within its MPA Program. New York University offers a sub-specialization in Arts and Policy Management as part of its Nonprofit Concentration.

Religious Administration. The University of Pittsburgh and the Pittsburgh Theological Seminary, which trains Presbyterian ministers, offer a joint degree program leading to a Master of Divinity degree and an MBA. The Azusa Pacific University in California offers a Master of Ministry Management degree, developed in cooperation with the Christian Ministries Management Association.

Management of Human Services. A number of schools offer master of human service degree programs, with an emphasis on applying modern management techniques to human service programs. The curricula combine management and social policy courses. While traditional social work programs have always included some administration courses in their community organization curricula, they typically do not incorporate quantitative and marketing courses. The Heller School at Brandeis University offers a Master's degree in Management of Human Services, and Springfield College in Massachusetts offers a Human Services and Administration degree. The School for International Training in Brattleboro, Vermont, offers a master's program in intercultural management with a concentration in international human service administration.

Master's programs in association management are covered in Chapter 10 in this book, "Associations as Employers and Professional Development Resources."

Nonprofit Management Education Programs. There are fewer than a handful of master of nonprofit management programs that stand on their own without being dependent on other preexisting curricula. These programs have developed a core of primary courses related to specific nonprofit subject matter.

The New School for Social Research in New York City has a master's program in nonprofit management, leading to a master of professional studies degree. This program grew out of a more narrowly focused master's degree program in fundraising management and still offers a larger-than-usual selection of professional courses in fundraising. Students are required to take several courses from the core curriculum in nonprofit management, general management, economics, finance, and quantitative and qualitative methods. In addition, there is a good selection of dedicated nonprofit courses including: public relations and communications in nonprofit organizations, trustee boards, volunteers and lay leadership in nonprofit organizations; and fundraising courses such as direct mail fundraising, corporate philanthropy, and the development of planned giving programs. Each student is required to complete a master's project.

The University of San Francisco's College of Professional Studies, with locations in northern, central, and southern California, offers a Master of Nonprofit Administration (MNA) degree. This well-established program for working professionals clusters its courses into the following major areas:

- resource development skills
- resource management skills (human resources, financial management, information management)
- legal issues management
- organizational behavior and management theory
- studies of the historical, social, economic, legal, and moral context within which nonprofit organizations have developed
- quantitative analysis

Students are required to do a directed research project or a thesis.

The Mandel Center for Nonprofit Organizations at Case Western Reserve University is offering a Master in Nonprofit Organization (MNO) beginning in the 1989–90 academic year. The degree is a joint offering of the Mandel School of Applied Social Sciences and the Weatherhead School of Management—two of the three professional schools that sponsor the Mandel Center (the third is the School of Law). The program is unique in engaging regular faculty from several professional and academic schools of the university in a new curriculum designed specifically for nonprofit managers and leaders. The MNO is a professional degree requiring

45 credit hours of coursework in a variety of management- and nonprofit-related subjects, including social context and history of the sector, legal framework of nonprofits, economic and quantitative analysis, financial accounting and management, human resources management, marketing and promotion, operations management, and electives in areas of special interest. The program also requires successful completion of consultative (practicum) projects carried out within nonprofit organizations.

Certificate Programs

The certificate program is a way for educational institutions to offer a cluster of specialized courses to meet specific training needs without requiring commitment to a degree. They are attractive to students because they are generally offered at a convenient time for working adults, and they are less costly and often less demanding than degree programs. They offer timely and practical professional development and a credential. Some certificate program courses can be taken for credit and applied toward the requirements for a degree, providing the student fulfills stipulated requirements. Others award CEUs—continuing education units— required by some professions and organizations. Certificate programs are offered at the baccalaureate, post-baccalaureate, master's, and post-master's degree levels.

Figure 4.4. shows a brief sample of certificate programs. It demonstrates the current level of interest in nonprofit management education and the diversity of program offerings to be found around the country. For more information about certificate programs in your area, consult the continuing education departments of local colleges and universities, newspaper advertisements, and the national *Independent Sector Resource Directory of Education and Training Opportunities and Other Services* (Gray, 1987). Certificate program listings are not generally found in standard college and university directories.

Doctoral Programs

Since its founding in 1976, the Yale Program on Non-Profit Organizations (PONPO), an interdisciplinary center, has stimulated research and scholarship to build a body of information, analysis, and theory relating to nonprofit organizations. Through its grants to faculty and doctoral students across the country, it has generated working papers and books that have provided the base for current research efforts in the sector. For more information about PONPO, write Program on Non-Profit Organizations, P.O. Box 154, Yale Station, 188 Trumbull Street, New Haven, CT 06520.

Since 1983, the national organization INDEPENDENT SECTOR (IS) has provided additional impetus to research and scholarship through its annual research conference as well as the papers presented there, and its yearly compendium, *Research in Process: A National Compilation of Research Projects on Philanthropy, Voluntary Action and Not-for-Profit Activity*. (See "Independent Sector" in Section 10, under Associations that Serve the Nonprofit Sector, General Service and Management Associations.)

The PONPO and IS initiatives, plus the activities of the newer academic centers, such as Indiana and Case Western, translate into opportunities for faculty and graduate students of

FIGURE 4.4. SAMPLES OF CERTIFICATE PROGRAMS IN NONPROFIT MANAGEMENT

INSTITUTION	CERTIFICATE PROGRAMS
American University Washington, DC	Certificate in Arts Management Professional Certificate in Volunteer Management
Azusa Pacific University School of Business and Management Azusa, CA	Certificate of Ministry Management
Case Western Reserve University Mandel Center for Non-Profit Organizations Cleveland, OH	Certificate Program in Nonprofit Management
Columbia University Graduate Schools of Business The Institute for Nonprofit Management New York, NY	Certificate in Not-for-Profit Management (for executive directors)
Community College of Allegheny County Pittsburgh, PA	Certificate Program in Volunteer Management
George Washington University Center for Continuing Education Washington, DC	Management Certificate in Fund Raising Administration Management Certificate Association Executive
Graduate Theological Union (a consortium of theological seminaries) Berkeley, CA	The Advanced Management Certificate Program
Metropolitan State College Denver, CO	Community Service and Development Program
New York University School of Continuing Education New York, NY	Certificate in Fund Raising Management
Rutgers University School of Social Work New Brunswick, NJ	Post-Master's Certificate in Human Service Administration
University of Denver and The Technical Assistance Center Denver, CO	Advanced Management Certificate Program for Nonprofit and Executives
University of Southern California School of Public Administration Los Angeles, CA	Executive Administration of Mental Health Programs
York University of Administrative Studies Downsview, Ontario, Canada	Summer Residential Faculty Certificate course in Voluntary Sector and Arts Management

public and social policy, economics, history, management, religion, and philosophy who want to contribute to existing knowledge in the field. A new nontraditional Ph.D. program "with emphasis on philanthropy and leadership" was launched in 1988 by the Union Graduate School of the Union for Experimenting Colleges in Cincinnati, Ohio. A number of academics have been instrumental in attracting students to this field. Dr. Burton Weisbrod, of the Department of Economics at the University of Wisconsin stands out for the number and quality of students he has motivated.

Continuing Education Offerings

Continuing education in nonprofit management is pervasive, with formats, cost, and length of courses and programs varying according to location, sponsor, and market. The continuing education umbrella covers certificate programs, workshops, conferences, institutes, and in-house training. Sponsors include higher education institutions but are more likely to be associations, technical assistance centers, consulting firms, private schools, as well as consortia of agencies and/or schools. (Association-sponsored training programs are described in Section 10.)

The advantage of continuing education programs is that they offer quick training for existing needs as defined by employers, students, or program providers. Faculty are drawn from a wide pool of expert practitioners, trainers, consultants, and academics. The following includes some examples of continuing education programs.

College and University. Some college and university continuing education divisions have found a market for nonprofit management offerings, particularly in skills development subjects. For instance, New York University sponsors an annual Summer Arts Management Institute; Tufts University sponsors an annual Management and Community Development Institute; and the University of Wisconsin, Madison, offers many half- and full-day programs on board management, fund-raising, marketing, budgeting, and strategic planning subjects. Case Western Reserve's Mandel Center offers periodic one- and two-day workshops to the public, as well as training programs for client nonprofit organizations. The Fuller Theological Seminary in Pasadena, through its Institute for Christian Organizational Development, offers management education workshops and seminars for its target audience, Christian pastors, executives, and organizational leaders. Check with your local colleges and universities to see what is available.

Fundraising Schools
The Grantsmanship Center. Since 1972 this Los Angeles-based organization has been offering short-term training programs in subjects of particular concern to nonprofits. The Center has trained over 40,000 agency employees in grantsmanship, fund raising, and nonprofit management. It offers a five-day grantsmanship training program, three-day programs in fundraising, grant proposal writing, and business ventures for nonprofits, and a three-day development officer training program at locations across the country. For information write: The Grantsmanship Center, 650 South Spring Street, P.O. Box 6210, Los Angeles, CA 90014.

The Fund Raising School. Founded in 1974, the Fund Raising School is a nonprofit national and international training organization based in San Rafael, California. In 1987 it became part of the Center on Philanthropy at Indiana University. The school offers three- and five-day basic or advanced fundraising programs at sites across the country. They will design on-site programs for organizations. For information write: The Fund Raising School, P.O. Box 3237, San Rafael, CA 94912-3237.

Technical Assistance Centers. Technical assistance centers have been operating in various parts of the country since the early 1970s for the purpose of assisting nonprofits with their management problems. Training is one of their major functions. The centers are nonprofits themselves and charge relatively low fees for their services. Among the centers that regularly offer training are:

Accounting Aid Society of Metropolitan Detroit applies business skills in accounting, management, and law to assist nonprofit community organizations. Their seminars for staff, boards, and members cover accounting, budgeting, general marketing, resource development, and related business and legal topics. For information contact: Accounting Aid Society, One Kennedy Square, Detroit, MI 48226.

Center for Non-Profit Corporations in Trenton, New Jersey, represents the interests of New Jersey's 9,000 nonprofits. It periodically offers workshops of interest to its members on topics as diverse as advocacy techniques, business venture strategies for nonprofits, and strategic planning. For information contact: Center for Non-Profit Corporations, 36 West Lafayette Street, Trenton, NJ 08608.

Funding Information Center of San Antonio, Texas, through its Management Assistance Program (MAP), offers workshops in accounting and finance, fundraising, general administration, board administration, law, marketing, public relations, and personnel management. For information contact: Funding Information Center, 507 Brooklyn, San Antonio, TX 78215.

Independent Community Consultants, Inc., a management support organization in Hampton, Arkansas, offers one- to four-day workshops in financial management, case management, fundraising, proposal writing, trainers' training, program evaluation, and consultation skills. For information contact: Independent Community Consultants, P.O. Box 141, Hampton, AR 71744.

Management Center of San Francisco provides nonprofit agencies in the San Francisco Bay Area with one-on-one assistance and training and peer group discussions for executive directors, as well as workshops on decision-making, board management, public relations, and working with consultants. For information contact: Management Center, 215 Leidesdorff Street, 4th Floor, San Francisco, CA 94111.

Nonprofit Coordinating Committee of New York was established in 1983 to help nonprofits meet common challenges and problems. Through its newsletter, *New York Nonprofits,* it alerts New York metropolitan area organizations to current education and training programs. The Committee sponsors workshops on legal issues, political lobbying, insurance questions, and other current topics. For information contact: Nonprofit Coordinating Committee of New York, 121 Ave. of the Americas, New York, NY 10013.

Support Centers of America is a national network of management accounting and fundraising assistance providers located in San Francisco, San Diego, Chicago, Boston, Newark, New York, Oklahoma City, Tulsa, Providence, Memphis, Houston, and Washington, D.C. They train staff, boards, and volunteers of nonprofit organizations (11,000 in 1986). For information contact:

Support Centers of America, 1410 Q Street NW, Washington, D.C. 20009. (Jonathan Cook, Executive Director of the Support Centers of America, is profiled in this book in Section 9, "Service Providers.")

Technical Assistance Center (TAC) in Denver, Colorado, founded in 1979, offers a year-round program of seminars on financial management, fundraising, human resource management, marketing management, information systems, governance, structure and systems, leadership, and personal development. In co-sponsorship with the University of Denver, the Center offers an advanced management certificate program for nonprofit executives. For information contact: Technical Assistance Center, 1385 South Colorado Boulevard, Suite 504, Building A, Denver, CO 80222. (Carol Barbeito, President, Technical Assistance Center, is profiled in this book in Section 9, "Service Providers.")

Volunteer Consulting Groups in New York City was founded in 1969 by the Harvard Business School Club of New York to provide professional management assistance to nonprofit organizations. Yearly, they sponsor a Non-Profit Leadership Seminar, a forum for trustees and staff. For information contact: Volunteer Consulting Group, Inc., 24 West 40th Street, New York, NY 10018.

In-House Training. A number of the larger and older national nonprofits conduct in-house education and training programs as a means of directing the professional development of staff and volunteers and improving their performance. Because of their large size and history, these organizations tend to have more predictable career paths, making them attractive to job seekers and career planners who want to make a commitment to one organization, and who see that organization's in-house and training programs as a benefit.

United Way of America has the best-known in-house program, the National Academy for Volunteerism (NAV), which has trained thousands of participants. The NAV program is available to United Way professionals, board members of United Ways and the agencies they support, and agency professionals. Its courses, workshops and seminars are offered at the NAV Training Center in Alexandria, Virginia, and at selected sites throughout the country. In 1988, NAV offered over 100 workshops on subjects including: communications, community problem solving, fund distribution, community resources, financial management, government relations, management development, management information systems, marketing, personal development and skill enhancement, resource development, strategic planning and market research, and the special needs of smaller United Ways. For information contact: National Academy for Volunteerism, 701 North Fairfax Street, Alexandria, VA 22314-2045.

Among the national organizations that develop their own training programs are the Girl Scouts of the U.S.A., Girls Clubs of America, Boy Scouts and Boys Clubs, American Red Cross, YMCA, YWCA, and others. Since their programs are designed for targeted groups of staff and volunteers and are not accessible to the general public, we mention them only to alert the reader to their existence. For many community volunteers who later become paid professionals, typically women, the leadership training they received as volunteers for organizations like the Girl Scouts, the YWCA, or the National Council of Jewish Women is the foundation for their later career development.

Volunteer Administration. In an emerging field of opportunity, volunteer administration programs of all sorts are surfacing at community colleges, colleges, and universities. A survey of higher education institutions, conducted by the Association for Volunteer Administration in 1987, revealed that 54 academic institutions offered credit courses, workshops, or certificate programs for managers of volunteers. For a list of volunteer management programs in higher education, contact: Association for Volunteer Administration, P.O. Box 4584, Boulder, CO 80306.

Shopping for Your Own Program

Finding a fit between your personal and professional goals and existing education and training programs requires some research and planning. Start by locating sponsors and offerings in your area. Read the program literature. Talk to faculty, administration, current students, or former participants of programs that interest you.

Before deciding on your next step, put together the following information about yourself:

- Field(s) of interest
- Area(s) of specialization
- Short-term professional goal
- Short-term educational goal
- Long-term professional goal
- Long-term educational goal
- Management role preference—decide whether you want to work in general management (operational side), program management (service side), or as a specialist in an area such as fundraising, public relations, membership, or finance.

The factors to consider in undertaking a commitment to an educational or training program include:

- relevance or adaptability of available programs to your needs/desires
- accessibility of program (location, days, time of day)
- cost of program—who will pay
- amount of time required to complete
- stage of life and career—whether the education or training is for career entry, a mid-career transition, reentry or preretirement
- personal objectives for education—these can include career advancement, the attainment of credentials or degrees, skills development, peer interaction, or simply a broader perspective on your field
- current employer's objectives for your professional development—including improved performance, credentials, or promotion
- plan of action—whether you want to pursue the education over six months, one year, or three years.

PART TWO

Career Profiles

Lilly Cohen

Who are these dreamers and doers we refer to in the title of this book? I have interviewed 25 men and women, managers of nonprofit organizations, who told me what they do, why their work is important, and how they got where they are today. The information and insights they reveal about their work life and their organizations give a representative if not exhaustive view of what the nonprofit sector is about and the caliber of people it attracts. We discover that people who are committed to the betterment of life in some dimension and who are prepared to devote themselves to such a purpose can indeed find satisfying and gainful employment in the sector.

Many of the people I interviewed are inspired by visions of service, but these visions are not lightly held. If you are looking for role models, examples of careers or career paths, and advice, I hope you will profit from the following profiles. No single lesson will be drawn from them, except that success appears to come from a combination of talent, opportunity, and determination.

5

General Managers

General Management Positions

Profiles in this group describe individuals who hold general management positions. They either manage a broad function or an entire organization. Some are leaders as well as managers.

In 1985, Dick Shubert, president of the American Red Cross and a former president of the Bethlehem Steel Corporation, noted that managing a nonprofit is tougher than managing a corporation. He cited three key reasons. Nonprofits must rely on volunteers, which means that managers cannot lead by simply giving orders. Nonprofits have difficulties in setting measurable performance standards, for they lack the "bottom line" so clear in the business sector. Third, nonprofits operate in a "fishbowl," under constant scrutiny by the public, the press, and government. Despite these differences, Schubert said, "I would not exchange my present responsibilities for anything."

For Further Information

Gardner, John
  n.d.   John Gardner has prepared a series of Leadership Papers for the Independent Sector, 1828 L Street, N.W., Washington, D.C. 20036

Mason, David E.
  1984   *Voluntary Nonprofit Enterprise Management.* New York: Plenum Press.

John R. Garrison

Chief Executive Officer, National Easter Seal Society (NESS)
Executive Director, Easter Seal Research Foundation

"If you have a sense of making a contribution you can do it in government. But what I like about nonprofit work, as opposed to government, is that there is more opportunity for experimenting, more flexibility and change. It moves very rapidly and is exciting. It gives you a greater opportunity to use your creativity."

What He Does

John Garrison summarizes his career interest as "the promotion of better health care and social services for the public good." As chief executive officer of the National Easter Seal Society (NESS), he heads the oldest and largest organization providing direct services to people with disabilities.

The Society operates through some 200 affiliates in 50 states. Over 1,100,000 disabled people and their families are served annually by a total of 5,500 staff members and 800,000 volunteers. The Society has a combined budget of $220 million. National Easter Seal Society's 1987 *Annual Report* offers an eloquent summary of what the organization stands for:

> Quality direct services. Preventive screening. Aggressive advocacy. Award-winning public education. Result-oriented research. Plus innovative techniques, skilled management, acknowledged leadership, and a commitment to constant improvement.

Garrison describes his job this way, "I am in charge of a large, far-flung organization of separate corporations. My role is to serve, motivate, and provide leadership to a very diverse group of volunteers and staff across the country. Our mission is to help people with disabilities to become more independent."

The Society provides a multifaceted program of direct services to people with disabilities through its affiliates. These services include: physical, occupational and speech language therapies, vocational evaluation and training, job development and placement, work centers, camping and recreation programs, psychological counseling, and stroke clubs.

Garrison compares the organization of NESS to that of a business franchise, because Easter Seal affiliates are licensed by the national society and must conform to their standards. Each affiliate is separately incorporated and works with its own staff and board of directors.

Garrison works with NESS's 25-member board of directors and the 150-member House of Delegates, a governing body representing the affiliates. He manages the national office with a budget of $14 million and a staff of 85. Key areas of staff responsibility include governmental affairs, communications, development, program services, direct mail, affiliate relations, Easter Seal systems, and internal operations.

When Garrison took over the management of the society in 1978, his mandate was to increase the productivity of the national office and to improve its relations with the affiliates. By creating a productive internal environment hospitable to innovation and change, and encouraging programmatic excellence and a businesslike approach to management, he has reached these goals.

Garrison is particularly proud of his influence on the quality of the organization's communications. By obtaining donated creative services from a national advertising agency, he has strengthened the Society's message and image. When a survey revealed that most NESS managers lacked formal management education, he contracted with several universities to provide it. Today, every national department head must use at least two days a year for professional development. Affiliate executives routinely participate in fundraising, program, and communications seminars.

Under Garrison's leadership, the national office generates considerable activity. NESS is actively involved in advocacy programs for people with disabilities and the agencies that serve them. Through its Washington-based Office of Governmental Affairs, the Society works on legislation, regulation, education, negotiation, and litigation. Also, since its founding in 1919, the organization has produced a stream of educational materials for people with disabilities and their families.

Recently, NESS has become known for its multimedia presentations designed to increase public awareness and understanding of people with disabilities. The Society has also developed Rehabware, a computerized management system for vocational and rehabilitation facilities. Strong market interest in the system and related consulting services may lead to the establishment of a separate business whose profits will benefit NESS.

Like any CEO of a major organization, Garrison must handle multiple problems and challenges. He is concerned that services be available to the growing number of people with disabilities. More babies are being born with birth injuries and more adults are living longer. He worries about the diversification of the organization's income base in a competitive environment.

The Society receives public funds, contributions, sells products from its workshops, and attempts to maximize income through effective fundraising and business operations, such as its computer software and consulting business for rehabilitation facilities. The Society's annual telethon continues to bring in the major portion of contributed income, maintaining viewer and donor interest by using sophisticated marketing techniques.

From Garrison's perspective, the most critical skills required for managing a complex organization like NESS are interpersonal skills—people skills. He says that his job carries no true authority in affiliate relationships and that you cannot be directive with affiliates, their staff, or with volunteers. "You have to lead by example. You have to motivate people. You have to deal with people from a variety of backgrounds. The challenge is trying to get these people moving, if not in step, at least in the same direction." He adds, "The rewards are worth the challenge."

How He Got There

For as long as he can remember, Garrison has been interested in politics and government and has been fascinated by American presidents. As a Harvard undergraduate, he majored in American government and was very active in Students for Kennedy and Harvard Young Democrats. He says that the Harvard education instilled a certain social awareness. He completed a master's degree in public administration at New York University while serving as a lieutenant in the Army, stationed in New York City.

His first job was as an administrative assistant in the New York State Banking Department. He was then employed as a senior planner, first by New Jersey's Department of Conservation and then by New York's Office of Regional Development in Albany.

In 1966, he phoned the office of Governor Nelson Rockefeller to ask whether he could work on the reelection campaign. They happened to be looking for a junior researcher, so he was called in for an interview. When the interviewers learned that he was an urban planner, they asked him to come back in a week with a report on what Rockefeller had done for the cities in New York State during his eight years as Governor. Garrison says this was a "take-home test." He was able to produce a factual report that could be turned into political profit— and got the job!

Garrison worked for five years for Governor Rockefeller and for two years for Lieutenant Governor Malcom Wilson. He was the day-to-day liaison between the Governor's office and the state's Health and Social Services departments. Garrison points out that, "This job taught me to deal with very high-level people, to work under pressure, and to meet deadlines."

In describing his next move, he notes, "When you are working with elected officials and in your twenties, you become a bright young man, but if you stay too long you run the risk of being labelled a political hack." Therefore, his next move was to an administrative job, which gave him an opportunity to learn hands-on management skills. He became Deputy Commissioner for Administration of the New York State Health Department. As the ranking lay member of a state department with a $240-million budget, his responsibilities included personnel, public relations, program planning, legal operations, data processing, and health manpower activities.

After 10 years in government, Garrison accepted a position in the nonprofit sector, which drew on his health and management experience. He became Vice-President for Operations and then Executive Vice-President of the Hospital Association of New York State, which represents more than 300 nonprofit hospitals and health facilities. Garrison's ambition to become the head of a major national organization was achieved when he became CEO of the National Easter Seal Society (NESS) in 1978.

Garrison believes that it is essential for managers at all levels to participate in professional development programs. Programs that have been helpful to him are: the American Management Association Course for Presidents, a University of Chicago seminar on the Winning Organization, and a Wharton School of Finance Program on Implementing Strategic Planning.

While his responsibilities at the Society take up a great deal of time, he says, "It is important for a CEO or any professional to have outside interests and see what is happening in the field." He currently volunteers as President of the National Health Council and as a board member of Independent Sector, and he has served on the Advisory Board on Standards and Revision of the National Charities Information Bureau.

Advice to Others

Garrison observes that there are no real career paths for managers of nonprofit organizations. At NESS, Garrison notes most managers have professional degrees in program-related specialties, and these people can and do become good managers. What they need, he says, is post-master's training in management, particularly in decision-making, strategic planning, and dealing with outside influences.

In department heads and other top people, he looks for "a creative, innovative, aggressive go-getter, someone who does not want much supervision. I tell them what the objectives are and stay in touch with them and see how well they are doing on the objectives, and then reward them appropriately if they accomplish them. But I let them do their own thing. I emphasize creativity, the willingness to take some risks and to go out on a limb."

On hiring people to work for nonprofits:

- He would like to get young people interested in looking at the sector while still in college—take some courses, do volunteer work, and experiment.

- Out-placement firms faced with a glut of middle managers from the private sector could channel some of these managers into nonprofit employment.

- Middle-aged and older people may be an untapped resource for nonprofit employers, who tend to think more about hiring recent graduates with low salary requirements.

Anne L. Bryant

Executive Director
American Association of University Women (AAUW)

"Success is much harder to measure in a nonprofit . . . you have to take a look at how the organization is serving the public."

What She Does

As executive director of AAUW, Anne Bryant manages a major national service organization. Founded in 1881, AAUW serves 150,000 individual members who are college and university graduates, 700 colleges and universities, and 1,900 local branches. Bryant is also executive director of the separately incorporated AAUW Educational Foundation and of the AAUW Legal Advocacy Fund.

AAUW's mission is "Equality for women, education and self-development over the life span, and positive societal change." Its Educational Foundation has for 100 years funded the scholarship and research of outstanding women including Marie Curie, Margaret Mead, and Judith Resnick. Since 1980, the foundation has spent more than $1 million annually in support of American and international fellowships, awards, and project grants. The Legal Advocacy Fund provides funding and a support system for women seeking judicial redress for sex discrimination.

Bryant works with the 20 members of the AAUW Board and the 14 members of the Educational Foundation Board. Eight department directors report to her and are responsible for: administration, finance, management information systems, membership, communications, program, policy, and the foundation. Her staff of 100 is based at the organization's headquarters in Washington, D.C. About one-third hold management positions; the balance are support staff.

As executive director, Bryant's responsibilities fall under four broad categories:

- Working with the presidents of the boards (of AAUW and the Educational Foundation) and with committees of the organization.
- Administration of the organization.
- Maintaining effective relationships and providing support services to state divisions, regions, branches, and members.
- External relations with government, the media, and other associations.

Historically, all AAUW members have been community activists and change agents. When Bryant took over as executive director, she familiarized herself with the organization and all of its local program activities. She realized that AAUW's programs were so diverse that the organization no longer had a recognized mission and its resources were stretched over too broad a span. Therefore, her first steps were to develop a more targeted and strategic interpretation of the mission of the organization and to streamline the operation of the national office. This required the support of the board and the cooperation of staff. AAUW's mission was narrowed to four major focus areas: education, equity issues for women, valuing women's work, and leadership development.

Recognizing that local chapters and members would always be responding to local issues, the national office had to confront the question of how to support local projects while limiting the national office's resources to concentrated work in the four major focus areas. The solution was to achieve total board and leadership commitment to this goal and to provide alternative member services.

One such example is the Helpline. When AAUW members call the national office for help with local problems not directly related to the four focus areas, the Helpline identifies other organizations and resources that can provide assistance.

Bryant and her organization are keenly aware of women's needs to grow personally and professionally and to receive recognition for their contributions to society. Sixty percent of AAUW's members work for pay; 40 percent work part-time or are involved in non-pay work. Bryant says, "In everything we do, we try to think how we can save this busy woman's time. We know she has nine other jobs. . . . We thrive on involving as many volunteers as possible. . . . If your goal is to develop the skills of women so that they are better able to cope and compete while still being active citizens, then you spread leadership." AAUW encourages breaking down leadership jobs, using co-presidents and co-chairs, and designing other functions more narrowly to enable women to volunteer despite competing demands for their time.

Bryant thinks that one of the real challenges of managing a nonprofit organization is dealing with change and turnover in the composition of the board. Bryant believes, "Once you change the ingredients of the governing board, you change the board. . . . I have new bosses every two years. . . . It means reviewing and rearticulating the goals every time you have a new group."

As a staff person working with volunteer leaders, Bryant is especially sensitive to maintaining the balance between the short-term goals of new leaders and a 10-year perspective on where the organization is moving. Her task is "to involve people and motivate them, while keeping them on a long-term thinking strategy."

How She Got There

Bryant has a bachelor's degree in English and secondary education from Simmons College. She continued her studies at the University of Massachusetts at Amherst, earning a doctorate in higher education.

As a doctoral assistant she worked for the Massachusetts State College System on a variety of projects including the development of a statewide admissions system. Then, as Assistant to the Academic Dean of Springfield Technical Community College, she developed funding proposals and cooperative projects between the college and the University of Massachusetts.

After receiving her Doctor of Education (Ed.D.) Bryant spent 12 years with the National Association of Bank Women (NABW), an organization with 30,000 members. She became the Director of NABW's Educational Foundation, which she helped establish to provide management and career development programs for people in banking.

For the NABW, Bryant organized national, state, and local leadership training programs, as well as seminars, state conferences, and three college-degree programs in banking. The foundation began with an annual budget of $100,000 and grew into an organization with an annual budget of more than a $1 million. During this period Bryant supplemented her experience-based management skills with courses offered by the American Society of Association Executives (ASAE).

In 1978, while still with the Bank Women's Educational Foundation, she also assumed responsibilities in a new multiple-association management firm. This company hires staff and provides management services to small associations. Its operating concept is that groups can share expertise and buying power. Bryant became vice-president of the firm's Professional Education Division. As the number two executive of a $5-million corporation with a staff of 70, her responsibilities included corporate planning, financial and strategic decision-making, leadership, management, training, and consultation with clients.

A fast-moving professional, Bryant has received a number of awards for academic excellence and contributions to the fields of education and association management. Her board directorships include Simmons College, the American Association of Higher Education, the Council for Adult and Experiential Learning, and the American Society of Association Executives. She is also an Advisory Commissioner of the Education Commission of the States.

An executive search firm recruited Bryant for the AAUW position. AAUW was looking for an executive director with association and management experience as well as a background in education and equity issues for women. Bryant was attracted by the job because she cared about the issues that AAUW addresses, and she saw the job as a challenge to her own professional growth.

Bryant says that while career paths in the public, nonprofit, and private sectors can be quite similar, she finds that:

> Nonprofits allow us to combine avocational interests and beliefs with all of the skills and experiences that are necessary to run any entity. And that commitment to a premise, whether it is a deeply held belief or one that you come to know and learn when you are there, that commitment to an organization and its mission, becomes a career, more than a job. It would be very tough to work for a nonprofit or an association whose mission you did not agree with—more difficult than working for a corporation whose product or service you did not totally endorse. I think the bottom line in a nonprofit is the cause, while in a corporation it is the job or compensation.

Advice to Others

As an employer, Bryant recognizes the difficulty of retaining staff in the face of the higher salaries generally offered by the government and business sectors. She believes that one of the positive effects of working in an organization with limited resources is that it fosters creativity. "You have to think of 900 new ways to do something without a lot of money. . . . We have to force ourselves to be innovative."

At AAUW, many of the management positions are filled by talented people from within. What she looks for when hiring people is "writing, thinking, energy, and commitment." She believes that good writing and speaking skills are essential for those seeking employment in the nonprofit sector because, "It is a sector that absolutely depends on communication skills."

Bryant emphasizes the importance of sales and marketing skills as well. She thinks that women in particular are both articulate and persuasive. "They are good at saying things in ways that touch the heart. Women who believe in what they are doing are absolutely the best salespeople in the world."

Bryant advises job seekers to use interviews as an opportunity to ask questions that elicit information about the organizational climate and the motivation of the boss—in her view the controlling factors in any work situation. She would want to know whether the boss is committed to the goals of the organization, willing to put in the long hours often required in nonprofit work, and to go the extra mile. Other considerations that should enter into a job seeker's assessment of a potential employer are whether the organization encourages skill development, creates a climate that fosters professional growth, and pays adequately.

John N. Bailey

President
American Association of Fund Raising Counsel (AAFRC)*

"Associations are wonderful places to work."

What He Does

As President of the American Association of Fund Raising Counsel, John Bailey heads an industry association that represents some of the large established for-profit fundraising consultant firms in the United States. He also manages the AAFRC Trust for Philanthropy, the association's public service arm.

For over 50 years, the American Association of Fund Raising Counsel has "devoted its energy, resources, knowledge and experience to maintaining and improving the quality of philanthropy." The Association is identified with setting standards for ethical fundraising, working with legislatures to develop laws to protect the public against fraudulent practices, fostering high levels of professionalism and training, and publishing *Giving USA*, a well-known annual reference that documents facts and trends in American philanthropy.

As chief executive officer, Bailey works closely with a board representing each of the Association's 33 member firms. Member firms are, by and large, the industry leaders, the firms that work with major universities, museums, hospitals, churches, and other large non-profit organizations. Membership in AAFRC is limited, because membership standards are very high. Bailey also works with the 18-member board of the AAFRC Trust for Philanthropy. He directs a staff of nine, including Vice Presidents for Administration and Public Affairs and support staff.

Bailey came to AAFRC with 25 years of association management experience. He sees no real differences between managing a small industry association and a professional association with thousands of members. The skills are the same—people skills, management skills, knowing how to work with an association's diverse public, understanding issues, communicating effectively, creating cohesive networks, being open to fresh ideas.

The AAFRC's Trust for Philanthropy is both a grantmaking foundation and an operating foundation that conducts its own studies and projects. The Trust works closely with a number

---

* Since this profile was written John Bailey has moved to the headquarters of the American Cancer Society in California, where he is Executive Vice-President.

of key organizations in the nonprofit sector on projects related to ethics, giving, and philanthropic trends. The Trust, in cooperation with the Association of American Colleges, recently funded 16 colleges and universities to develop and teach undergraduate courses in philanthropy. This initiative grew out of AAFRC's concern that the history and unique contribution of philanthropy in America are not known to the public.

Bailey loves the challenge, the dynamism, and the broad interaction with people that characterizes association management. He believes that changes in the board of directors every year or two are revitalizing. "They (the board members) don't care what you did last year. They are concerned with what you are doing this year. And it is fun."

How He Got There

Like many association executives, John Bailey started out in journalism. A language arts major at California State University, Sacramento, he worked as a reporter and newspaper editor for five years. When he began looking around for something more challenging to do, he stumbled into the field of association management. Bailey was hired by the California State Employee's Association as a junior writer. In 10 years he was deputy general manager, having served as an assistant editor, managing editor, editor, legislative advocate, public relations director, and administrator of the communications division.

As deputy general manager of the 115,000-member California State Employee's Association, Bailey had a chance to learn all aspects of association management. Highlights of this period in his career were his initiation of a campaign that resulted in 5,000 new members in one week and his participation in a lobbying effort that resulted in a state constitutional amendment.

His next position was president of the International Association of Business Communicators, a professional society serving individuals in the public relations and communications profession. Bailey had taken on a struggling organization that had a declining membership of 2,200, only 58 chapters, and a budget of less than $100,000. During his 11-year tenure, he transformed the organization into an international association with 126 chapters, a membership of 12,400, a budget of over $3 million, and a staff of 26.

Under Bailey's direction the association did such outstanding work that it won more American Society of Association Executives awards for high-caliber programs than any other association in the country in a 10-year period. The association distinguished itself in research, professional education, chapter relations, public relations, publications, book publishing, membership development, and awards programs.

Bailey came to New York in 1984 as executive director of the Financial Analysts Federation, a 16,000-member professional society of investment managers and financial analysts. He has been described as someone who "creatively and aggressively contributes to an organization's growth through solid goal setting and skilled management of human and financial resources." Bailey believes that an association's reason for being is to provide services to its members and to "put services out the door." He drives himself and his staff hard to reach this goal. During his three years with the Financial Analysts Federation, his initiatives included surveying membership in detail for the first time, setting up an international affiliate, building membership, establishing strategic planning, instituting zero-base budgeting, and revamping the communication program.

Years of committed volunteer work on behalf of the American Association of Association Executives (ASAE) and the American Cancer Society have been a source of personal and professional growth for Bailey. As a board member of ASAE and as its former national chairman, Bailey has devoted a great deal of time to the leadership of his own profession. He says, "I'm selfish. I never went to a meeting without getting more out of it than I returned to it. You get a sharing of ideas and information."

In 1986, Bailey received ASAE's top honor, the Key Award. He was voted Association Executive of the Year by his peers. He has also been active in the American Cancer Society for many years at local, state, and national levels, serving on executive, finance, personnel, communication, and public information committees. Bailey's credentials include a CAE (Certified Association Executive), and an ABC (Accredited Business Communicator). An accomplished writer and speaker, Bailey has written many byline articles, contributed to books, and spoken to hundreds of groups internationally.

Advice to Others

Bailey says he looks for the following when hiring association staff: "I want doers. I want bright, intelligent people, self-starters, people who are creative and don't have to be told what they should be doing. I want people who can write, who can put words on paper. It is important to communicate in this business. . . . Association management is a people-dealing job."

He says that people tend to come to association management from a variety of backgrounds—journalism, education, and law are common. Association work offers a real career potential for beginners because it is easier to break into as a beginner than at mid-career. Entry-level jobs do not pay much, but benefits often are good. Compensation at the top can be excellent. The field attracts a lot of women and is very opportune for them. Association management is a satisfying business, and people who get into it tend to stay.

Bailey says that those who work their way to the top are usually generalists who branch out and get an overall feel for the mission of the organization. They are the people who can concentrate on the big picture. He emphasizes the need to acquire management skills as one moves up the career ladder, especially time management skills. While it is possible to work your way up in a large organization, Bailey believes that those who move ahead in association management tend to change employers. Overall, he believes that association management is a significant field—and opportune, for to the general public it is still unknown.

Lois Blume

Director of Community Services
Bon Secours Hospital, Villa Maria Nursing Center

"You have to understand power and politics in order to make change."

What She Does

In 1987 Lois Blume was hired by the Villa Maria Nursing Center in North Miami to manage and build up its Adult Day Care Program and to create other new community outreach programs. They were attracted by her impressive history as an entrepreneur, builder, and manager of innovative programs, both in government and in academia.

Established in 1959, Villa Maria is one of nine voluntary hospitals operated by the Sisters of Bon Secours, a Catholic nursing order that provided the first visiting nurses in the United States. Villa Maria is now a 212-bed long-term care and nursing center and a 60-bed rehabilitation hospital. The Sisters' recent decision to provide outpatient services for the elderly and the poor was prompted by several factors: available operating surpluses, which could be invested in community programs; the desire to develop more aggressive marketing practices in a competitive environment; and the need to build better name and quality recognition for Villa Maria within its service area. The Adult Day Care Program is the first of these community services.

Blume manages the Day Care Program with a nurse, two aides, a social worker, an activity therapist, and a secretary. The Adult Day Care Program offers nonresidential care to adults experiencing declining health, memory impairment, or isolation. Services include transportation, meals, socialization, nursing, health monitoring, therapy, recreation, and social services and support to care givers. A weekend Alzheimer's Program provides support to this special population and their families.

During her first year at Villa Maria, Blume concentrated on managing and expanding the Day Care Program, making sure that client and family needs were met; she also concentrated on building working relationships with the staff of the hospital and nursing center. Determined to increase the use of Villa Maria facilities by expanding outpatient use, Blume recognizes that some reeducation of her colleagues is necessary because they previously concentrated exclusively on the care of inpatients.

Blume faces several frustrating dilemmas. She has insufficient time to develop new community services because of her Day Care Program responsibilities. Like other professionals, she often finds herself caught between institutional values that have the potential to be conflicting—caring, human values on one side and financial concerns on the other. There is emerging precedent for entrepreneurial activity at Villa Maria, and Blume is slowly beginning to obtain venture capital and other forms of institutional support.

The resistance of fellow professionals is another obstacle. Despite her frustration and impatience, Blume understands that institutions change slowly and that growth is incremental. She believes the Adult Day Care Program will ultimately be the nucleus of other new services for the noninstitutionalized elderly.

Blume has formulated plans for several initiatives. Convinced that working people would benefit from having a place to bring their elderly charges during the day, she hopes to set up a second adult day care center in a church in the downtown Miami business district. From her prior contacts with the Miami corporate community, she has reason to believe that they would be supportive of an adult day care facility, for it could reduce the loss of productive work time for employees with elderly relatives.

Blume's agenda for other new community services includes a child care center for Villa Maria employees, a day care center and camp for special-needs children, and an income-producing exercise program for older patients who have completed physical therapy and need a supervised follow-up program. Her goal in developing these projects is to take advantage of the institution's existing expertise and equipment for the benefit of other client groups.

(Note: Several months after this interview, Blume reported that her entrepreneurial efforts were succeeding because of solid support from management. The Adult Day Care Center has a waiting list. The State of Florida now provides support for the Alzheimer's Respite Program. Income from fees, grants, and contracts has increased, as has her staff. Joint research and service projects with the University of Miami's Center on Aging and the Easter Seals Society are under way, resulting in the development of additional initiatives.)

Blume's ability to identify needs, visualize solutions, and get programs off the ground and funded is well known. She believes, "Power and politics is how you get things done." She thinks it is important to understand:

> How people behave, why they do things and how they think. You have to figure out what is going to move an institution and what's in it for them, and what's in it for somebody else. Then you have to do the moving from there. I must have it in my gut, because it always works! The first thing is to bring in some income. Do something that will make a bit of money fast and then use that to get more support. You can't get a grant until you have done a lot of work and can show people that you know how to use it and can get something going.

How She Got There

Blume was raised in a sheltered middle-class environment. While attending Hunter High School in New York City, she realized that she had been "walking through life with blinders on." As she woke up to the real world, she developed a social conscience and an interest in political science. She studied political science at Hunter College and graduated with honors. Although she won a scholarship for graduate study at the New School for Social Research, like many women of her generation, she received no support from husband or family for graduate study or career interests. Abandoning her goal, she settled down to raise a family instead.

Her involvement in the League of Women Voters and school board politics became an outlet for Blume's community interests. When her youngest child started nursery school, Blume returned to Hunter College as a graduate student in political science. She received tremendous encouragement at that time and throughout her career from her political science professor and mentor, Dr. Ruth Weintraub.

Dr. Weintraub encouraged Blume to apply for a Ford Foundation internship in state and local government, at a time that no woman had ever been selected for this honor. Dr. Weintraub believed that Blume was the perfect candidate and that she would be selected, as indeed she was. Because of family responsibilities, Blume arranged her internship on Long Island, and she was assigned to the office of the newly elected Supervisor of Nassau County, Eugene Nickerson. It was an exciting time, for Nickerson led a new Democratic administration after years of Republican control of this large suburban county. It was also the beginning of the Johnson era, a period of profound change for local governments. Blume was assigned to the public relations office, and her first assignment was to write captions for press pictures. She says, "I found out that public policy is made in the public relations office. It was a great place to learn."

During her internship, Blume also researched and wrote her master's thesis. Her topic was the impact of federal aid on Nassau County, a subject that no one knew much about. She focused on how new federal funds would help shape local government and what local government could do with the money. At about this time Supervisor Nickerson was called to a meeting on federal aid in Washington, D.C. with Vice-President Hubert Humphrey and the National Association of Counties. When he returned he asked for data on federal aid to Nassau County, and Blume had just written her thesis on the subject. As no one in the Nickerson administration was as well versed as Blume on this subject, she was appointed State and Federal Aid Coordinator of Nassau County.

Blume lobbied and testified about pending legislation. She went to Washington and became a spokesperson for urban counties in Congress. She found out how to get money and obtained millions of dollars for Nassau County. Blume remained with the Nickerson administration for 10 years, the last two years as executive director of the Nassau Drug Addiction Commission. She says, "I started out at the top. A lot of people would be glad to have that kind of power position. I happened to be in the right place at the right time."

After leaving government, Blume began a 14-year career in academia. She started at Hofstra University as Director of the Center for Business and Urban Research and was then invited to become Dean of Continuing Education at Adelphi University. At Adelphi she quickly developed a series of innovative new programs—for-credit and noncredit, undergraduate and graduate, on-campus and off-campus. Her programs brought new adult and part-time students to the university and millions of dollars in additional income.

Then Blume moved to the New School for Social Research, a nontraditional university for adults in New York City, and she built a variety of innovative new graduate degree and certificate programs for the Graduate School of Management and Urban Professions. Blume was Director of Programs in Health Services Administration, Gerontological Services Administration and Fund Raising Management, responsible for 900 students. When she relocated to Florida, she obtained funding to direct a Corporate Initiatives Project for the Southeast Center on Aging at Florida International University. From there she went to Villa Maria.

Blume says she is driven by challenge. She believes that she has not deviated from her lifelong ambition to contribute to the social good and that the intuitive and professional skills she brings to her work have not changed, only the context has. She derives great satisfaction from the fact that, wherever she has built programs and services, these programs and services continue to thrive under new leadership.

Blume has been an active member of many volunteer boards and professional associations in Long Island, New York City, and Miami. She has served as a consultant to government and community agencies, taught graduate courses, and has completed the course work towards her doctorate in political science.

Advice to Others

Blume believes that the nonprofit sector is a good place for an idealistic young person who wants to make a difference, who is interested in social and political change, and who wants to make the world a better place to live. She advises against working for a very large organization, because it is hard to demonstrate what you can do in such a setting.

From her experience in academia, where she advised hundreds of students, she knows that people develop more than one work role in life. She notes that, "Not too many people start out where they end up." A proponent of mentors and networking, Blume is also a strong believer in periodic participation in professional management education programs as a way to broaden understanding, to develop nuts-and-bolts skills, and to give direction to a career.

Albert W. Garrison

Director of Finance
Synod of Southern California and Hawaii
Presbyterian Church U.S.A.

*"I came here almost by accident, and now that I'm here I want to
stay, because there is such a need for strong financial management."*

What He Does

As Director of Finance of the Synod of Southern California and Hawaii, Albert Garrison
manages an annual budget of $5 million and assets of about $30 million. The Synod, a
nonprofit corporation, includes 311 churches, 123,000 church members, and eight Presbyteries
(local administrative units that work with about 40 churches each). The Presbyterian Church
has a vertical system of management, with the local church at the base, the Presbyteries at
the next level, then the 16 Synods and the General Assembly at the top. (There are 11,000
Presbyterian churches in the U.S. with a total membership of over 3 million people). The
income of the Synods, Presbyteries, and General Assembly comes from donations at the local
church level; approximately ten cents of every dollar collected is provided to the other three
units.

As an intermediate administrative agency, the Synod's responsibilities include: coordination,
communication, fundraising, consultation, technical assistance, joint action with other de-
nominations, and the provision of services and programs that can only be offered from a broad
regional base. For example, the Synod is deeply involved in outreach and programs for special
populations including the elderly, women, and Asian, black, and Hispanic Americans.

Garrison reports to the Synod Executive. As one of only two Synod managers who is not
an ordained minister, he interacts with 15 Associate Executives who are ordained. He reports
a good working relationship based on mutual respect for special expertise.

Garrison describes his role as being similar to that of a corporate controller, treasurer, or
vice-president of finance of any firm. He deals with banks and investments, overseeing the
management of the Synod's money. He buys and manages real estate, and he handles insurance, financial reporting, and computerization. Garrison also provides financial advice to
the Synod's churches and Presbyteries. He emphasizes that budgeting and financial planning
is a year-round process that involves a volunteer budget committee that acts on all budget
requests.

How He Got There

Garrison was born in Montana and raised in the Middle West. He graduated from the University of Missouri with a degree in business administration. He went to work for the General Electric Company in Syracuse, New York, where he rose through the ranks by assuming a variety of financial management responsibilities. In 1968, while living in Cleveland, he accepted a position with TRW as a corporate controller and relocated to Redondo Beach, California, to head up a new unit, the Industrial Operations Group, which acquired small companies outside of the aerospace industry. When TRW later wanted to move him again, he decided to leave the firm and stay in California. Over the next several years he was corporate controller for one firm and manager of product support for another.

Garrison began to learn about church and nonprofit management in 1976 when he became treasurer and controller of Pacific Homes in Los Angeles, a group of seven nursing homes and seven retirement homes owned by the Methodists. The Homes had filed for bankruptcy. They had been operated by pastors with no background in financial management. Inflation, high costs, and poor management of the funds turned over by the residents in return for lifetime care, had caused severe problems. A trustee appointed by the bankruptcy court had taken over the administration of the Homes. The reorganization lasted five years, and when Pacific Homes was back in financial good health, Garrison's job was finished.

At that time the Presbyterian Synod of Southern California and Hawaii was looking for a Director of Finance. A Presbyterian, Garrison interviewed for the job with some uncertainty as to whether this was what he wanted to do. He had, after all, spent his entire career working on large projects for large organizations. After a lengthy and complex employment intake process, he was offered the job, and Garrison accepted it with the thought that it would do nothing until something else came along. He says:

> One of the things I didn't like, and I think others don't necessarily like about church work, is that the compensation is not good. I had been used to making a lot more money. One of the reasons I could take this job is, that several years before, my wife and I had started a Baskin Robbins Ice Cream franchise. Income is not a big deal with me, and it still isn't, but obviously I am used to spending more money than I make here. I was able to take this job because we had something else. The church has benefited from that.

Garrison is active in an association of Presbyterian business administrators. He does some training on business management and auditing for the Methodists in Southern California. He wishes he had time for more professional development activities but notes that, like other managers in the church, he is "busy all the time."

Advice to Others

Garrison is very concerned about compensation in church management positions. He points out that salaries are low, noting:

> Ordained employees do not have high salary expectations. . . . When they go into this work, they have to say to themselves it's not going to be a big paying job. For the most part people don't complain, and nobody leaves. Nobody has left the Synod because of pay. We're so busy, we don't have time to fret or pout about it. It is true that some pastors, particularly in the West, make a lot

of money. Those individuals who do administrative work for low pay are not necessarily less competitive or aggressive; they would just rather do this kind of work. There is a lot of power in an office like this.

Garrison's three grown children all work in some aspect of business or management. Despite the tremendous satisfaction that he personally derives from his work, he has not encouraged them to work in a nonprofit environment, "because the money isn't there." He believes that only those who are financially independent or have outside income can afford to take church management positions. That often means older people or retirees. He therefore sees a problem both for the church, which may not be able to recruit the kind of talented people it can use, and for people who are drawn to this work but cannot afford to work for the salaries the church can pay.

Evaluation is another matter of concern for Garrison. He says, "I think we church workers, at least the Presbyterians, are not supervised or managed very well. We kind of do the things we like to do, when we want to do them. And the things we don't like to do, we don't do. Maybe we're not doing what we ought to be doing. . . . We're not measured very well, even though we go through a rather complex performance review process with our personnel committee. Our performance report in this office is pretty much based on what we think we do. . . . In other words, the office allows us to pretty much evaluate our own performance."

6

Managers of Philanthropy

Dispensers of Philanthropy

Americans are a generous people, willing and eager to support the causes and institutions they believe in and that affect their lives. *The Charitable Behavior of Americans* (Independent Sector, 1986) reveals that 89 percent of Americans reported giving an average of $680 a year for charitable purposes. Motivations for giving are varied and complex. They may be based on personal and emotional considerations, on rational decisions, or on a combination of the two.

Professionals make an interesting distinction between charity and philanthropy. Charity is characterized as a spontaneous response resulting from emotion; while philanthropy is a planned response involving thought before action. The decision to give may be stimulated by the savings that accrue to the giver because of the tax deductibility of the contribution. Whatever their reasons for giving, research studies confirm that Americans at all income levels exercise their nobler impulses and make contributions.

Since 1955, estimates of total charitable contributions to nonprofit organizations have been compiled annually by the American Association of Fund-Raising Counsel (AAFRC). In 1955, estimated giving was $7.7 billion, and giving has increased every year since then, reaching $92 billion in 1987. Individual donors are the source of most of these funds, and the rest comes from bequests, foundations, and corporations.

Table 6.1 illustrates who the donors are and how much they gave in 1987.

TABLE 6.1. TOTAL GIVING 1987

Contributions in 1987	Amount in Billions	As % of Total
Individual	$86.70	83.1
Bequests	6.79	6.79
Foundations	6.13	5.9
Corporations	4.75	4.6

Source: *Giving USA: The Annual Report on Philanthropy for the Year 1988,* AAFRC Trust for Philanthropy.

Annual giving has averaged about 2 percent of the gross national product over recent years. Several hundred thousand nonprofit organizations depend on donations as a critical source of income. Given this dimension of giving, the philanthropic enterprise must be viewed as a significant industry and, by extension, as a provider of jobs.

According to Jack Schwartz, former President of AAFRC, "The three forces that make up the philanthropic enterprise are the donor, the donee, and the enabler—otherwise known as fundraising manager." In this section we describe some of the management opportunities that exist on the donor side. This is a small, sophisticated work force operating in what is known as "organized philanthropy," which includes foundations, corporate giving programs, and federated philanthropies such as United Way agencies. The people who staff these organizations are dispensers of philanthropy—professionals charged with the responsibility of managing and giving away large sums of money. Acting as intermediaries between donors with largesse to give and applicants who need their help, grantmakers give away money that is not their own.

We will be discussing here the 10 percent of philanthropy that is carried out through formal organizations. In fact, individual gifts and bequests account for approximately 90 percent of total annual contributions, but because these are essentially private transactions, it is difficult to ascribe specific job opportunities to them. This is not to overlook the fact that in the process of making their gift, individual donors may work with lawyers, accountants, insurance brokers, planned giving specialists, and trust officers.

Working in Foundations

What is a foundation? The *Foundation Directory* defines a foundation as a "nongovernmental nonprofit organization with its own funds (usually from a single source, either an individual, family, or corporation) and program managed by its own trustees and director, which was established to aid educational, social, charitable, religious, or other activities serving the common welfare primarily by making grants to other nonprofit organizations."

There are approximately 25,000 foundations in the United States. Figure 6.1 describes the four types of foundations: independent foundations, community foundations, operating foundations, and company-sponsored foundations.

FIGURE 6.1. THE FOUR TYPES OF FOUNDATIONS

Independent Foundation: A fund or endowment designated by the Internal Revenue Service as a private foundation under the law, the primary function of which is the making of grants. The assets of most independent foundations are derived from the gift of an individual or family. Some function under the direction of family members and are known as "family foundations." Depending on the range of their giving, independent foundations may also be known as "general purpose" or "special purpose" foundations.

Company-Sponsored Foundation: A private foundation under the tax law deriving its funds from a profit-making company or corporation but independently constituted, the purpose of which is to make grants, usually on a broad basis although not without regard for the business interests of the corporation. Company-sponsored foundations are legally distinct from corporation contributions programs administered within the corporation directly from corporate funds.

Operating Foundation: A fund or endowment designated under the tax law by the Internal Revenue Service as a private foundation, the primary purpose of which is to operate research, social welfare, or other programs determined by its governing body or charter.

Community Foundation: In its general charitable purpose, a community foundation is much like many private foundations; however, its funds are derived from many donors rather than a single source, as is usually the case with private foundations. Further, community foundations are usually classified under the tax law as public charities and are therefore subject to different rules and regulations under the tax law than those which govern private foundations.

Source: *The Foundation Directory,* 12th Edition, 1989. New York: The Foundation Center.

Foundations are a very diverse group of organizations, differing in type, size, mission, and *modus operandi.* Their individual mandates express the wishes of their founders. Their on-going policies are determined by the boards of trustees that govern them, with these policies executed by staff, if there is a staff. About 20 percent of all foundations hold 97 percent of total foundation assets and account for 92 percent of the awards made.

Recent surveys of foundations suggest that about 1,500 foundations employ staff. Estimates vary, but they suggest that there are on the order of 5,000 to 7,000 foundation jobs. These include full- and part-time professionals as well as support staff. Large foundations, community foundations, and corporate foundations are the most likely to employ staff. The smaller foundations are often managed by lawyers, accountants, family members, or corporate executives with other responsibilities.

People who work in foundations think of themselves as generalists without any particular qualifications. Major job categories in foundations include chief executive officer, program officer, administrative assistant, and executive secretary. A 1984 Council on Foundations survey resulted in a detailed classification and definition of foundation jobs. This listing is included at the end of this text as Appendix B.

Opportunities for women in foundations differ markedly from those available to men, reflecting current patterns in the general work force. Women make up 66 percent of foundation employees, but two-thirds of these women are employed in support positions, and female professionals earn 59 cents for every dollar earned by men. Foundation heads tend to be men with advanced degrees from elite institutions, and they tend to hire program officers with similar backgrounds. These staffing patterns are slowly changing in the foundation world, largely as a result of advocacy groups like Women and Foundations/Corporate Philanthropy (WAF/CP), which fosters greater awareness of the roles and needs of women. WAF/CP sponsored the research that led to the definitive portrayal of work in this elite occupational field, *Working in Foundations: Career Patterns of Women and Men,* by Odendahl, Boris, and Daniels. This book is required reading for anyone who wants to work in foundations.

Foundation heads come from many different backgrounds, generally significant positions in academia, government, or business. Some have built a career in foundation philanthropy and have moved from smaller foundations to larger ones. Others are chosen for their eminence, sometimes at the point of retirement from a prestigious position in another field. Career patterns tend to be different for female chief executives. Some may have come from significant full-time volunteer jobs, while others may have started in foundations as ambitious administrative assistants and worked their way to the top.

There are no educational programs to prepare foundation staff for the challenges they face. A few colleges and universities started to offer undergraduate courses in philanthropy in 1987, as a first step in creating greater awareness of the history of philanthropy and the significance of the nonprofit sector. The Council on Foundations (the association of foundations) and regional associations of grantmakers periodically offer professional development programs for foundation staff.

Paul Olson, President of the Blandin Foundation, summarized the problem of preparing for foundation work in a *Foundation News* article as follows, "I can think of no other industry handling such great financial resources that has so little training as the foundation professional staff. We have no curriculum, no body of knowledge, no prescribed competencies that suggest we are qualified." Among his recommendations for overcoming these problems, he suggests that every foundation institute a personal development policy and require each staff member to develop their own personal development plan.

Since the majority of foundations that have staff employ only one to three people, career ladders are short. The fact that opportunities for advancement are limited is offset by the prestige and high interest level of the work. There is a constant flow of new people and ideas to deal with, and the opportunity to influence board policies and funding decisions. Career advancement is possible, sometimes within the foundation field, often by a move into related fields.

In this section, the profiles of Steve Minter and Barry Gaberman describe management positions in two very different foundations. Steve Minter came to foundation work from a distinguished background in social service and government. He heads a community foundation dedicated to supporting one specific area, greater Cleveland. Barry Gaberman, on the other hand, has spent his entire working life at the Ford Foundation, the largest foundation in America. Its mammoth resources are used to address fundamental human problems in the United States and in the third world.

Working in Corporate Contributions Programs

Corporate giving is another growing and complex area of philanthropy. Corporate philanthropy is part of a corporation's external relations with its communities and markets. It is a way for business to exercise its social responsibilities and to return something to the communities from which it benefits. It offers the corporation an opportunity to generate visibility and good will. Corporate contributions are made in one or more of the following three ways:

- A corporation may set up a separate company foundation as a vehicle for its giving programs.
- A corporation may allocate funds annually for corporate contributions on the basis of the company's profits.
- Donations may be charged to corporate expense budgets instead of the contributions budget.

Corporate giving programs provide cash assistance and noncash assistance, which may include loaned executives, surplus equipment, vehicles, land, buildings, meeting space, writing, printing and secretarial services, and almost anything that a corporation can spare or share.

Figure 6.2 is an excerpt from the Pillsbury Company's Community Relations Annual Report, 1987, illustrating a corporate philosophy about meeting community needs.

FIGURE 6.2.

THE PILLSBURY WAY

Corporate philanthropy has new rules. They weren't written by a committee. They evolved from significant economic forces that have changed every state, city and neighborhood in the country: cutbacks in government spending for human services, the growing gap between the rich and the poor and the restructuring of American business.

As a major food company, Pillsbury is creating distinctive strategies for funding, suited for our particular businesses, to respond to this new reality of critical need. In that sense, "charitable giving" for Pillsbury may be a misnomer. We would suggest, perhaps "charitable investing" because that is what we do—invest the best that we have to offer—in cash, technical expertise, employee-volunteers, donated product and facilities—in the future of those non-profit organizations whose clients can benefit most from our partnership. If that partnership is to prosper, we must:

[　] Listen.
[　] Focus on important issues where we, as a total food company, can make a difference.
[　] Build community relations priorities into our business.

[　] Respond creatively and sensitively.
[　] Take advantage of our resources throughout the company.
[　] Constantly evaluate the efforts of our programs, to be certain we *are* making a difference.

Source: The Pillsbury Company Community Relations Annual Report, 1987

The corporate contributions function may be administered by the chief executive's office or assigned to another key executive. Where a staff person is assigned to handle this responsibility, it will most likely be a professional in the public affairs department. A 1982 Conference Board survey of top 1,300 *Fortune* companies revealed that only a few hundred major corporations operate full-time staffed contributions programs and that more than half of contributions executives have other responsibilities. The Public Affairs Office typically serves as an umbrella for a broad array of functions, and the person handling corporate contributions may also be handling functions like public relations, government relations, political action, strategic planning, stockholder relations, and issues management. Where full-time contributions programs do exist, they generally consist of one or two people.

The career profile of Cecile Springer exemplifies the corporate executive with dual responsibilities, corporate contributions and community relations. Liz Sode, on the other hand, is a corporate executive who devotes most of her time to the corporation's business and only a part of her time to the management of a corporate foundation. Both women are creative, entrepreneurial, and productive, and their careers illustrate opportunities for service in corporate jobs.

Employment in Federated Campaigns

Federated or combined campaigns were established by groups of nonprofit organizations for the purpose of sponsoring a joint annual fundraising campaign for the benefit of the participating organizations. Federated campaigns were introduced in the late nineteenth century by businessmen tired of being bombarded by community organizations seeking donations. They believed that there must be a better way to handle appeals and donations and sought an organized system for evaluating the merits of requests for contributions and for reducing the competition among needy groups. Over time, the unified appeals came into use in many communities as a system that benefited both donors and recipients.

Recently, federated fundraising has been closely identified with work-place fundraising, especially since the introduction of the payroll deduction system—a refinement developed by United Way, the largest welfare federation. This 100-year old organization sponsors drives in 2,200 communities nationwide.

There now are a variety of other joint appeals operating in the philanthropic market place. Some, like the National Catholic Campaign for Human Development, the Protestant Welfare Federation, and Federation of Jewish Philanthropies/United Jewish Appeal, have a common denominational interest. Others, such as the Combined Health Appeals, United Arts Funds, International Service Agencies, Black United Funds, and the United Negro College Fund, serve special interests.

Alternative funds have also been organized as a counterpoint to United Way to serve newer, more controversial organizations and grass-roots groups. By virtue of their number and size, the United Way agencies are the major providers of jobs in this field. The profile of Jack Sage, a United Way career professional, describes the challenges associated with raising and distributing funds in the local community. Appendix E, United Way of America, 1987, Summary of Position Classification offers an overview of United Way jobs.

For Further Information

How you go about locating these depends on where you live. Look for a library, technical assistance center, local nonprofit association, or academic center. If you live in the greater New York, Washington, D.C., Chicago, San Francisco, or Cleveland area, your first step should be at one of the Foundation Center's libraries. The Foundation Center is a service organization which provides information about foundations, primarily to grantseekers. They also maintain an outstanding collection of materials about nonprofit organizations and nonprofit management. Their extensive, well-organized resources and knowledgeable librarians can also be immensely helpful to job seekers and career changers. In addition to its four main libraries, the Foundation Center has a nationwide network of cooperating libraries that house some of the Center's major current directories. See Appendix D for a complete listing of these libraries.

Once you have identified a resource, you should:

- Identify the foundations in your area by consulting *The Foundation Directory,* or state and local directories.

- Find out whether there is a regional association of grantmakers. They may publish a bulletin listing jobs or circulate position announcements on behalf of their members. (The New York Regional Association of Grantmakers does both.)

- Check position listings in *Foundation News* and other periodicals and bulletins in the field of philanthropy. The Foundation Center posts position listings on its bulletin boards. Local nonprofit resource centers may do so as well.

- Try to find printed materials like the Foundation Center's fact sheets on *Finding Work with Grantmakers and Other Nonprofit Organizations* and *Corporate Fundraising Sources.*

- Attend workshops and conferences in your area that attract both grantmakers and non-profit agencies. Networking is a critical component in the job search process.

Additionally, the authors recommend the following titles as being particularly useful while conducting a job search in foundation work.

Daniels, Arlene Kaplan
  1988 "Career Scenarios in Foundation Work," in *Educating Managers for Nonprofit Organizations.* New York: Praeger. (This chapter is a further expansion of information developed for *Working in Foundations*, see below.)

Joseph, James A., Elizabeth T. Boris, and Carol A. Hooper
  1984 *Foundation Management Report.* Washington, DC: Council on Foundations. (The biannual survey of over 500 foundations contains detailed information on staff compensation, employee benefits, and personnel policies.)

Odendahl, Teresa, Elizabeth T. Boris, and Arlene K. Daniels
  1985 *Working in Foundations: Career Patterns of Women and Men.* New York: The Foundation Center. (An exhaustive, well-documented study and analysis of work in foundations.)

The Foundation Center
  1989 *The Foundation Directory,* 12th edition. New York: The Foundation Center. (This biannual directory is the most comprehensive resource on America's 6,700 largest foundations. A lengthy introduction provides the most up-to-date information on all aspects of foundations, including staffing patterns.)

Steven Alan Minter

Director
The Cleveland Foundation

"Look forward. Keep investing in yourself. Learning never ends."

What He Does

As chief executive officer of the oldest and second largest community foundation in the country, Steven A. Minter operates at the intersection of community needs and philanthropic investment. In 1987 the Cleveland Foundation managed a $427 million pool of bequests, gifts, and special funds. The earnings from these funds—$25 million in 1987—are allocated annually to Cleveland's nonprofit organizations. The foundation makes grants for civic affairs, cultural affairs, economic development, health, social services, and special purposes. It works closely with Cleveland's public, corporate, and nonprofit sectors, acting as a "funder, catalyst, convener, educator, and philanthropic leader."

In the Foundation's 1986 *Annual Report*, Minter writes:

> What the Cleveland Foundation is ultimately investing in is people: their ideas, their energy, their commitment, their imagination. For if this community is going to have a future marked by opportunity and grace, it first has to be imagined. And then it has to be invested in, with all the resources, all of the commitment, all of the energy we have.

As chief executive, Minter works with an 11-person Distribution Committee that makes policy and allocates funds and a five-person Trustee Committee, which consists of the chief executive officers of the foundation's trustee banks.

As chief operating officer, Minter formulates the foundation's broad objectives, policies, and programs for approval by the Distribution Committee. He must "chart a suitable long-range course of action for the foundation." Minter works with a staff of 35, including program officers for each area of interest, functional managers—who administer donor relations, community relations and publications, financial services, and grant services—and backup staff.

How He Got There

In 1956, with $200 and encouragement from his high school teachers and principal, Steve Minter began his studies at Baldwin-Wallace College. In the summer of 1960, his teaching certificate in physical education and history did not open any employment doors in communities "not yet ready for black teachers." Therefore, Minter found work as a caseworker at the Cuyahoga County Welfare Department (CCWD).

The day he began work was, coincidentally, the day that the CCWD's first group of employees was leaving to participate in a funded master's degree program in social service administration at Case Western Reserve University. Minter was inspired by CCWD's send-off celebration for its future leadership. The location of his desk at this first job, next to the administrative offices, afforded him direct view of the organizational management process and of different leadership styles. In June 1963, with both a master's degree in social service administration and civil service status in hand, Minter began a six-year climb up the ranks to become the youngest director of the Cuyahoga County Welfare Department.

In 1970, Minter moved to state government as Commissioner of Public Welfare for the Commonwealth of Massachusetts, a cabinet position, with responsibility over a $500 million budget and 5,000 employees.

A change in Massachusetts political administration in 1974 coincided with Steve Minter's desire to broaden his experience. He returned to Cleveland in 1975 as a Social Services and Civic Affairs program officer of the Cleveland Foundation, evaluating proposals and recommending projects receiving approximately $5 million per year. In 1980 he took a leave of absence from the Cleveland Foundation to help organize the new Department of Education in Washington, D.C., as Under-Secretary (chief operating officer). He returned to the Cleveland Foundation in 1981 and was selected to become its Director in 1984.

Minter currently serves as a director of the Goodyear Tire and Rubber Company, the Ohio Bell Telephone Company, and the Society National Bank and Corporation. He is also a trustee of the College of Wooster, the Independent Sector, and the American Public Welfare Association, and he continues active participation at the Council on Foundations and the Presbyterian Church USA. He has published journal articles and holds honorary doctorates from Oberlin College, Kent State University, Baldwin-Wallace College, and Findlay College.

Advice to Others

Minter pinpoints the following career advancement strategies that have worked for him:

- Seek mentors; use mentors.
- Expect much of yourself; give much of yourself.
- Listen to others. Their stories of how "they got there" offer models for success.
- Ask questions. It takes a degree of comfort and self-confidence to say, "You know, I'm really a novice at this."
- Be responsible for your own professional growth. Invest your own time and money in professional association memberships, subscriptions, and conference attendance. Make up the time you miss from the regular work day by working late.
- Volunteer for in-house and related community activities.
- Assume that there is a fabulous network for people "out there" who will give you advice and assistance. Ask them.

- Know and respect your constituents: clients, the public government, funders, the business community, and professional colleagues.

Steven Minter does not think that any one kind of professional education necessarily offers the best preparation for becoming a nonprofit manager. However, he emphasizes the need for a direct service background and the value of the hands-on program experience, particularly "when you are in a position of making decisions about what people do or how programs are run."

Having worked at all levels of government, as well as in the nonprofit sector and with business, Minter is an expert on transferring skills. A generalist who is able to work effectively in many specialized areas, he attributes his success to "maintaining a broad view of the world" and "a constant searching for perspective."

Barry D. Gaberman

Deputy Vice-President
United States and International Affairs Program
Ford Foundation

*"I try to make people understand that we don't do anything. We are
a grantmaking organization and we try to exercise judgement in the
things we choose to support, but the guts of what we do is to give
money to someone else to do something."*

What He Does

In his 17 years with the Ford Foundation, Barry Gaberman has been a program officer in the Third World and in New York, the head of the office of Program-Related Investments, and he is now a top-level manager.

The Ford Foundation is a unique institution. With an asset base of over $5 billion, it is the largest private grantmaking foundation in the United States. According to a recent *Annual Report*, the foundation's purpose is "to advance human welfare," more specifically "to identify and contribute to the solution of problems of national or international importance that give promise of producing significant advances in various fields." The foundation's global concerns are targeted to the United States and Third World countries. Support is given to people and projects grappling with critical human problems.

The United States and the International Affairs Programs, which is Gaberman's current domain, oversee six major program offices: Urban Poverty, Rural Poverty and Resources, Human Rights and Governance, Education and Culture, International Affairs, and Program-Related Investments. The Division employs over 100 professionals and support staff and spends about $160 million annually on some 600 grants.

As Deputy Vice-President, Gaberman works closely with the U.S. and International Affairs Vice-President. His responsibilities are largely supervisory and managerial. He sets internal administrative and program priorities, evaluates the constant flow of information that comes from program officers and directors of the division's substantive programs, and he monitors a number of large grants.

The direct intermediary between the Ford Foundation, its grantseekers, and its grant recipients is the all important program officer who serves as a broker or entrepreneur in bringing many diverse interests together. At Ford a program officer is responsible for a budget of about

$4 million and covers 30 to 60 active grants of two- or three-year duration. Gaberman offers insight into the complexity of a large foundation's work by describing what a program officer does everyday:

- Read, review, and respond to a number of proposals within their subject specialties. The response may be a phone call, letter, or a site visit. Apparently the maybe's—the proposals that elicit neither a positive, nor negative reaction on first reading—are the most difficult proposals to deal with. Gaberman cautions that "you may become isolated from the hopes and aspirations that people have when they put together a proposal, because you are deadened by so many requests for funds."
- Monitor a set of grants that are already in place.
- Conduct telephone conversations with people who have ideas and need instruction about what sort of descriptive letter and materials to send in for preliminary review by the foundation. Ford is open to unsolicited proposals, recognizing that good ideas can come from anywhere. The foundation takes a more active role in established interest areas where they not only have in-house staff expertise but also years of research and field experience. In these instances they are in a position to identify gaps, commit resources to get things started, and bring in other organizations as partners in large-scale projects.
- Prepare convincing presentations and support documents for the in-house review of each proposal being recommended for funding.
- Collaborate with colleagues at Ford on projects that fall into more than one interest area.

Ford Foundation program officers also travel a great deal and are expected to maintain a range of professional relationships and activities that will keep them at the forefront of their subject areas and in close touch with the outside world.

Gaberman says that in his line of work you have to keep asking yourself, "What is it that we are collectively learning that is of use in designing better programs for the future, that allows us to have an impact on larger numbers of people?" He emphasizes that foundations can do things that are harder for public institutions to do. Foundations can risk failure and find out that an idea is not workable, they can fund controversial experiments, and they can concentrate a lot of money on a single demonstration project. Also, they can take chances, such as funding a small organization without a track record.

How He Got There

Barry Gaberman was born in China, and although he was raised in the U.S., he always maintained an interest in Asia. Because of an uncle who settled in the Philippines, he became particularly interested in South East Asia. After high school, he enlisted in the army, and while he was stationed in Europe the problems in Vietnam began to surface and he became increasingly concerned about them. This intense interest continued after he completed military service and enrolled in the University of Wisconsin. Gaberman planned to study political science as an undergraduate in preparation for law school. In his senior year, however, several courses in comparative politics and politics of the Third World were so stimulating that he decided to defer law school and pursue graduate studies in political science. Ultimately, he focused on Indonesia as his special area of interest.

After completing his master's degree in political science at the University of Wisconsin, he continued in the doctoral program, preparing for a university career in comparative politics. He became a teaching assistant for courses in American foreign policy, Chinese politics, and the politics of poverty and social welfare.

In the summer of 1968, Gaberman completed an intensive Indonesian language program at Cornell, which subsequently turned out to be helpful to his application for a position at the Ford Foundation's Indonesian Field Office. During a proposed two-year stint in Indonesia, he hoped to develop a research topic for his doctoral thesis and to stay on to do field work. Funds for academic research were tight at this time and this appeared to be a good plan.

Actually, Gaberman stayed four years in Indonesia with Ford. He was promoted and assumed both program and management responsibilities. These included monitoring, evaluating, and developing programs in population, agriculture, renewable resources and social sciences, and helping to manage a large staff.

He returned to New York in 1975 to the foundation's Asia and Pacific Office. As an Assistant Program Officer and then as Program Officer, he was responsible for developing new programs as well as monitoring and supporting all of the Asian field offices. Although he completed his doctoral course work, he decided to continue his work at Ford. He says, "I discovered something about myself that made the foundation more appropriate than academia. . . . I was not terribly well suited to the somewhat lonely and isolated research and writing experience. . . . I prefer to work on 25 different things and am willing to sacrifice some of the depth for the variety."

In 1979, the Ford Foundation went through a period of reorganization. New opportunities opened up and Gaberman spent the next three years working on management and financial projects. As an advisor to the Vice-President for Organization and Management, he worked on the review of information and data-processing systems, and he provided staff support to the Trustees Committee on Audit and Management. As the head of the Office of Program-Related Investments, he charted the direction of a $50-million revolving capital investment fund, upgraded their portfolio, and hired and supervised staff.

Since 1982 Gaberman has been part of the top management of the foundation's United States and International Affairs Programs, first as Program Officer in Charge, and now as Deputy Vice-President.

Gaberman's own professional development is a product of achieving increased levels of responsibility in a collegial organization that fosters growth by the very nature of its work. Gaberman has participated in a Wharton School Program in Finance and Accounting for the Nonfinancial Manager. He says, "Like most people who get involved in the sector, it was an accident. . . . I had no idea what the foundation world was about. . . . I have been here for 17 years now, in an institution where as program officers you can expect to be here for 4 to 5 years. There is no tenure, and everybody here, including me, is on a one-year contract."

Advice to Others

Professional opportunities in foundation work are somewhat limited. Employment by a foundation is largely a matter of luck. It helps to be known in the network of organizations and institutions that interact with the foundation world.

People who hold professional jobs in foundations have a strong academic background, intellectual curiosity, and a global perspective on issues and ideas. Creative thinking, critical analysis, and the ability to communicate and interact with other professionals are essential. At Ford, Gaberman says, they value people who understand the art of decision-making. The practical question is, "How do you make the decision about who to support, given the fact that you don't have the time nor the resources to have all of the information that you need to make the decision?" Timely decision-making is so important because if you take too long, the issue is past. Ideally, foundation people will understand not only what it means to come up with a powerful idea but also what all the necessary steps and tactics are that will put that idea to work.

Jack J. Sage

President and Chief Professional Officer
United Way of Long Island

*"We feel that we are part of the problem-solving mechanism of
the community and we have a responsibility to raise money and
stimulate generosity."*

What He Does

As head of United Way of Long Island, Jack Sage leads and directs his agency's two key
functions: workplace fundraising, and allocations to the 135 human service agencies that
participate in the United Way campaign. His job demands the management competencies
required of any CEO and, in addition, a high degree of skill in working with the local business
and human services communities.

United Way of Long Island is one of 2,200 United Ways across the country. Nationally,
United Way is a 100-year-old movement that now raises $2.5 billion annually and helps to
support 37,000 service organizations. As articulated by the national association, United Way
of America, the organization's mission is "to increase the organized capacity of people to care
for one another."

United Ways have a systematic approach to community fundraising. By combining the
appeals of many organizations into one annual appeal, a United Way offers employers and
employees a simple way to make contributions and eliminates some of the competition for
funds among local agencies and institutions.

Participating employers—typically those with over 100 workers—institute a payroll deduction program. Payroll deduction is a relatively painless way of giving and by making one
donation, a giver supports a variety of human service organizations. Volunteer review panels
decide how to allocate the funds collected this way, as well as funds from employer and
individual contributions. Every year a number of review panels are charged with the task of
evaluating applications for refunding and new applications for funding. Allocations are made
on the basis of continuing need or new needs and take into account agency performance,
financial health, and leadership.

Each local United Way agency has its own character. The United Way of Long Island,
founded in 1965, serves a complex suburban area with a population of 2.6 million residents.
Long Island is 100 miles long, spans two counties, and has 875 government units. Long Island

is affluent, and small business, light industry, high technology, and service firms dominate its economy. Fundraising is a challenge because the area has no central core and residents' loyalties and interests are fragmented. Also, Long Island charitable organizations often compete with New York City for the charitable dollar, because many residents live on Long Island but work in New York City.

As president, Sage works with an independent voluntary board of up to 36 members plus numerous other volunteer committees, and a 25-member staff, supplemented by a large loaned-executives program. His top staff consists of an Executive Vice-President/Campaign Director and Vice-Presidents for Allocations and Planning, Marketing and Communications, Finance and Administration, and Management Information Systems. (For further information about United Way jobs, see Appendix A at the end of this text, *United Way of America, 1987 Summary of Position Classifications.*)

In 1986 United Way of Long Island received $8.7 million in pledges—about 72 percent from employees, 23 percent from corporations, and 5 percent from individuals. Total funds distributed in the year starting July 1987 was $7.6 million. These funds helped support 135 Long Island agencies and hospitals, benefiting 1.25 million people. Only $.12 of every dollar donated was spent on overhead.

Since taking over the direction of the agency in 1983, Sage has increased its fundraising income by 56 percent, its allocations by 60 percent, and the number of participating employers from 500 to over 1,000. He has also eliminated the agency's long-term debt, and, by establishing an area-wide Agency Executives Council, he has improved his organization's credibility and visibility. Cooperative agreements with other local funds, a new planned giving program, and greater emphasis on marketing and long-term planning are among the initiatives that Sage points to with pride.

Because of its central role in helping to support member agencies, United Way has many opportunities to improve the human service system. One of the ways to help, Sage says, is to bring together and coordinate agencies providing innovative services. Such agencies often do not cooperate. Sage says, "We will try to make a network out of a care system, linking agencies through technology." An example is the FIRST CALL FOR HELP, a United Way project that offers information and referral about care services on Long Island and in other parts of the country.

As he looks ahead, Sage plans to reach out for contributions from another 350 Long Island employers with over 100 employees, and to make contact with some of Long Island's 72,000 smaller employers through their business associations.

How He Got There

Since childhood Sage has been a constant reader, with history always a compelling interest. He pursued a liberal arts program at St. Francis College in Milwaukee. While he was in college, the plight of Mexican farm workers in Wisconsin came to his attention and led him to volunteer. One summer he ran an education program for migrant children.

He was shocked by conditions in the migrants' camp. Not even reading Steinbeck's *Grapes of Wrath* had prepared him for what he saw. When he returned to college in the fall, he volunteered to work at the Hispanic Center of the Catholic Archdiocese in Milwaukee. He spent a second summer at the migrant camp, and these experiences led Sage to his decision to become a social worker and to enroll in the Master of Social Work (MSW) program at the University of Wisconsin in Milwaukee.

In graduate school, his first-year field placement was in the Child Protection Unit of the Milwaukee County Department of Welfare. Sage says, "It was dreadful to see children abused. . . . I wanted to change the world not just help individuals. . . . So in the second year, I changed my major to community organization." His second-year field placement was at Milwaukee United Community Services (now Milwaukee United Way). The agency was at that time the subcontractor for the War on Poverty Programs, and Sage found his work there very rewarding. A United Way of America recruiter talked to him about planning a career in the United Way system and circulated his résumé around the country. By the time he completed his MSW, he had received several job offers.

Sage began his career with United Way in 1967 as an associate executive in New Haven, Connecticut. It was an exciting time to be there, for United Way was a partner with the city administration in the War on Poverty. Mayor Dick Lee's efforts to create real change in his community were well publicized, and there was Ford Foundation support for experiments in social change. Sage was assigned to an interracial neighborhood during a confrontational period. He says, "Unfortunately when I got there it was all winding down. The Ford Foundation grant had stimulated a lot of quick successes, then some failures in the methodology began to appear. It was a great learning experience because I was there for all of the failures."

A trained community organizer, Sage was primarily interested in United Way planning and allocation functions. But, at the New Haven United Way, their professionals had a chance to do everything. To his surprise, he found that he had a flair for public relations. He also learned that the route to becoming executive director or president of a United Way agency was through fundraising. Sage wanted to rise to the top, to be in charge, to become a leader, and to have influence.

Sage says, "I liked everything about United Way . . . the whole process." He loved the challenge of working with the brainiest and toughest volunteers in the community, often successful business leaders. The fact that salaries and fringe benefits were quite high in comparison to those of other human service agencies was another inducement to building a career at United Way.

His next job was as associate director of United Way of Duluth, a number-two position that carried with it major fundraising assignments, particularly with big companies. Under the tutelage of an accomplished executive director, Jay Hess, he learned, "Fundraising is not a ruthless exercise of putting pressure on an individual, but a great educational effort—turning people on to generosity."

With eight years of experience behind him, Sage moved to his first executive directorship at United Way of Greater St. Joseph, Missouri. During his four years there, he increased the funds raised by 30 percent. The career path of United Way executive directors is to move to increasingly larger communities, and so, after four years in St. Joseph and four years in Rockford, Illinois, Sage came to Long Island, an area whose population exceeds that of 21 states.

Sage has completed the Executive Management Program at the Harvard Graduate School of Business, and the Management Skills Program at United Way's National Academy for Voluntarism. He served on the National Fund Raising Advisory Committee of United Way of America and is President of the Long Island Chapter of the National Society of Fund-Raising Executives. Sage also serves on various boards and committees.

Advice to Others

With 20 years in the system, Sage has the following suggestions for people interested in United Way employment:

- United Way of America operates a good personnel service out of its Alexandria, Virginia, headquarters. They no longer use recruiters but have a competitive internship program designed for entry-level people—college graduates and those with advanced degrees. These internships consist of two six-month placements at different United Way agencies. One placement concentrates on teaching allocations, the other on teaching fundraising. For additional information about United Way opportunities, see Section 11.

- For the professional development of United Way staff, other nonprofit managers, and volunteers, United Way of America operates continuing education programs through its National Academy for Voluntarism.

- The entry-level management jobs for which Sage and other United Way executives recruit are generally fundraising positions, with college degree and a year or two of experience required. What Sage looks for, in particular, is a candidate's volunteer experience. Sage says, "Volunteering is the most important career development I know." He wants to know if applicants have been activists, have commitments to human services, have a flair for organization, and whether they can communicate.

- As people move up in the ranks, the preferred credentials are the MSW, the MBA, or comparable management degrees.

- The scope of the United Way system and the existence of specific job titles create a number of career paths. Sage's career path exemplifies moving from smaller to larger United Way agencies. Another route is to start on the campaign side of a large United Way and try to become the chief professional fundraiser, and from there move on to executive directorship. Because of the complexity and sophistication of its systems, United Way tries to develop top managers from within. When it comes to recruiting for positions requiring technical expertise, such as marketing, communications, finance, and planned giving, Sage says they do hire from outside the system.

- Sage emphasizes the importance of acquiring good management skills—not only to ensure personal and agency effectiveness, but also to earn the respect of the business community. United Way works closely with corporate leaders. Sage says, "You are working with people who are highly organized . . . and they won't respect how their generosity is going to be handled unless they see in your organization the same skills they see in theirs." However, he cautions, "There is a tremendous temptation to forget human services and their values. Try not to pick up that arrogance."

Reflecting on his own growth, Sage says, "I began by really wanting to change the world . . . the world and individuals resist change with enormous resourcefulness. . . . The key to my satisfaction is that I have a much more realistic view of the world. I have become pragmatic and am happy with small individual gains towards long-range goals."

Lizabeth G. Sode

President
Beatrice Foundation

"Nonprofit managers must act from their heads as well as their hearts."

What She Does

As vice-president of a major corporation with over $4 billion in annual sales and president of a corporate foundation with assets of $20 million, Liz Sode shoulders both business and philanthropic responsibilities. Not the typical corporate public affairs person, she devotes only 10 to 20 percent of her time to philanthropic work. Her major responsibility is directing communications for the Beatrice Company, a U.S. food company that has recently gone through a number of major restructurings.

She says, "I consider myself a business person first, and, to the extent that I am a philanthropist, it is not my money, it is the stockholders'." She believes her dual responsibilities are complementary. The common element in both roles is an emphasis on communications and effective management.

Sode has helped shape the foundation's philosophy and direction for some 17 years. The Beatrice Foundation defines its mission today:

> To provide philanthropic investments to nonprofit organizations primarily in the Chicago metropolitan area that can demonstrate effective and efficient services to their clients.
>
> The Foundation particularly encourages effective management within nonprofit organizations. Well managed organizations can provide a higher quality and greater quantity of services and, thus, are able to make a greater impact in their neighborhood and communities.

Sode is convinced that the same management principles that guide the corporation are adaptable and appropriate to the nonprofit sector.

She reminisces, "When corporate public affairs became an industry in the seventies, I happened to be the resident guru because I had been paying attention. People used to write all these proposals and requests. It was almost like junk mail. One day out of boredom I started to read some of this stuff. . . . I became enthralled. . . . It's an incredible world that a lot of people don't know exists. . . . I was the first executive director of the Esmark Foundation [forerunner of the Beatrice Foundation]. I had the chance to build it and create it. It was a thrill."

"We looked for a program that could be on-going . . . and one where we felt there was a real need." The foundation now commits two-thirds of its funds to the improvement of nonprofit management. The centerpiece of this effort is the Awards for Excellence program, an annual competition among Chicago's nonprofit organizations resulting in substantial cash awards to organizations that are "Models of Management Effectiveness." Of the nearly 200 applicant organizations in 1987, four organizations were chosen. Applicant organizations must complete an extensive self-study questionnaire developed by the foundation. The review process evaluates organizations on their human resource management, program management, financial management, and organizational planning. The competition has not only served as a spur to Chicago organizations but has also inspired similar programs in the Twin Cities, as well as in Nashville and New York.

As president of the foundation, Sode works with a six-person board of directors and a staff of three, consisting of administrative assistants and a secretary.

How She Got There

As a communications major at the University of Illinois, Champaign-Urbana, Sode's goal was to go into television production. Instead, she obtained a public relations job at Swift & Company. Except for one year as Director of Corporate Communications at Quaker Oats, she has spent 16 years with the same corporation and with the same management team, through several reorganizations. She says, "I have had a chance to create my own job. I took myself where I wanted to go. I didn't have a job description. Somewhere along the way we arrived at a mutually agreeable role for me to play."

She notes that a "good corporate public affairs person must be a good business person first. A good public affairs person is one who understands the company and environment in which it operates first and foremost. I was ill equipped . . . I didn't know the first thing about business . . . I had to go back and get an MBA at night." She believes hard business skills are essential to advocating philanthropic policy effectively in the corporate context.

Advice to Others

Sode says that philanthropy changed her life. "It certainly gave me a much bigger perspective on the world than I would normally have had. There is so much information that passes one's desk when one distributes money . . . so many ideas and issues I would not have been exposed to."

An active volunteer for many years, Sode is a board member of Junior Achievement of Chicago, the Center for Rehabilitation and Training of the Disabled, and she is chairperson of Travelers and Immigrant Aid of Chicago. She has been chairperson of the Donor's Forum of Chicago and is director of the Public Affairs Council and of the National Charities Information Bureau.

She says that her volunteer experiences have been critical to her development and her ability to be sensitive to the nonprofit sector.

I don't think you can be a good donor unless you have rolled up your sleeves and had a first-hand experience working with nonprofit fundraising. When someone comes asking me for money, I know how tough that is. When someone is orchestrating a development campaign, or doing a strategic plan for their board, or trying to recruit board members, or doing financial analysis or program evaluation, I know first-hand what it is like!

Sode's views on planning for a job in public affairs are that "in many cases you have to go in and create the position." She says, "The successful corporate public affairs programs have been run by problem solvers." In her view future opportunities will not be with the blue chip companies where these functions have been established for many years. Her advice is, "Go find yourself a company that is in the next tier down, that is aggressive, ambitious and wants to be competitive in terms of its image, and has no formal giving program. Go and create something there."

Cecile M. Springer

Director, Contributions and Community Affairs
Westinghouse Electric Corporation

*"In any environment you should not only know where you are, but
where you have to go. That begins to define the skills and tools that
you need to be personally successful."*

What She Does

Westinghouse Electric Corporation is a Fortune 500 company operating at over 200 sites
across the United States and abroad. As Director of Contributions and Community Affairs,
Cecile Springer's work affects the corporation's interaction with its communities as well as
the public's perception of the firm.

Westinghouse Giving: 1986, a report on the corporation's philanthropic activities, explains:
"We at Westinghouse believe that our continuing health, education and prosperity are inter-
woven with the health, education and prosperity of the communities in which we operate."
Springer says her job is to "demonstrate that Westinghouse is a leading corporation and that
we have the tools to be good problem solvers as well as good decision makers in everything
we do, including how we relate to the community."

In 1986 Westinghouse gave $16.5 million in funds, goods, and technical support to a broad
array of organizations and causes—United Ways, hospitals, health services, youth and recreation programs, education, civic, and social programs. The support of engineering, science,
and math education is a high priority, given the corporation's need for technical professionals.

As Director of Contributions and Community Affairs, Springer manages a corporate social
responsibility program that encompasses both donations and the support of employee involvement in community and educational affairs. Springer conducted a Community Involvement Survey at 30 Westinghouse sites in 1981 and found that 47 percent of Westinghouse
employees volunteer, with 22 percent volunteering more than eight hours a month.

To maximize the impact of their employees' volunteer work, Springer designed a Volunteer
Training Program for Westinghouse people and their families. The program teaches management, leadership, communications, planning, and problem-solving skills. Springer says:

> What this does is to make everybody's productivity improve personally and in an objective way,
> so that they can apply the skills and use them back at the job also. They go through all of these
> exercises, and they know how to take better minutes, they learn to be better listeners, they know

how to articulate what is bothering them. They understand everything requires a plan. A plan that you put together to achieve a personal objective is the same as a business plan. So, what we are really doing is imparting management skills to nonmanagement types.

This program illustrates what Springer often tries to achieve—a benefit to the community, a benefit to the individual, and a benefit to the corporation.

Another outcome of the Community Involvement Survey was the expansion of the corporation's matching gift program. Traditionally corporations match an employee's donation to his or her alma mater. By matching donations to hospitals and other nonprofits, Westinghouse, in effect, has extended the same benefit to employees who are not college graduates.

Springer is especially proud of her initiatives to recruit and prepare minority students for scientific and engineering careers. Ten years ago she determined that the people best suited to help Westinghouse achieve this goal would be minority engineers already working for the corporation. She recruited a group of black and Hispanic engineers who had been nominated by their bosses and who were willing to donate their time. Westinghouse paid for this group to be trained in public speaking and in the art of handling the media and controversial environments.

Springer now had an effective cadre of Westinghouse spokesmen to go out to schools and elsewhere. The corporation got back much more than it expected. Springer says, "You just need to know how to do a little bit of investment to make things move. Very few of the people we have ever trained have left the corporation, and this is the tenth year. And they are all viewed with respect by their management. They all have had at least one or two promotions since they have been in the program." Springer's strategy is to "leverage everything I can get my hands on" and "to make sure everything I do mirrors right back to the corporation."

During her nine years in the job, Springer has devoted her energies to increasing the corporation's philanthropic allocations budget. She has integrated management into the grant awards process, and giving outside of Pittsburgh, the headquarters city, has been expanded. Local site managers have received support from Springer's office for their community activities and have learned how to take advantage of the corporation's contributions policy. Additionally, the three existing Westinghouse foundations have been merged into one. Springer manages a staff of five, including one professional and one manager.

How She Got There

Springer studied chemistry at Manhattanville College and obtained a master's degree in chemistry from Wellesley. She loved her first jobs as a research chemist. Later she decided to enroll at the University of Pittsburgh and obtain another master's degree in urban and regional planning. She wanted to learn how public policy was made, what the ingredients of good public policy determination are, and what is involved in the financial aspects of municipal decision-making.

After completing this degree, Springer decided to use her urban planning and chemistry background to get into environmental planning. Her next job as Principal Planner for the Southwestern Pennsylvania Regional Planning Commission gave her the opportunities she wanted and helped her to develop financial and administrative skills. While she found her work in planning fascinating, she decided to move on again. She wanted to see how she could use her physical science, public policy, and planning background in a profit-making institution.

She went to work at Westinghouse as Manager of Product Development for Advanced Energy Systems. She became involved in marketing the nuclear side of the corporation's business, and she learned the corporate strategic planning skills essential to being effective in her new setting. An ambitious manager, she was determined to move ahead.

Springer says she was suggested for the position of Director of Contributions and Corporate Affairs because she had always made her commitment to nonprofits a visible part of her persona at Westinghouse. She was an active board member in voluntary organizations like the United Way, League of Women Voters, and local colleges. It had been Springer's practice to make a contract with each of her supervisors at Westinghouse that allowed her to take two days a month to fulfill her volunteer commitments, as long as she made up the time and her work did not suffer.

Springer serves on the boards of many local and national organizations, among them: Pennsylvania State University, Carlow College, Family Service America, the Conference Board Contributions Council, the Heritage National Bank, and the Business and Professional Women's Foundation. She has published, and recognition for her work includes a Doctor of Humane Letters from Seton Hall College.

Advice to Others

Springer says, "Design a long-term strategic plan for yourself. Decide where you want to be in five years and figure out an ambitious plan to get you there. Identify a mentor. Try to find someone who is in a position to see where the world is going. For women this may be difficult. Keep trying. Take a mentor to lunch!"

7

Fundraising and Development Managers

Fundraising/Institutional Development

Our country's first fundraising effort dates back to 1641—when the Massachusetts Bay Colony sent three clergymen to England to raise money for Harvard College. The practice of fundraising, as we know it today, began in the latter part of the nineteenth century. A body of expertise began to accrue in three interrelated areas—community development, public relations, and fundraising. This was largely an outgrowth of the work of Young Men's Christian Association secretaries, who systematically organized fundraising drives in communities all over the United States, following the westward movement of the railroads.

Between 1900 and 1918, the application of these and other sophisticated planning and promotion techniques produced astonishing results for organizations including the American National Red Cross, the YMCA, and the United Fund. They collected unprecedented sums of money, and not just from the rich! The "experts" who developed and managed these campaigns gained widespread recognition and began to consider other ways of applying their talents. In 1919, several of the YMCA's most distinguished secretaries formed Ward, Hill, Pierce and Wells, the first of a number of fundraising consulting firms that would be organized in the coming years. This marked the official beginning of fundraising as a small, specialized occupation and as a business (Cutlip, 1965; Cohen, 1984).

Most nonprofit organizations depend on several kinds of income: notably, fees for service, dues, endowment earnings, profits generated by for-profit ventures, and fundraising from individual, foundation, and corporate donors. Fundraising management (also known as development, resource development, institutional development, and stewardship) is a vital function for 501(c)(3) nonprofit organizations. It requires highly skilled professionals who are adept at working with the chief executive and volunteer leaders of an organization and who are knowledgeable about several of the more common strategies for raising funds. These strategies include grantsmanship, annual campaigns, capital campaigns, major donor cultivation, direct mail, special events, and planned giving.

There are two kinds of fundraisers, those who work within an organization and those who are outside consultants. The consultant business is divided among regional and national firms, small local firms, and independent consultants, with staff fundraisers and consultants often working together in a productive team relationship.

Because the nature of the fundraising enterprise is not well understood by the public, and occasionally hurt by the dishonest practices of outsiders, the industry's associations have established and promulgated high standards for the profession through ethical codes of practice, training programs, and credentials. The associations leading the development and promulgation of high standards (described more fully in Section 10) are:

AAFRC—American Association of Fund-Raising Counsel

CASE—Council for Advancement and Support of Education

NAHD—National Association for Hospital Development

NSFRE—National Society of Fund Raising Executives

NCDC—National Catholic Development Conference

Fundraising may be the part-time function of the executive director of small nonprofits, or it may be the major work of a large staff, as is the case at the New York Public Library described in the following pages. In addition to the four fundraising careers described in this section, the work of Jack Sage, Michael Seltzer, Sally Baines, and Penny Stoil, described in other sections, also involve some aspects of fundraising.

In 1988, the 10,000-member National Society of Fund Raising Executives conducted a Membership Career Survey of fundraisers. The survey offers a representative compilation of facts and figures that describe the age, sex, ethnic background, education and employment history, type of employing institution, job title, salary, fringe benefits, and other job-related characteristics of development professionals. The survey is recommended reading for those planning a fundraising career or those currently in career entry positions. Among the survey's findings in this rapidly growing profession are:

- females are entering the field at twice the rate of men, and that they outnumber men

- salaries are going up, particularly for men

- educational levels of chief development officers are high—9.4 percent have some college credits, 28.3 percent graduated college, 16.3 percent attended graduate school, 27 percent have a master's degree, 10.2 percent have done postgraduate work, and 7.6 percent hold doctoral degrees.

For Further Information

Graduate Programs:

- MPS in Nonprofit Management, with a concentration in Fund Raising Management
  Graduate School of Management and Urban Professions
  New School for Social Research
  66 Fifth Avenue
  New York, New York 10011
- MS in Management, with a concentration in Fund Raising Management
  Lesley College
  29 Everett South
  Cambridge, MA 02138

Certificate Programs in Fundraising Management:

- Fund Raising School
  (Indiana University
  Center on Philanthropy)
  P.O. Box 3237
  San Rafael, CA 94912-3237
- George Washington University
  Division of Continuing Education
  801 22nd Street, N.W.
  Washington, D.C. 20052
- Grantsmanship Center
  650 South Spring Street
  P.O. Box 6210
  Los Angeles, CA 90014
- New York University
  SCE/Management Institute
  48 Cooper Square
  New York, NY 10003

Heidi Weber

Research Coordinator
Office of Development and Public Affairs
The New York Public Library*

"I'm a super sleuth for a good cause. I'm doing research in a library, for a library and that's just a researcher's dream come true. Because the fundraisers here are good at what they do, they have a true appreciation of how important research can be to a successful fund- raising campaign."

What She Does

Heidi Weber holds a critical staff position in the Office of Public Affairs and Development of the New York Public Library. Weber does all the research on donors and prospects who have the propensity and ability to make major gifts to the library. Supporting the work of 10 development officers, she prepares background profiles on individuals, corporations, and foundations.

The New York Public Library, a major New York City and national institution, is currently experiencing a renaissance due largely to the dynamic leadership of its recent President, Vartan Gregorian, who restored the library to its position as an educational, social, and cultural center. (Dr. Gregorian resigned in September, 1988, to become president of Brown University.) The library, a nonprofit organization, was originally set up in the first years of this century as a unique three-way partnership comprised of the philanthropist Andrew Carnegie, the New York Public Library, and the City of New York.

To this day the library depends on a combination of city, state, federal, and private support. The library has 86 facilities, a $120-million annual operating budget, and 3,000 employees. Its branch libraries in the boroughs of Manhattan, Staten Island, and the Bronx circulate nearly 10 million items among one million library card holders. The four research libraries include the Central Research Library on Fifth Avenue, the Annex, the Performing Arts Research Center, and the Schomburg Center for Research in Black Culture. These libraries contain 33 million non-circulating materials, and they served 1.2 million visitors in 1987, plus 125,000 users who communicated by mail and phone. In addition, the library sponsors thousands of

---

* Since this profile was written, Heidi Weber has moved to the New School for Social Research in New York. She is Manager of Research and Prospect Tracking.

public education programs, concerts, exhibits, and special events at the main library and at the branches.

The Library's current five-year campaign seeks to raise $307 million in private and public funds for capital and endowment purposes, operating funds, and special projects. Support is needed to expand and renovate facilities, to install modern technology, to preserve holdings, and to maintain the library's leadership position.

All fundraising campaigns start with questions. Who are our current donors? Can we ask them to give again? Are they capable of making substantial donations? Who do they know? Who are other attractive prospects? How can we reach them? How can we interest them in what we do? What are the possible links between the prospective donor and the library? How much has the prospective donor contributed to other charitable organizations?

The list of questions is long, and before any strategy for a prospect or donor cultivation can begin, information must be gathered and assembled. That is Heidi Weber's job—collecting, organizing, analyzing, and shaping information into a coherent donor profile that provides clues to fundraisers and the volunteers who participate in the solicitation process. Weber's reports identify the links that can be established between the library's needs and the donor's interests and motivations.

Weber says, "A prospect researcher is doing all of the legwork, the homework for the fundraisers themselves and for the people who go to ask for the money." Except for the summer, when she trains and works with an intern, Weber works by herself. She uses different formats for preparing reports on individuals, corporations, or foundations, always mindful of what information is critical to the fundraiser.

For example, in preparing a comprehensive report on an individual, Weber will look for his or her address, business affiliation, primary professional affiliation, other corporate affiliations, ties to nonprofit organizations, and relationship to any public library. She will also research major gifts to other institutions, birthplace, school, family structure and relationships, sources of wealth, and any other information that can be helpful to the understanding of a prospective donor.

Weber uses a broad array of resources, starting with donor files and references in the Development Office, going through the general and specialized source books of the library itself, and taking trips to the Foundation Center, the Probate Court, the Securities and Exchange Commission, and wherever else experience has taught her that she will find what she needs. The information she tracks down is all public information. It is simply a matter of knowing where to look. She says:

> In this business, accuracy and comprehensiveness are the name of the game. If your information cannot be trusted, you've had it, because you're as good as the information you provide. And the rest is instinct. It's the feeling that if there is one last shred of information out there to be gotten, I've got to get it. The difference between a good researcher and a superb researcher is that gut instinct—that desire to get the nth detail.

Weber enjoys analyzing and shaping the information and writing the reports. Her satisfaction comes when someone says, "Heidi, you've made that person come alive for me." She says that, because of the team spirit and close professional interaction at the library, she participates in the satisfaction of the ultimate outcome—a major gift. She notes that this may not be the case in other organizations where researchers remain in the background.

Because the library encourages its staff to be creative, Weber recently initiated a Japanese philanthropy project and conducted a study on Japanese private and company-sponsored foundations. She hopes that her findings will help the library obtain support from these newly identified sources.

How She Got There

After graduating from Dartmouth with Departmental Distinction and a degree in philosophy, Weber decided to go to work rather than graduate school. Her first job was at a cancer institute doing clerical work. After a year or so, Norman Fink, a family friend and then Vice-President for Development at Brandeis University, suggested that there was a future in prospect research. He encouraged Weber to talk to the researcher in his department to see whether the work would interest her. Weber had been exposed to a good library at Dartmouth and had enjoyed the process of finding, reading, and analyzing information for her course work. Therefore, the description of the research position appealed to her, and she was hired by Brandeis as a Research Assistant in the Development Office.

Weber says that she was fortunate in this first job to be working for a "phenomenal" researcher who trained her thoroughly in the basics of development research. When Fink moved to New York to become Deputy Vice-President for Development at Columbia University, he invited Weber to join his staff. She started as a foundation researcher and was soon promoted to Manager of Research, a challenging job for she supervised and trained a staff of 10 researchers and edited their work.

After two and one-half years at Columbia, Weber decided to try front-line fundraising and joined CARE as Assistant Director of Planned Giving. While she loved working for CARE, she did not feel at home in the planned giving business, and after a year and a half she applied for the position of Research Coordinator for the New York Public Library. "It was a job description that was designed for me," Weber says. "I came for the interview and got the job."

Weber foresees continuing her career in prospect research either at the library, at another major institution with a large fundraising staff, or as a consultant, because she has found that there is indeed a small but growing demand for her specialized skills.

Advice to Others

Weber believes prospect research is a good entry-level position, because it exposes the beginner to many areas of fundraising. For those who are attracted to this work, it can be the beginning of a well-paid career with a future. She notes that this is a good field for generalists who have broad interests, lots of curiosity, and the ability to work well independently. The work requires persistence, imagination, and good conceptual and writing skills.

Steve Rose

Director of Development
Miami Jewish Home and Hospital for the Aged at Douglas Gardens

"In the brokerage business I did the same thing I do today. Both are people businesses. You develop a relationship, get to know people and help them to grow. I always had the feeling in brokerage sales that the customer was going to buy something. You just had to find out what made the customer tick. This is true in fundraising. The key is to offer lots of different programs and services."

What He Does

Steve Rose is one of a small but growing group of development directors employed by geriatric facilities. As the first Director of Development of the 43-year-old Miami Jewish Home and Hospital for the Aged, commonly called Douglas Gardens, Rose has had the opportunity to plan and build a complex fundraising program for a high-growth, multi-service facility serving the elderly.

Douglas Gardens is located on a 17-acre site that includes attractive buildings and tropical gardens. The Home offers a broad spectrum of care. At the center is the nursing home and hospital, which cares for over 500 patients. In addition, outpatient and off-campus services include ambulatory health, mental health, senior employment, home health care, adult day care, adult congregate living, Alzheimer's respite care, and short-term rehabilitation. These services also include case management; meals; transportation; information and referral; physical, speech, and occupational therapy; outpatient medical services; and research, training, and planning.

Rose's job is to create the financial resources necessary for new buildings, capital improvements, and new programs. Although "aging" is considered a "hard sell" among fundraisers, Rose has been able to raise $31 million for Douglas Gardens in five and a half years. Rose has found that:

A lot of people in this community have the capacity to give, and many of them are seniors themselves. Some feel that "There but for the grace of God go I." Others feel that since these kinds of services were not available to their parents, they want them to be available to someone else's parents. . . . We don't ask people for money. We put them into a frame of mind. We create the environment. Then they can make their own commitment after considering the various opportunities available.

When he first came to Douglas Gardens, Rose prepared a detailed marketing plan that specified both the groups of people he wanted to reach, by level of giving capacity, and the cultivation process he would use to convert each category of prospects into donors. With minor changes, he has followed this plan, building a staff of five professionals plus support personnel along the way.

Rose has a four-stage system of donor cultivation: identification, education, involvement, and commitment. Douglas Garden donors are classified by level of giving. Humanitarian Founders give $250,000; Founders give $50,000; Guardians give $15,000; Next Generation, $10,000; Honor Thy Father and Mother Society, $1,000; Alzheimer Notables, $1,000; and Friends of Aging, $50 a year. Rose is particularly proud of the fact that he has over 450 Founders, donors of $50,000 or more. Additionally, seven auxiliaries raise money for the capital expansion of Douglas Gardens. These are geographically based except for the Latin and Men's Clubs. Finally, two thrift stores owned and operated by Douglas Gardens earn over $1 million annually.

Each of the Home's donor and volunteer groups is carefully organized, supported, and acknowledged. A heavy calendar of social, cultural, and educational events assures maximum involvement of all constituencies in the life of the institution. There are monthly dinners at the Home for major donors, as well as art exhibits, performances, and joint projects bringing together residents and members of the auxiliaries. Each undertaking is backed by the necessary staff work and a beautifully written, elegantly designed piece of literature. The writing and art work are done in-house.

Rose and the other development and public relations staff are sensitive to the nuances of writing about aging and services for the elderly. They seem to understand that public relations and fundraising materials for geriatric facilities must be written with delicacy, humanity, and warmth. A true marketer, Rose is attentive to what people want and need. Rose reports to the executive director of Douglas Gardens and works closely with the board and its development committee. Because of his success, he has been called in as a consultant by other nursing homes planning to incorporate a development position in their top management.

Rose is an active and contributing member of his professional association, and, as a certified member of the National Association for Hospital Development, he was chosen to chair their 1989 Regional Conference.

How He Got There

Rose spent 13 years in the financial services industry before changing direction. A business administration graduate of Boston University, he worked for Bache and Co., first as a stockbroker in New York City and then as resident manager in Dallas. Along the way he obtained an MBA in finance. When Rose moved to Texas his Jewish identity became a matter of concern to him, and he involved himself in several Jewish community organizations. In 1973, while serving as president of his B'nai Brith chapter, he went to Israel on a group tour. He loved the experience and suddenly realized, "My avocation was more enjoyable than my vocation in life."

When he returned to Dallas he consulted a vocational services agency. Their tests suggested that he should be the administrator of a social service agency! Determined to change the direction of his work life, Rose resigned his job, reorganized his finances, moved his family into a smaller house, and began to concentrate on building a new career. He started by doing some community organizing. This soon led to the position of Director of the B'nai Brith Foundation of the Southwest. While his job was to raise funds for youth services, Rose really knew very little about the fundraising process. Fortunately, a professional from the national office of B'nai Brith gave him a three-day crash course on how to organize fundraising dinners and continued to serve as his mentor during the following year.

Rose learned by doing. He knew how to sell himself and how to cultivate people. He was adept at finding out what people were interested in. He says, "I knew enough about business to be able to talk to them [the prospective donors] about their businesses." After about a year of crisscrossing the South to raise money, he was offered a similar job with Israel Bonds. By this time, Rose had acquired some confidence in his new role and was pleased with the direction his new career was taking. A year later he was offered a campaign position at the Greater Miami Jewish Federation. The new job did not require traveling and appealed to him because he would again be in a setting that fostered continuity in working relationships and "growing givers."

At the Federation he managed the annual campaigns of several divisions, such as the accountant's division and the attorney's division, as well as the campaigns at 20 high-rise apartment buildings. Since he had capital fundraising experience as a volunteer in Dallas, he was asked to assist one of the Federation's member agencies with a capital campaign. The success of this particular project led to his promotion to Director of the Federation's Foundation.

The mission of the Foundation of the Federation of Jewish Philanthropies of Miami is to build a body of long-term gifts. In this role Rose was really able to use his investment background, and he started an Investment Committee. He recalls the reactions to this new committee:

> Now you are not dealing with charity any more. This is not just a social service agency. You're dealing with business. We know how to invest money. We will make money on the money that you, the donor, give us—invest it wisely and create another pool of dollars which we can use for programming. . . . My investment know-how gave me credibility with the donors. The Investment Committee, which continues today, was made up of high-powered businessmen and bankers, people who could volunteer their time and feel good about what they were doing. It wasn't that they came to a typical board meeting and said, "We ought to have this program or that program." Here they were really using their expertise. . . . It was business.

By the time Rose left the Federation after five years to take the newly created position at Douglas Gardens, the Foundation's asset base had grown from $3 million to $21 million.

Advice to Others

Rose's professional skills in fundraising management were self-taught. He says it has been a struggle. He has learned a great deal by talking to people and by reading professional management and fundraising materials. Rose is a strong believer in education and training programs for fundraisers and has made some efforts to initiate such programs in the Miami area, as well as in his national professional association.

Rose believes that you have to use whatever attributes you have in whatever you do, that you have to capitalize on what you can do best. His financial expertise has worked well for him, but in training his own staff he has found that he cannot replicate himself, nor does he want to. It is better to find out what a person's strongest attributes are and to work from that base. As to career planning, Rose recommends looking for growth areas, such as aging services and fundraising. The blend of the two has worked for him.

Gwinn H. Scott

Director of Development
The Baldwin School

"In development there are more no's than there are yes's. You are asking people to do things all the time, to serve as volunteers, or to give money. A development manager has to be able to overcome the no. For me to get over the no, I have to believe that somewhere along the way I have persuaded somebody else to say yes, because he or she felt the same way I do. I love the Baldwin School!"

What She Does

The Baldwin School in Bryn Mawr, Pennsylvania, is a 100-year-old independent preparatory school for girls, from kindergarten through twelfth grade, with an enrollment of 500 students. Gwinn Scott probably knows and understands the school better than anyone else. Not only were she and her mother educated there, but she has also served the school as an active alumna, board member, and president. She has been a member of the staff for 18 years.

The Baldwin School is dedicated to excellence. It aspires to creating in each student, "The ability and enthusiasm to continue growing as a scholar, a woman and a human being." The school continuously develops innovative curricula and educational processes designed to foster curiosity, moral awareness, responsibility, independence, and imaginative thinking. One hundred percent of its socioeconomically diversified students go on to four-year colleges. Additionally, the school has been recognized for its outstanding program by the U.S. Department of Education.

As Director of Development, Scott is responsible for all fundraising, public relations, publications, and alumnae and parent activities. She has a staff of four full-time people and three part-timers. The department is responsible for an annual campaign of $310,000 and is currently working on a $4-million capital campaign. The department publishes two alumnae magazines, three newsletters a year, as well as other printed materials. Scott attends all Board of Trustees meetings as well as Finance and Development Committee meetings. She loves the variety of her work and that feeling when success is in hand. She remembers vividly the pleasure of receiving a six-figure gift and taking the check to the bank to pay off the mortgage on one of the school's buildings.

How She Got There

After one year at Salem College and a year at the University of Pennsylvania, Scott married and had two children. She became an active alumna of The Baldwin School while she was in her twenties. Becoming alumnae president gave Scott an opportunity to exercise and develop leadership skills, and representing the alumnae association on the board gave her insight into how policy and decisions are made. She attended conferences with alumni association presidents from other schools, broadening her outlook. When her term of office was over and her marriage ended, she needed to look for paid work.

Scott consulted with the head of The Baldwin School, who, knowing that she was good with people and had leadership and secretarial skills, offered her a full-time position as assistant to the Alumnae Director. It was the beginning. Scott immersed herself in the details of alumnae work and learned the rudiments of an alumnae development office. She compiled mailing lists, mechanized systems, and organized groups of volunteers to help her get more work done. In 1972 when the school embarked on a capital campaign, she was asked to be the secretary to a professional fundraiser brought in to manage the campaign. When Baldwin was forced to close its boarding school, the capital campaign came to a halt, and Scott went back to the alumnae office. The Alumnae Director became ill shortly thereafter and Scott was appointed to the job. In this position she was responsible for the annual campaign, alumnae programming (Career Day, College Day, Alumnae Council, Alumnae Association, Executive Board and Reunions), and maintaining data on 4,000 alumnae, 450 current parents, 1,500 parents of alumnae, and 500 grandparents and friends.

In 1974 the school hired its first director of development and reestablished the capital campaign, and then in 1977 the school received a challenge grant with the condition that twice as much money be raised within a year. An outside consultant was brought in again to look at the school's fundraising problems. The development director resigned, and suddenly, much to her surprise, Scott was asked to take on the job.

Scott was reluctant to leave her position as Alumnae Director but was finally persuaded to make the change to development. Apparently, everyone who knew the school and knew her agreed that she was exactly the right person for the assignment. She notes, "My reservations about taking the job are classic, particularly for women. It is an enormous responsibility, fraught with politics. It's taking the responsibility for leadership, win or lose. Dollars are the bottom line. Specific goals have to be met every year, and in accepting the job, I was accepting that responsibility." The outside consultant stayed to provide backup and became her mentor. She says, "We raised the second million dollars and went over the top. We had a marvelous, successful campaign!" Scott has continued to exceed the school's development goals every year.

Scott is one of the founders of ADVIS, a consortium of 75 independent schools in the Delaware Valley. She has further developed her professional and leadership skills through active participation in the work of the Council for Advancement and Support of Education (CASE). She has been a District II Board Member and Program Chair as well as Trustee-at-Large for Independent Schools in the national organization. She has served as chair of both the Independent School Advisory Committee of the CASE board's Nominating Committee and she has been a member of the Presidential Search Committee. In 1986 CASE recognized her service to The Baldwin School, to CASE, and to independent schools in general by presenting her with the Robert Bell Crow Memorial Award.

While her longevity at Baldwin has been an asset both to her and to the school, Scott recently concluded it was time to move on. Marts and Lundy, a leading fundraising firm, has invited her to join them as a consultant, and she made the change in the fall of 1988. Scott has already had two consulting assignments for her new employer and feels very confident about her future as a consultant.

Advice to Others

Scott loves the development business, and she enjoys interviewing job candidates. Asked what she looks for when hiring, she says, "I am one of those people who takes risks. I will hire somebody because of character traits, personality, and enthusiasm—regardless if they know anything about fundraising. I can teach that. But I can't teach someone to be naturally enthusiastic, or to be gracious or assertive. Those things either come with the package or they don't, and I'm interested in those qualities. I am looking for someone with a good heart and genuine interest, who asks important questions and has energy and enthusiasm." Scott hired a staff member with these qualities two years ago, someone familiar with the academic environment, but not with fundraising. Scott is pleased to report that this woman has done a "remarkable job . . . bringing in more people and more money than ever before."

C. Arthur Littman

Executive Director
Robert Wood Johnson University Hospital Foundation

*"If you can raise money for education, or hospitals or cause agencies
or symphony orchestras, you can raise money for anybody. It is a people business. People give money to people. Few, if anyone, ever gives
to just a cause. The first thing they do is give it to somebody. You
don't get money if you don't ask."*

What He Does

As executive director of the Robert Wood Johnson University Hospital Foundation, Arthur
Littman heads a separately incorporated 501(c)(3) nonprofit organization, established for the
purpose of raising funds for the hospital. In recent years, legislated rate-setting restrictions
have forced many nonprofit hospitals to restructure in order to protect their assets. A separate,
independent foundation permits a hospital to raise funds or undertake entrepreneurial activities
without a negative effect on reimbursement formulas.

The Robert Wood Johnson University Hospital, a 416-bed acute care hospital, is affiliated
with the Robert Wood Johnson Medical School. Together, the two institutions form a major
academic medical center serving central New Jersey. Both the hospital and the medical school
have had long histories under different names. Today they carry the same name but maintain
separate identities and a close working relationship. Despite misconceptions, the hospital is
not affiliated with the Robert Wood Johnson Foundation, a large nearby philanthropic foundation that is generous to the hospital but does not endow it. Littman says he spends a great
deal of his time explaining the differences and relationships among these three institutions
whose names honor the same man.

Since coming to the Robert Wood Johnson University Hospital Foundation in 1985, Littman
has transformed it. He works with a small backup staff, in offices located outside of the hospital,
and runs a full-scale development program that includes annual campaigns, planned giving,
special events, corporation and foundation proposals, and the solicitation of major gifts. Littman's job is to raise money for the hospital and its clinical services. The job is challenging
because the Robert Wood Johnson Medical School also does fundraising for research purposes.
While the two institutions do not compete, they sometimes target the same constituencies.
Littman reports to the chairman of the board of the Hospital Foundation. He also works closely

with the hospital's president and chairman of the board. He notes that the hospital board cooperates fully with the foundation in the fundraising enterprise.

With 27 years in fundraising, Littman sees his current responsibility from the perspective of the future. "I am not raising a lot of money, I am building bridges. . . . When I walked into this door three years ago there was nothing but a fine institution. What I have been doing for three years now is to build a fundraising base."

Littman has had considerable experience both in educational and hospital fundraising. He sees hospital fundraising as a much more dynamic undertaking because hospitals are constantly generating new services and programs and meeting new needs. He says, "Hospitals, unlike colleges and universities, have people who get very hot about the institution and very involved, very dedicated and very anxious to give to you at a particular juncture in their life, and then all of a sudden they are gone and they never come back." Littman attributes some of this loss of donors to the mobility of Americans. When people move to a new community, they do not maintain their loyalty to a hospital, whereas loyalty to one's school is a lifelong affair.

Littman describes himself as a people person. He believes in getting people involved and in building strong personal relationships. He says he still maintains and periodically renews all the professional contacts he has made over the years. They can still call on him and he can still call on them. He also pays close attention to the needs of donors, noting:

> One of the most important words in fundraising is recognition. I spend more time in the office saying thank you to people and recognizing them than I do prospecting for new people. I find that if you treat people well and remember who they are, and why they have given and what they have given, they are going to give again. That is what makes my job easier and easier.

A driving, dynamic man, Littman says, "I have never regretted a day in this business, and there have been thousands of frustrating days in 27 years. . . . I am enthusiastic and involved in what I do."

How He Got There

Art Littman came to Widener University in Chester, Pennsylvania, as a Navy veteran. He majored in economics, obtained teacher certification, and taught high school history and economics classes while he was still a student. After graduating near the top of his class, he took a job as a sales correspondent at du Pont, in his home town of Wilmington, Delaware.

Littman returned to Widener for his first college reunion. In a conversation with the president of the university, a former dean who had known and encouraged Littman as a student, he was asked about his reaction to the reunion. Littman brashly informed the president that he would never come back to Widener because the college only cared about its affluent, older alumni and was short-sighted in its treatment of young alumni. He indicated that he could have done a much better job of organizing the reunion! These comments led to a job offer at the university.

He started as Assistant Director of Admissions. The president hoped to move Littman into alumni relations as soon as an opening occurred and Littman recalls, "That is how I stumbled into fundraising!" After two years of doing admissions work and learning about alumni relations, he became Director of Alumni and Parent Relations. With a staff of eight he managed social and fundraising events and public relations, edited parents and alumni magazines, and worked with the alumni and parents associations. At the same time he was working for his MBA degree at the University of Delaware. His thesis was on marketing as a tool of alumni relations.

Littman's next move was to the Montclair Academy Foundation, as Associate Headmaster for Development and Administration for two private day schools with over 600 students. His responsibilities there were to complete a $5-million capital campaign and to handle annual giving, alumni relations, public relations, and publications. He established an Endowment and Deferred Gifts Program, which brought in $4.5 million. Five years later he moved on to become president and chief executive officer of the Lankenau School in Philadelphia. During his tenure at this private school, Littman planned and found financing for the first phase of an expansion and building program.

After leaving Lankenau he worked as a consultant for the Academy for Educational Development, a nonprofit organization that provides consulting services to educational institutions. He provided long-range planning, institutional development, and financial management services to clients. One of his clients, Bloomfield College in New Jersey, brought him in as Vice President for Resources and Public Affairs. He was charged with managing the school's admissions, development, and public affairs functions. During his three-year stint there he developed a master plan for the college's short-term and long-range general and capital fund campaigns.

Littman moved on to become Vice-President for Development of the Hackensack Medical Center in Hackensack, New Jersey. For six years he was responsible for all aspects of fundraising, including initiating and completing a $6-million capital campaign and setting up and managing a separate nonprofit entity, the Hackensack Health and Hospital Foundation.

Littman's career is typical of many fundraisers in that he has moved around a great deal, bringing his expertise to many institutions either as an in-house executive or, in many instances, as an outside consultant. Longevity in fundraising positions is the exception rather than the rule. Industry studies have shown that fundraisers stay in jobs 18 to 24 months. This has been attributed to the rapid growth of the industry, lack of qualified professionals, and the unrealistic expectations of employer organizations, which often do not understand that fundraising takes time.

Littman says that for a fundraiser his career has been fairly stable, for he has stayed with each position for several years. Because he enjoys a fine reputation, new opportunities that take him to the next step in his career have always come his way. The lateral and vertical moves that Littman has made during his career have led him from education to health, from smaller institutions to larger ones with more diversified needs—with each job requiring increasing levels of professional skills.

Littman is a committed and active member of all three major professional fundraising associations, NSFRE, NAHD, and CASE. He has been credentialled by all of them because he has worked as a general fundraiser, a hospital development officer, and an educational fundraiser. He believes that the credentials establish a person's level of expertise and credibility.

Each association has developed a rigorous credentialling process, and candidates earn credentials only by satisfying a number of objective criteria and passing an examination.

Littman has served as a teacher, trainer, and mentor to many young fundraisers and to this day uses university interns and tries to get them interested in the profession. Currently, he and his wife, also a fundraiser, produce the *Mitchell Guide to New Jersey Foundations, Corporations, and Their Managers.* He is also involved in church and community affairs and is a retired Lieutenant Commander in the Naval Reserves. Littman has been honored for his work as Executive Director of the Navy Bicentennial.

Advice to Others

Littman says, "Too many young people come into this business thinking that it is a stepping stone to something else. I think that is a mistake. I think if you get into this business you have to learn it and should stick with it and become a practitioner. We are not members of a trade, we are members of a profession."

Despite the fact that Littman has raised some $150 million during his career, he is a great believer in keeping up with whatever is going on in the profession. He keeps a weekly folder of professional materials to read and makes a point of attending conferences. He says if he picks up one new idea, the conference was worth attending. The networking is critical as well, but, most importantly, he finds that conference attendance, "Recharges my fundraising enthusiasm battery."

8

Marketing, Public Relations, and Membership Managers

Working with the Organization's Publics

A critical task for each nonprofit organization is to communicate with people on whom it depends. Those who run the organization must define its essential message about who it is and what it does and then communicate this message to the world. Periodically, there are other messages that must reach the public. Every nonprofit must also interact appropriately with its identified constituencies, including both internal constituencies, such as staff, boards, committees, and volunteers, and external constituencies, such as members, audiences, clients, funders, and media.

The people who handle these functions in a nonprofit may be managers of marketing, membership, communications, public relations, public information, community relations, media relations, or publications. How their organization is viewed may depend on how they analyze its political, economic, and social environment, with whom they interact, what they communicate to the world, and how they package and disseminate materials about the organization.

Jobs of this sort call for people with a college education at minimum. A liberal arts major or a major in communications, journalism, or public relations is helpful. According to the *Occupational Outlook Handbook* ('86), in 1984 140 colleges reported undergraduate degree programs in public relations, 25 reported graduate programs, with another 300 colleges reporting at least one course in public relations. Internships, part-time or summer employment, membership in the Public Relations Student Society, and a portfolio of clippings are helpful to the job seeker.

According to the 1986–87 editions of the *Occupational Outlook Handbook,* the essential skills required for people who are interested in communications occupations are:

- acute powers of observation
- ability to think clearly and logically

- an excellent command of language, oral and written
- being well informed about a particular subject or area.

The following profiles illustrate not only the wide variety of skills and tasks that may be needed to work with a nonprofit organization's publics, but also the contrasts among the settings in which these skills can be put to work.

For Further Information

Fry, Ronald
    1988   *1988 Public Relations Career Directory,* 2nd edition. Hawthorne, NJ: Career Press.

Public Interest Public Relations, a division of M. Booth Associates
    1987   *Promoting Issues and Ideas: A Guide to Public Relations for Nonprofit Organizations.* New York: The Foundation Center.

Catherine R. Fallon

Associate Director, Alumni Relations
Brandeis University

"The rewards in alumni relations are often personal rewards. . . .
You don't get paid very well. That's not what motivates me. I am
really not driven by profit. There's more . . . endless opportunity. I
don't know where else I could go and find that."

What She Does

As Associate Director for Alumni Relations, Catherine Fallon's efforts focus on helping Brandeis University and its alumni to maintain contact and to provide meaning and enrichment to one another. Brandeis is a research university in Waltham, Massachusetts, known for its high-quality liberal arts college as well as its graduate programs in arts, sciences, and social welfare. Brandeis was founded in 1948 by the American Jewish community. A nonsectarian university with a diversified student body of 4,000, the university is proud of the outstanding academic reputation it has earned during its 40-year existence.

Fallon reports to the Vice-President for Alumni Relations and Development and works closely with several professional colleagues in the department; she also works with the faculty, the Alumni Association and its chapters and committees, and with the university's administration and support services. Fallon's responsibilities are governed by the department's three-year strategic plan and operational calendar, a document that grew out of a participatory planning process to which she contributed her ideas and work goals. In addition to fulfilling her defined responsibilities, Fallon has the freedom to undertake additional projects and initiatives that seem appropriate.

Management skills are essential to her job because of the planning, logistics, marketing, and communication required to handle a calendar of special events and the staff support functions required in working with both the administration and the Alumni Association. Budgeting and cost control are important. While the university supports the department and subsidizes some direct costs, most of the programs and services provided by the alumni relations office must pay for themselves. Fallon says it is almost like running a small business.

Fallon has direct responsibility for administering three alumni class reunions a year with the help of backup staff and volunteers. She designs and administers special events such as Homecoming, Third World Reunion of minority alumni, and many receptions, dinners and awards programs. She does considerable writing and has produced an alumni directory, articles, and brochures. Fallon has been especially active in developing the university's adult education programs for alumni. She has found that alumni are hungry for intellectual stimulus and that there is an increasing demand for educational programs and a desire for continued contact with the university and the faculty. Faculty in the Field is one such program. It brings faculty to the alumni chapters for a one-session guest lecture. Another popular program is the Alumni College, a three-day annual event that brings alumni back to the campus. Fallon conceived of the theme for the second Alumni College, "Civil Liberties and the Constitutions: Old Rights in a New Age," selected the faculty, and managed all aspects of this successful undertaking.

Fallon's creative and entrepreneurial talents are not only dedicated to planning programs, services, and publications but also to finding new links between the needs, talents, and resources of individual alumni and what the university can offer. She says, "If I have any talent at all, it is to be able to find out what people always wanted to do and what their secret desire is."

Fallon has been able to help some alumni achieve their dreams by helping them find a satisfying connection to the university. Some have returned to lecture or to develop and teach a course. One has returned to become an artist-in-residence, to study and redirect his life. Another has found an audience for her art collection. Fallon finds personal satisfaction in using the university as an agent for change in the life of an alumnus. Strengthening the bonds between the university and its alumni often results in concrete benefits for the university. For this reason, Alumni Relations and Development work together in one department.

How She Got There

Fallon studied American literature at Middlebury College and was editor of the school paper. As a young woman she was unclear about her career goals and taught English for a time before settling down to marriage and caring for a large family. Always a cause person, she became very active in the political and educational life of her community during the 1970s. She was an elected Town Meeting Member, School Board Member, and President in Winchester, Massachusetts. She served on the board of a regional mental health association and also became an active volunteer for Middlebury College. Working her way through the ranks, she became a trustee of Middlebury College in 1981 and, during her on-going board service, she has chaired several key committees. Her major role at Middlebury was as National Chairman of Alumni Giving during the first two years of a $60-million capital campaign. This experience was pivotal in helping her to realize that she loved working in academia.

In 1981 she began to work as an independent contractor for the Center for Public Service at Brandeis, the Department of Urban Studies at M.I.T., and the Center for Research on Women at Wellesley. During this period, she says, "I invented opportunities and created jobs for myself wherever my interests took me." She wrote grant proposals, coordinated conferences, edited papers, and worked on publications. Middlebury's recognition of her alumni leadership strengths together with the success of her consulting initiatives translated into a professional goal—working in alumni relations. In 1985 she started working full-time at Brandeis University as Assistant Director of Alumni Relations, and she was subsequently promoted to Associate Director.

Advice to Others

Fallon's career path is one followed by many experienced community leaders and volunteers who transfer their enthusiasm, capacity for dedicated work, and volunteer management background to a professional job in nonprofit management. Fallon says that her "aggregate experience is so rich that she qualifies for an MBA in life experience." She says, "It is too bad that there is so much turnover in development and alumni relations because you lose the whole constituency when you leave. It takes time to build the kinds of relationships and the trust that you need to make this job work."

Asked about how people typically get into alumni relations, Fallon says that one route is through volunteering. She has also observed that many alumni relations officers are graduates of the institution—and just do not want to leave. A third model is the professional who returns to the university after another career.

Albert J. Sunseri

Vice-President, Education and Member Services
Healthcare Financial Management Association (HFMA)

*"I like the umbrella perspective. In any national association you can
see all the players, all around the country. That's the real benefit to
me, seeing the whole field."*

What He Does

The Healthcare Financial Management Association is a personal membership organization for
26,000 financial management professionals who are employed by hospitals, public accounting
and consulting firms, long-term-care facilities, and related health care organizations. Its members include: chief executive officers, chief financial officers, controllers, patient account managers, business office managers, accountants, consultants, insurance executives, lawyers,
internal auditors, professors, and students.

Founded in 1946 as the American Hospital Accounting Association, HFMA is based in
Westchester, Illinois, near Chicago. It has 74 chapters, organized into 11 regions. It also
maintains a Policy and Government Relations Office in Washington, D.C. The organization
is membership driven, with a 17-member board and nine functional councils and committees.
HFMA states that it, "Represents its members and meets their needs by providing opportunities
for professional development and growth, influencing health-care policy and communicating
information and technical data." Since health care is the nation's largest industry, accounting
for 11 percent of the gross national product, providing quality support for its financial managers
is a daunting task.

As Vice-President of the Division of Education and Membership Services, Albert Sunseri
supervises a complex set of services, products, and relationships. He reports to the president
and supervises a staff of 24. The organization also has Vice-Presidents for Finance and Administration, Communications, and Public Policy and Government Relations. Sunseri manages
an annual budget of $7 million out of a total association budget of $8.25 million and is
responsible for 83 percent of the association's income. His responsibilities encompass:

- *Education.* Every year HFMA sponsors a five-day Annual National Institute plus hundreds
  of conferences and workshops around the country. The organization can respond quickly
  to new topics of concern (Medicare Cost Reporting or Medicare Payment Methodology,
  for instance) and is also free to co-sponsor programs or to use audio conferencing or video

teleconferencing for educational purposes. Sunseri reports this department handles some 2,500 registrations annually. He is proud that HFMA education programs provide an important service to the health care industry and are also a profit center.

- *Certification.* HFMA offers two levels of certification, Fellow (FHFMA) and Certified Manager of Patient Accounts (CMPA). There is also a recertification maintenance program. The association publishes study guides and schedules and monitors the entire process.

- *Computer Services.* HFMA develops and markets computer programs and services under the umbrella of *Hospital-Data Plus.* These services have set the standard for hospitals to analyze profit and loss ratios based on national norms.

- *Marketing.* Sunseri is alert to members' needs and perceptions. He uses membership market surveys to assess the members' satisfaction, their familiarity with products and services, and their priority needs. The results of market studies are reported in the monthly journal *Healthcare Financial Management* and are used for planning purposes. The organization has a 90 percent membership renewal rate and a 1 percent growth rate annually.

Sunseri credits HFMA's strength to the strong interaction between chapters and the national office. He works with chapter leaders on skills and management techniques, and chapters assist the national office in member recruitment and retention and in long-range planning. "They talk, we listen," says Sunseri.

Sunseri truly loves his work and is energized by the diversity of his job. He relishes the planning and says, "What satisfies me is seeing it happen. . . . We do something right here. We are bottom-line oriented. I run a successful business for the association. We are accountable." Despite the seeming emphasis on providing sophisticated products and services, Sunseri says that the essence of his job, and of association work, is people and their interactions.

How He Got There

Sunseri prepared for a teaching career in higher education. He has a B.S. in biological sciences, an M.Ed. in science education, and a Ph.D. in curriculum and supervision, all from the University of Pittsburgh. He spent four years as a college professor at Point Park College. His expertise in educational research, particularly behavioral research, led him to a Rhode Island school district, where he wrote his first grant proposal. He received $90,000 for an interdisciplinary mental health project to humanize the school district. With help from the Harvard Center for Humanistic Education and the University of Massachusetts, his team came up with an approach to behavior change that transformed the district.

In 1975 he went to work for the Chicago Heart Association, which had been looking for a professional who had experience in behavior education, to direct a preventive cardiology project. This was his introduction to management in a nonprofit association. He started fundraising, working with volunteer and membership programs. "I ended up being an association manager doing research in an association." The heart project received national recognition and is still in place. After nine years as executive officer of the Heart Health Curriculum Project and director of education, Heart Attack Prevention Program, he left to become executive director of the 32,000-member American Dental Hygienist Association.

Sunseri updated the business functions of the Dental Hygienists Association. Within three years of his arrival, he had trebled the percent of total income from non-dues sources, and while revenues increased, expenses and cost of sales decreased. With sound business operation, the association could direct its energies toward its mission of improving the functions of hygienists.

Having spent 10 years in academia as a student and professional, and 14 years in association management, Sunseri finds association work far more satisfying. There is not the tension between teaching and research and the competition for funds and advancement. Instead he finds the association environment gives him both the freedom and the resources to respond to problems quickly, with all the creative energy and entrepreneurial skills he can mobilize.

Sunseri is a Certified Association Executive (CAE) and an active volunteer in the American Society of Association Executives. He has served as consultant to the National Cancer Institute, National Institute of Dental Research, American Heart Association, American Cancer Society, the Veterans Administration, and the National Heart, Lung, and Blood Institute.

Advice to Others

In addition to his own enthusiasm for association work, he has found that children of association executives tend to follow their parents' footsteps. His wife works for the American College of Surgeons, and his son, a college student, spends his summers as a research assistant for the American Medical Association.

Entry-level management jobs in associations are for program managers who handle specific projects. At the next level there are directors in charge of a specific function, and top managers have the most diversified roles. People come into association management from varied backgrounds. Sunseri has come to believe that, "People can learn this field. They don't have to have any particular preparation. They can move from department to department and find their own niche."

Association work settings tend to differ according to the size of the organization. In small associations with a staff of three or four people, the top executive has to be able to do everything. Associations with budgets of over $5 million are considered large and have more specialized staffing. Major groups like the American Medical Association, with a staff of around 1,000 people, are in a different league.

Sunseri stresses it is critical for an association manager to understand that credit for an association's successes goes to the voluntary leadership. Professional staff must understand that they are facilitators and must know when to stay in the background.

Sandy Stumbaugh

Associate Manager, Media Relations*
San Francisco Ballet Association

"You have to be thinking constantly in terms of how a journalist thinks . . . I know that if it's a story that interests me, if it automatically catches my ear, that it's to be that way for the journalist as well and then to their audience. . . . In the arts you're at an advantage because they want to do things for you."

What She Does

The San Francisco Ballet is the oldest professional ballet company in the United States. As Associate Manager, Media Relations, Sandy Stumbaugh works with the media in promoting a ballet company that has recently experienced considerable growth in size and stature. Stumbaugh's efforts have helped the company receive national and international attention and acclaim from critics and audiences.

When Stumbaugh came to the Ballet in 1983, it was still a small organization. Under the tutelage of her boss and mentor, the Director of Marketing and Media Relations, she was encouraged to try her hand at a variety of assignments. This has enabled her to develop her professional expertise and take on greater responsibility. Since she began work there, the Ballet has celebrated its 15th anniversary, moved into a brand new building (the first completely new facility created to house a major dance institution in the history of the dance in America), brought in an outstanding artistic director/choreographer, Helgi Tomasson, and initiated a rotating repertory program.

Stumbaugh's job is to keep the Ballet's multiple activities before the eyes of the press and ultimately before the public. Her work flows in relation to the company's performance schedule in San Francisco, San Diego, and Hawaii; its national and international tours, its gala openings every season, its new productions and stars; its major donors and donations, and its professional ballet school and other educational activities. Stumbaugh identifies stories and pitches them to the press. She cultivates and develops contacts with the local, national, and international press.

---

*Following this interview, Sandy Stumbaugh was appointed Director of Media Relations of San Francisco's Museum of Modern Art. She will be marketing and managing the museum's image as it expands, undertakes a $70-million capital campaign, and builds a new, world-class home.

During a summer sabbatical in 1986, she helped to coordinate public relations at the Jacob's Pillow Dance Festival in the Berkshire Mountains of Massachusetts. She also used this opportunity to establish strong East Coast press contacts for the San Francisco Ballet. Stumbaugh writes releases, and when she has the time, stories for the company's program guide, a large magazine format. She maps out advance publicity and press opportunities for the tours, tries to get reporters to accompany the tours, and travels with the company to handle press relations wherever they perform. Stumbaugh supervises a staff of four, including a writer.

How She Got There

Stumbaugh majored in French literature and minored in journalism at Penn State University. She also spent a semester at the University of Strasbourg and did some traveling in Europe. She says, "I was just one of those all-around liberal arts students that loves everything. I loved the performing arts."

She got a lot of hands-on work experience as a reporter, columnist, and editor at the *Daily Collegian*, Penn State's daily newspaper. She says she learned to write under pressure at the *Collegian* by covering the trustee meetings of the local school district:

> It was a great and also frightening experience. I would go to these meetings with no background. They were very political. On occasions there would be an enormous amount of information just sort of dumped on me in a very short period of time. They would always end late, about ten o'clock at night. I would go back to the paper and I would have to write copy and have it in by eleven or eleven thirty. So, I would have to crash it out.

An internship with The Artists Series, an organization that presented major performing arts groups on campus, gave her the opportunity to do public relations for the arts. She learned how to write press releases and how to contact newspapers to get coverage for events—and she discovered she loved this kind of work.

After graduating with honors, Stumbaugh moved to San Francisco. She found a job there that drew both on her knowledge of French and her journalistic experience—press secretary of the French Consulate in San Francisco. Her primary duties were in public information, i.e., dealing with the information needs and fears of French visitors to San Francisco and of Americans going to France. She reviewed the French and American press and periodicals to provide information to the French government and to the American public. She developed contacts with the American and French Bay Area media to promote special events, prepared French and English press releases about consular activities, and set up interviews for visiting French dignitaries. Additionally, she made contacts for the French press, and she arranged meetings between the French Consul and newspaper editors on difficult current issues.

After three years, Stumbaugh decided that she wanted to do more writing and public relations work and therefore began consulting. She worked with a freelance dance critic on promotional materials for a dance-related travel tour to France. Through this contact, she learned that there was an opening at the San Francisco Ballet for a media relations associate. Although she had a great interest in ballet, she did not know a lot about it, but her background was sufficient to get her the job.

Advice to Others

When Stumbaugh hires public relations staff, this is what she looks for:

- Writing skills are paramount. She wants to see writing samples, clippings, and releases. She wants to know that a job candidate can produce a good release or pitch letter in an afternoon.
- Personality, good manners, grace, and style are essential. Abrasive or shy people do not belong in a business that depends so much on good interactions with people.
- Motivation and energy are equally necessary. She looks for people who are outgoing and get involved in extracurricular activities.
- Flexibility—being able to go with the flow.

Theresa M. Nelson

Director of Membership
Sierra Club

"At the Sierra Cub membership is the key, not only financially but organizationally. Everything flows from that—power, income, lobbying and activism."

What She Does

As Director of Membership of the Sierra Club, Theresa Nelson maintains and develops the Sierra Club's membership roster of some 500,000 people. Since membership dues account for about one-half of the Club's $28-million budget, and 10 to 15 percent of members are active volunteers, her membership management role is pivotal to the success of the organization.

The Sierra Club is a grass-roots conservation organization, founded in 1892 by John Muir, a naturalist and writer concerned about preserving the vast open spaces in the West from encroaching development. The organization wields considerable influence, with 57 chapters in the U.S. and Canada (each organized into local groups) and with 338 local special interest groups. The Sierra Club's stated purpose is, "to explore, enjoy and protect the wilderness." The Club believes that exploring and enjoying the environment are necessary for understanding it. As Nelson says, "You begin to realize that, unless you personally do something, this might not be around for your children and your grandchildren."

The Sierra Club's mission is "to influence public policy and its implementation at all levels of government." It reaches these goals through its network of members, concerned citizens, and staff, "using legislative, administrative, electoral and legal approaches" and by influencing public opinion. The Club advocates through education, lobbying, and litigation.

The Club maintains a stronghold in the West where most of the U.S. national parks are located and where many of its early battles were won. Saving the Yosemite and preventing the damming of the Grand Canyon were two historic victories. The Club's headquarters are in San Francisco, and one-third of its members are Californians. The Club's issues attract a national interest. These issues include clean air and water, toxic waste control, and the protection of forests, parks, and wildlife habitats. An active effort is currently underway to increase membership in other parts of the country, through greater attention to urban concerns, particularly the public health aspects of environmental hazards.

Nelson reports to the Director of Development, who manages a staff of 42. She herself supervises two professionals and three support people. She confers and consults with other Sierra Club professionals because, "Membership is very important in everything that we do. Membership provides a market for the outings, the recipients of public information and a volunteer work force for conservation issues." She also works closely with the board and with a volunteer National Membership Committee of 17 people.

Nelson stresses, "Getting people involved is the key to keeping them in the Club." She notes that the organization's structure comes from the bottom up:

> The members at the local level are the real power and strength of the Club. There is a consensus style of management here and at the volunteer level. It takes a little longer to do things, but it keeps people involved, keeps them committed to a project and gives them ownership of the project. It's not dictated from the top. I'm sure that is one of the reasons it's so successful and so many people stay involved. They spend an enormous amount of volunteer time on these issues. They can be active in a way that is personally satisfying and also make a contribution. Their opinions are respected and listened to.

Nelson says volunteer involvement is strengthened because the Club's several hundred national committee members are brought to San Francisco or Washington, D.C., twice a year for national meetings. Membership costs $33 a year. Benefits include: *Sierra* magazine, discounts on books, calendars and outings, a direct voice in the election of local and national leaders, and, most important, the opportunity to participate in the local and national leadership of the organization.

Nelson's overall goal for membership is to have a moderate rate of growth that can be absorbed by the organization's infrastructure. A high priority is to increase the number of activist members. In the past, the Club's growth spurts resulted from public reaction to specific events. Today their stance is more proactive. For example, they train hundreds of volunteers as lobbyists to work on specific issues in the state capitals and in Washington, D.C.

The Sierra Club acquires new members by using a variety of marketing techniques: direct mail, exhibits at trade shows, package and magazine inserts, brochures, outreach to other nonprofit organizations like the Boy Scouts, or to special groups, like teachers. Nelson's unit conducts four direct mail campaigns a year. She is very involved in the writing, research, and testing of various direct mail packages. She develops brochures and campaign strategies, hires consultants, and does a lot of "number crunching."

Nelson points out, "It is expensive to get new people in but less expensive to retrain them through renewals. We shoot not only for growth but for renewal. A higher renewal rate means you don't need as much growth, and that means more net income. . . . Our renewals are primarily through direct mail, and the renewal rate varies according to the number of years that people have been involved. The average renewal rate is slightly over 70 percent and we focus on making that rate higher. People who have been involved for four or more years renew at a rate of about 86 percent and that's healthy."

How She Got There

In high school Nelson was an interested student, a musician, a debater, and an actress. She enjoyed organizing and teaching and consequently decided to take a business program in college, in order to develop practical skills that she could then apply to her areas of interest. She attended Michigan State University and the University of Illinois, majoring in marketing and minoring in the humanities.

Nelson worked during her entire college career. Before graduating in 1978, she made the decision to go into nonprofit work on the basis of her experience as a volunteer. Unfortunately, because she lacked professional experience, the large cultural institutions in Chicago were not interested in hiring her fresh out of college. She decided to get a corporate job, instead, while continuing to develop her interest in nonprofit organizations through volunteer work.

Her first job was with a Chicago-based conglomerate in the energy, chemical, and mineral-processing business. As marketing and communications associate, she gained practical experience in advertising and public affairs and did some traveling. She was soon hired by a competitor, Envirotech, a pollution control firm in California. As their Director of Marketing and Communications, Nelson had a large professional staff to manage and achieved increasing levels of responsibility. At the same time, both in Chicago and later in San Francisco, she spent her spare time as a volunteer manager of small arts organizations, trying to apply business practices to voluntary organizations. She was 23 years old!

When Envirotech was bought out and broken up, Nelson decided to return to school full time, and to support herself as a consultant. She enrolled in the Golden Gate University MBA program because it had a strong concentration in nonprofit administration. In her consulting work she was now able to combine her volunteer and professional experience by providing membership management services to a number of local museums.

When she completed her MBA in 1984, she again found a tight job market. She returned to private industry as a marketing and communications director, this time for a food-processing equipment firm. She learned about the Sierra Club position in the fall of 1987 and was hired after a four-month interview process with 12 people and with the volunteer leadership. She says, "It was very helpful to meet with the volunteer leadership before I was hired because they felt they were part of the decision and I'm working very closely with them now."

Advice to Others

Nelson is unusual in that she knew from the start that she wanted to be a nonprofit manager. She sought both the volunteer experience and the specific graduate training she needed. It took her nine years to achieve her goal, and she loves what she is now doing.

Her volunteer experience has been a great help. "I've been on both sides of the fence. . . . Volunteers understand that I know what it means to give your advice as a volunteer and have it not taken by staff. I have some special sensitivity to working with volunteers and try to get the best out of them, getting their advice so that I can do my job better."

Nelson recommends the academic study of nonprofit management, although she thinks a certificate program plus board or volunteer service is sufficient for most people, particularly if they already have business experience.

9

Service Providers to the Sector

The following profiles describe individuals whose business is to provide services to nonprofit organizations. The services range from management of volunteers to fundraising, marketing, training, employment information, and general management assistance. All of these people have worked with or for nonprofits all of their lives and seem to enjoy the autonomy of creating and being in their own business. They have developed a market for their services without abandoning their interest and commitment to causes. Some have set up private for-profit firms; others have created new nonprofits. This is a group of visionary, creative entre-preneurs, willing to take risks. They have been able to take advantage of the sector's growth. They contribute to its success.

Carol Barbeito

President
Technical Assistance Center (TAC)

*"I think we should train every professional in management skills.
Whatever you are, social worker, physical therapist, school teacher,
you ought to have management classes because you are going to be a
manager some day or work in a management system."*

What She Does

Carol Barbeito heads a unique management consulting firm in Denver. The Technical Assistance Center, founded in 1979, is a nonprofit organization that serves other nonprofits. Its mission is:

> To provide nonprofits—arts and culture, education, health, human services, environmental, civic service—with the most appropriate management assistance so they can serve the community needs effectively and efficiently.

The services TAC offers include: workshops as well as conferences and an Advanced Management Certificate Program with the University of Denver; on-site contract training; consulting services; information services; Community Cash Flow Fund; and Board Placement Services.

TAC's services are organized around specific management topics including: financial management, financial development, human resource management, management information systems, marketing, governance, organizational structure and systems, leadership, and personal development.

Barbeito's major responsibilities are to represent TAC and its cause to the business and professional community, to obtain resources for the Center, and to work directly with clients as a consultant and trainer. Her duties include general management, budget and fiscal oversight, marketing, and publications. She also is a director of TAC's for-profit subsidiary, the Management Assistance Center, which provides related consulting services and publications to business, government, and other nonprofits who are not 501(c)(3) charities.

Barbeito's small staff includes a vice-president of program, a volunteer and training coordinator, a business manager, and support staff; two of her people hold an MBA degree. TAC's use of contract consultants and a large volunteer staff of professionals and retired executives expands its abilities to provide services. Under Barbeito's guidance there has been considerable growth in fee income as well as programs, agencies, and individuals served.

How She Got There

As an undergraduate, Barbeito looked for a program of study that would hold her interest, help people, and lead to employment. She found it in speech pathology and audiology and obtained her BA and MA from Indiana University.

Barbeito began her career as the first director of a speech and hearing department in a Detroit hospital just starting a new Department of Physical Medicine and Rehabilitation. She was told she was free to do whatever was necessary to start the program. She remembers an early administrative initiative, a series of phone calls around the city to find out who was doing what, in retrospect, an "instinctive market survey." Three years later, she had a diagnostic center for southeastern Michigan and an alternative school program for primary students severely handicapped in language.

She quickly realized that her clinical training was excellent and had prepared her well for helping people. However, she often found herself thrown into situations that called for management training and experience, which she did not have. Barbeito says, "It was really terrible to try to do good things in a bad management system. You could do some good, but your overall ability was hampered if you didn't have good supervision and an adequate budget. . . . My naivete slowed me down and hurt my effectiveness."

"I had what many of our TAC clients have, which is no administrative training whatsoever." She learned management techniques as she was doing them, scrounging for information, reading, taking seminars. Now she believes people should learn something about management before they have to do it. The technical assistance movement is important to her because she believes that the know-how it disseminates can greatly improve an organization's ability to succeed and help individuals in their job performance.

Barbeito's success in working in multi-ethnic neighborhoods and with school systems in Detroit led to her next job as a maternal and child health consultant for southeastern Michigan, where one of her tasks was to help develop the first neighborhood health clinic system in the country. She was now operating in a much broader arena, and her interests extended way beyond her original specialty.

After receiving her Ph.D. in speech and hearing at the University of Denver, Barbeito began her 15-year career as a nonprofit executive in Denver. She has been the first executive director of the Mile High Child Care Association, then director of the Department of Community Services, Mile High United Way. Subsequently, as executive director of the Colorado Affiliate of the National Mental Health Association, she became active in designing and testing a national training program for volunteer staff, and became a trainer herself. Her next move was to the Technical Assistance Center. She says, "I have had everything from a two-and-a-half-million dollar budget with 200 regular employees and 250 contract employees in the day care program, to TAC, which is a small, highly professionalized service company.

Barbeito has been an active participant in the technical assistance movement and in the Nonprofit Management Association. She explains that the Great Society programs in the 1960s resulted in a proliferation of new nonprofits and an expansion of established ones. In the beginning, government tried to offer technical assistance to these organizations directly or through their grant programs, but this support dwindled.

By the 1970s, the Mott Foundation commissioned a study to determine whether donated dollars would make more of an impact if nonprofits could manage themselves better. The study showed that nonprofits had management problems and needed help. This finding led to the establishment of a few management assistance groups. The movement has grown and there are now some 40 or 50 organizations across the country offering these services. Barbeito has been among the handful of professionals at the forefront of this development.

Advice to Others

As a manager, trainer, and consultant, Barbeito has a broad view of work in the sector. She says that there is no clear path to career advancement. Many people job-hop to get ahead—from small agencies to larger ones; from community, to regional, to national organizations. This seems to be the way to get more money and a better title.

She says, "Find a way to become a star in what you are currently doing. . . . In a career change it helps to be a success in the previous career. No matter where you start, management training is absolutely critical."

"Becoming involved in professional societies and accepting a leadership role has been very helpful in terms of my learning . . . it is both a contact and a vantage point. . . . You have to be willing not only to be a member but to get involved, make yourself known and take some risks." Barbeito advocates getting out into the community, volunteering, being on boards. She also recommends a practice that she has followed, systematically setting new learning goals for herself every year.

She believes that technical assistance is a growing area with room for both specialists and former managers of 501(c)(3) organizations who have multiple areas of expertise. She says, "Most nonprofits are run by people that have excellent education in the area of service they are delivering, but are not trained managers. They often cannot hire the managers they need or afford the price of private consultants."

Jonathan B. Cook

National Executive Director
The Support Centers of America

*"I identify with people who find more meaning and enjoyment in life
in giving than in having security and physical possessions. I turn back
virtually all of my salary to the organization. I live inexpensively. I
have a simple life-style. It is a matter of choice."*

Who He Is

Jonathan Cook heads a national network of management, accounting, and fundraising assistance centers for nonprofit organizations. Cook founded and built this nonprofit organization, the oldest and largest of its kind, which now operates 12 centers in 10 states. The centers are all part of the same corporate structure and, while interdependent, also have significant local autonomy. Cook works from the organization's national office in Washington, D.C., where the first center started in 1971. The Support Centers' 1986 *Annual Report* describes his organization's mission as follows:

> Support Centers provide high-volume, low-cost management resources to America's charities. Our professional, reliable management assistance strengthens nonprofit organizations and saves them time and money. By increasing the effectiveness and efficiency of nonprofit agencies, Support Centers also serve the interests of the corporations, foundations and individuals whose generous philanthropy makes the American nonprofit sector possible.

The Support Centers' services include: training for nonprofit managers and board members, information and referral services on management and accounting questions, diagnostic and direct management assistance, and volunteer programs. Services are provided by staff or volunteers. Cook and his staff now write and edit a monthly section on management for a widely disseminated paper, *The Nonprofit Times.*

Cook says his main job as national executive director is to plan and work with his national and local boards and with a nationwide staff of 40 people. He also spends a great deal of time writing about planning, fundraising for his organization, acting as a consultant and trainer, and, he says, as a "gadfly to the rest of the nonprofit sector."

How He Got There

Cook spent seven years at Harvard. He attended Harvard Law School with the idea that he wanted to manage a nonprofit organization. Since childhood he had been interested in causes and in watching how "cause people" operated. He says, "I kept thinking it could be done better. I had the notion that I was going to be involved in those things for the rest of my life." After law school he went into a federal management intern program and then left to go into commercial management consulting. This proved to be uncomfortable for him because he disagreed with the firm's ethical standards. He left and took off some time to travel across the country, to read management books, and to work in a political campaign.

In 1971 he set up the Philanthropic Information Service, which ultimately became the Support Centers of America. He says he wanted "to set up an infrastructure of management resources that could help any not-for-profit organization work better." He started the organization without any capital or significant connections. He says the centers grew and survived because of his "dogged persistence." He believes the Support Centers fill a gap between the large market-driven fundraising consultant firms that act as a resource to large organizations, and the small independent consultants who offer valuable services but do not build organizations to last after their own retirement. What the Support Centers do is assist in "an articulation of process, methodology and knowledge that can be brought down to succeeding generations."

Advice to Others

As a student of the organizations and people who work in the sector, Cook offers thoughtful and personal perspectives on what it means to work and build a nonprofit sector career. Both an idealist and a pragmatist, Cook places himself in the middle between selfless altruists like Mother Theresa and Ralph Nader and more mainstream leaders of the sector whose concerns for effective management and personal recognition and rewards tend to be similar to those of corporate executives.

Compensation is a critical issue for Cook. He believes that we should help young people coming into the nonprofit sector understand that working in the sector is probably going to hurt them financially for the rest of their lives. His staff knows that they can make more money elsewhere, but they choose to stay, knowing they are making a sacrifice. He is well aware of the pressures to increase salary levels in the sector. However, he believes that there are many people like him who are willing "to take less from the organization in order for the organization to have more" and that these people will continue to keep salary levels down.

Another concern for Cook is advising young people who are in the process of making life choices. He tells them it is difficult to move from management or finance positions in a nonprofit organization to a similar job in a for-profit organization. On the other hand, it is always possible to move from business to nonprofit employment. Public relations, personnel, and community relations jobs, however, are less subject to these sectoral distinctions.

Regarding education, Cook believes that "graduate training in nonprofit management right after college makes no sense at all," but "continuing education programs for nonprofit managers makes sense." He is against MBA-type programs in nonprofit management. He does think that college and graduate students bound for business careers should learn something about the nonprofit sector and how it intersects with the private sector, in preparation for the board leadership roles they may play in the future.

Cook suggests that financial management is an area of opportunity, for good comptrollers are in demand. He notes that, while the principles of financial management are the same for all sectors, the conventions are different for nonprofits, and not enough accounting firms and financial managers know how to do good nonprofit accounting.

Susan J. Ellis

President
Energize Associates

"Most volunteers are a totally underutilized resource."

What She Does

Susan Ellis is an expert in the management of volunteers. Through Energize Associates, the consulting, training, and publishing firm she founded in 1977, she offers services to organizations in designing and administering effective volunteer programs. With a small organization, consisting of one secretary and several part-time associates who are brought in as needed, Ellis has built an impressive roster of clients in the United States and Canada. They include national, regional, and local voluntary organizations, state and local units of government, and corporations.

Ellis says, "One of the exciting things for me is to work in a field that isn't entirely formed, that you can make a dent in, and that has room for contributions." With a growing national interest in the effective involvement of volunteers, in their training and in volunteer–staff relations, there is a market for her services and products. When Ellis first started working in volunteerism in 1971, there were only five books in the field. Today her Volunteerism Resource Center houses over 5,000 items, including 150 books, periodicals, and journals.

Ellis has contributed to the body of professional literature with more than 30 articles and with pamphlets about current volunteer issues and practices, and she has produced five books: *By the People: A History of Americans as Volunteers*, 1978 (with Katherine H. Noyes); *From the Top Down: The Executive Role in Volunteer Program Success*, 1986; *Children as Volunteers*, 1983; *No Excuses: The Team Approach to Volunteer Management*, 1981; and *Proof Positive: Developing Significant Volunteer Recordkeeping Systems*, 1980 (both also with Katherine N. Noyes). An entrepreneur to the core, Ellis publishes and markets her own books. She has also written, produced, and marketed two videotapes for trainers: *Colleagues: The Volunteer/Employee Relationship* and *Together: Volunteer-to-Volunteer Relationships*.

Ellis's consulting and training business is directed to helping organizations start, develop, or improve their volunteer programs. In her view, "The skills and methods of working with volunteers are generic. Volunteer projects don't succeed by themselves. It takes careful planning, attention and time to mobilize volunteers. Above all it takes knowledgeable, creative leadership to manage superior programs."

In her book, *By the People,* a director of volunteers is defined "as an individual (salaried or not) who takes responsibility for coordinating a group of volunteers. This includes recruitment, training, supervision, evaluation, recognition and planning." Ellis says that the director of volunteers is in fact the personnel director for the organization's unpaid staff. The job is unique because volunteers are all part-timers and diverse in age, background, and amount of time they can give to the organization. Some volunteer assignments require specific skills. For others, the major criterion is "the kind of person you are." It is therefore important for the director of volunteers to determine whether a prospective volunteer has the personal qualities to do a given job.

Ellis believes, "The single most important skill required of a director of volunteers is the ability to do task analysis. It is not easy to design jobs for somebody to do two hours a week, and a lot of volunteers are underutilized for that reason." She sums up the essential tasks for the volunteer manager: analyze the job you need done, write a job description, advertise it, screen candidates, give them a place to sit, tell them who is going to supervise them, keep records on them, evaluate them, and accommodate them in your system." Also, "Recognize that you never 'direct' volunteers: you *enable* them to participate."

The following are examples of consulting services Energize Associates has provided.

- for a family counseling agency, the firm conducted a needs assessment that produced 61 recommendations for ways volunteers could be incorporated into service delivery.
- for a large rural school system, the firm developed a pilot program placing community volunteers into special education classrooms.
- for an agency serving people with disabilities, the firm gave individualized training to key staff on how to integrate volunteers into client services.

Ellis's multiple activities and those of her associates reinforce and intensify their manifold expertise in volunteer management and the capacity of her firm to take on an increasing variety of assignments. Ellis's many professional activities have included: six years as editor-in-chief of *The Journal of Volunteer Administration;* serving as Chairwoman for Professional Development of the Association for Volunteer Administration; and teaching graduate and undergraduate courses in volunteer administration at Temple University and Pennsylvania State University.

How She Got There

Ellis studied liberal arts at Temple University and obtained a master's degree in folklore and folklife from the University of Pennsylvania. A keen interest in juvenile delinquency, sparked by a job in the welfare system, led Ellis to apply for a position in the Philadelphia Family Court after graduate school. She wanted to work as a delinquency prevention counselor. Instead, to her surprise, she was offered the opportunity to start and direct a volunteer program. The court had just received a federal grant for this purpose and Ellis appeared to have the necessary qualifications. Ellis accepted the position, hoping it would be a stepping stone to something else.

Despite a lack of clear goals for the project, and with little personal experience to guide her in the start-up phases of her work, Ellis spent the next five and a half years setting up the first comprehensive justice volunteer program in Philadelphia. As Project Director of Special Services of the Philadelphia Family Court, she developed and managed all aspects of a system that used 1,000 volunteers and supervised a paid staff of five.

Among the projects that her department instituted through volunteer efforts were: a community resource information bank that probation officers could use for client referral, the assignment of volunteers to work on a one-to-one basis with hard-core cases, locating specific resources such as camp placements or tutors for individual probationers, and employment programs for juveniles on probation. Her success in attracting, inspiring, and organizing volunteers was recognized both by the Pennsylvania Juvenile Court Judges Commission and the Voluntary Action Council of Greater Philadelphia.

During her stint at the Family Court, Ellis became active in professional associations because "they provide you with an umbrella to do things beyond your own job." At one of the conferences she attended, a particularly effective trainer stimulated her interest in training. She says, "I thought it was the most exciting thing I had ever seen. I spoke to her afterward and asked her what do I have to learn to do what you are doing? She said to go to a lot of conferences. She also said publish—there's not enough written in this field."

Within three years of that conversation, Ellis and associate Katherine H. Noyes were doing training workshops on volunteer subjects. "I was never a wallflower when it comes to public speaking. . . . I love sharing and talking to other people." The two women also began work on their first book, *By the People*. As Ellis's visibility and reputation grew, she was called on to do outside consulting and training. She reached a point in her career where she had to choose between promotion within the court system to another management position or continuing her outside work. A consulting job for ACTION, involving on-site evaluation of volunteer programs in four states, gave her the impetus to leave the court.

Within six months, Ellis was not only doing training programs for ACTION, but also teaching a graduate course in volunteer management, directing a volunteer program for a cultural group, continuing work on her book, and doing enough training and consulting work to set up her own business. She says, "I'm a for-profit consulting firm, and that was purposeful. . . . I want to know if what I do is effective for people. I've been in business for 11 years, and I like to believe that what I do is of value because the actual recipients of my services pay me for it. I like that accountability."

Advice to Others

Ellis is dedicated to disseminating information about volunteer administration as a career field and to professionalizing its practice. While the field is starting to come into its own, she says, "It's a profession that is not clear to people, even to people in it." She attributes this to the fact that more than half the people who manage volunteer programs—an estimated 60,000 people—do not do it as a full-time job but as a part of another job, such as social worker or probation officer. This makes it hard for practitioners themselves to view volunteer management as a profession.

Ellis's concept of what a director of volunteers can do is very broad. It includes training members of the board of the organization and finding non-cash resources in the community, functions that are generally associated with fundraising. To reflect the expanded potential she foresees for this job, she would like to change the job title, from director of volunteers to director of community resources.

Thus far no particular credentials are required to work in volunteer management, but a BA or MA degree is preferred. A peer review certification program is available through the Association for Volunteer Administration. People, planning, organizing, and communicating skills are important generic competencies. A background in a specialized field, health or art for example, can be helpful.

Ellis believes that the best people in the field are those "who love the creativity of it." While the field is not well paid, Ellis believes it can offer opportunities for lateral movement, since skills are the same regardless of setting. The field also offers opportunities to move up to director of development or executive director, if one has demonstrated outstanding management and leadership skill.

Ellis points out that new opportunities for directors of volunteers are available in the court systems, because of the increase in court-ordered alternative sentencing programs that require offenders to do voluntary community service.

Michael Seltzer

Independent Consultant to
Nonprofit Organizations and Foundations

*''For many of us there is no substitute for that sense of being able to
do something that has social value.''*

What He Does

During his 20-year career in the nonprofit sector, Michael Seltzer has used his considerable
talents and his passion for justice and action in many roles. As a fundraiser, foundation
grantmaker, executive director, consultant, trainer, and writer, he has had an unusual opportunity to learn what nonprofits can do and how they can do it, as well as to provide help
to thousands of organizations. Since 1981 Seltzer has worked as an independent consultant,
giving him the freedom to manage many complementary roles.

Fighting AIDS is now the major, though not exclusive, focus of Seltzer's work. He has been
helping AIDS-related organizations since the early years of the epidemic by providing counseling and technical assistance on every aspect of the problem. At the same time he has become
the bridge and the natural link between AIDS efforts and organized philanthropy. A major
thrust of his effort has been to encourage foundations and corporations to fund AIDS-related
initiatives.

In 1987, the Ford Foundation retained Seltzer to prepare an internal report for their trustees,
to show the scope of the epidemic and what other foundations were doing about it. His report,
Meeting the Challenge: Foundation Responses to Acquired Immune Deficiency Syndrome (1987),
generated so much interest that the Foundation Center distributed it to the country's 1,000
largest foundations.

In 1988, the Allstate Insurance Company published *AIDS: Corporate America Responds* in an
effort to generate greater corporate interest and involvement. Seltzer coauthored the section
of the report on the role of corporate philanthropy. Concurrently, in association with a number
of colleagues including Joyce Bove, Vice-President of the New York Community Trust, Seltzer
was active in establishing Funders Concerned About Aids, an affinity group of the Council
on Foundations. The group compiled *A Funder's Guide to AIDS Grantmaking*, published by the
Council on Foundations in 1988. All of these initiatives served to build interest, and Seltzer
notes that by 1988 hundreds of people attended their special sessions during the Council on
Foundations' annual conference.

Because of the increasing volume of requests for his services, Seltzer is considering an affiliation with a consulting firm. In the long-term, he foresees the possibility that his work on AIDS may take up all his time.

How He Got There

Seltzer is a New Yorker. He attended the prestigious Bronx High School of Science, where his early interests were biology and the environment and where his social conscience was ignited by the civil rights movement. His years at Syracuse University from 1964 to 1968, a period of social unrest and social change, also influenced him profoundly.

In the summer of 1966 he decided to participate in Operation Crossroads Africa in Cameroon, where he and a group of other students from the U.S., Canada, and Cameroon built a school. This program gave Seltzer his first exposure to fundraising, since he raised $1,000 from a group of civic organizations in order to go to West Africa. To carry out the Crossroads philosophy of furthering understanding of Africa in America, he prepared a slide presentation and talk about his experiences and gave speeches to 25 groups after he returned.

Following his African experience, he changed his course of study to international relations with a minor in African studies. While in Cameroon he began to oppose the Vietnam War, and his opposition became stronger during his last two years at Syracuse University. He spent the summer of 1967 as a VISTA Associate in West Virginia, working in a Job Corps Center. When Martin Luther King, Jr., died, he made up his mind to reenlist in VISTA after graduation, a way to give alternate service to his country while avoiding a war he opposed.

VISTA sent him to Hawaii where he worked among poor Polynesians. His group's project was to redesign the curriculum and teaching materials used in the Hawaiian public schools so that they would incorporate Hawaiian images that had meaning for Hawaiian children, replacing the mainland focus with a Hawaiian focus.

When he returned to the mainland, Seltzer attended a United Nations International Affairs Conference. A speech about the American Freedom from Hunger Foundation, whose purpose was to educate the American public about world-wide hunger and development in the Third World, caught his attention. Seltzer was so inspired by the speech that on a subsequent visit to Washington, D.C., he knocked on the door of the Freedom from Hunger Foundation. Within an hour and a half their executive director offered him a job as East Coast Regional Director.

The Freedom from Hunger Foundation had recently brought the walk-a-thon to the U.S. It was a new fundraising device then popular in Europe. Seltzer traveled from Maine to Florida helping high school and college students to raise money for domestic and international projects. He says the walk-a-thons "were vehicles for youthful idealism at the time." The Foundation raised $2 million a year, and the walk-a-thons were so successful that the March of Dimes ultimately took them over. Seltzer remembers this as an energizing and exciting period of his life, which gave him both fundraising and foundation experience.

After a short stint with the McGovern campaign, Seltzer became involved with an art auction to raise funds for rebuilding hospitals in North Vietnam. Once again he realized how much he enjoyed fundraising, which few others enjoyed. He heard of a job opening in Philadelphia with the People's Fund (now called the Bread and Roses Community Fund). Because he and another candidate were both so well qualified for the position, they were both hired to share the job. Seltzer and Linda Richardson ran one of the first alternative foundations in the country. Its purpose was to raise money from the public to support organizations working for social change.

Seltzer found a second half-time job in Philadelphia with the American Friends Service Committee, which hired him to raise money for reconstruction projects in Vietnam. He was now fundraising for two different organizations—and loved it. During this period, Seltzer and Bill Taylor, a financial secretary for the Friends, originated the idea of starting an organization called the Philadelphia Clearinghouse for Community Funding Resources, which became one of the early nonprofit technical assistance centers. Its goal was to help community organizations, particularly in minority communities, by teaching fundraising and management skills. Seltzer notes:

> We didn't realize we were pioneering management support organizations. All our assistance was provided free. We did counseling, which is now called consulting, we ran workshops, we produced a newsletter, we ran a drop-in library. We serviced about one hundred requests a month.

Again, Seltzer and Linda Richardson co-directed this organization. As he now recalls, "It was one of the most special relationships in my professional career. I didn't then realize how many people thought it unusual for a black woman and a white man to work together as colleagues and co-directors."

After six years in Philadelphia, Seltzer decided to move back to New York. As one of the founders of the Funding Exchange, a network of social change funds, Seltzer became a grantmaker again. After two years with this organization, he decided to establish his own consulting practice. The New World Foundation retained him on a part-time basis to provide technical assistance to their grantees, and this affiliation continues today. Other clients included Amnesty International USA, WNET Thirteen, the Foundation for Independent Video and Film, and the Center for Family Resources.

Seltzer started writing and an article about the impact of Reaganomics on nonprofits, "Fundraising Strategies for the Eighties," led the Foundation Center to suggest that he write a comprehensive guide to fundraising strategies. With a grant from the Ford Foundation, Seltzer wrote *Securing Your Organization's Future: A Complete Guide to Fundraising Strategies*, a definitive reference work that enhanced Seltzer's growing reputation in all areas of nonprofit management.

Advice to Others

Seltzer is not a careerist. That is, he is not someone who carefully plans each step toward an ultimate goal. Instead, his life's work has been generated by an interest in social causes. Through that work, he has achieved both gratification and success, and he believes that others can do so as well. He says, "Social movements are not formed by people whose primary motivation is 'how do I succeed in life.' Social movements are formed by people who care about other people. They want to do something that makes a difference."

Penny Stoil

Co-Director
Projects Plus, Inc.

"Managing special events is a business that calls for diplomacy and tact, because what you are really doing is dealing in power. You are selling power, and you have to understand who has it and how it is translated into money for charities. When someone lends you their name they are lending you the gift of their power. You have to know how to use it."

What She Does

Penny Stoil is Co-Director of Projects Plus, Inc. (PPI) in New York City, a special events management firm that she operates with her partner Fran Liner. Since its founding in 1972, the firm has created and handled major fundraising events such as dinners, dinner dances, sporting events and dinners, charity balls, concerts, auctions, premieres of movies, opening nights of plays, and organization anniversary celebrations. These events are sponsored by the nonprofits that are PPI's clients for the purpose of raising large amounts of money, gaining visibility, and honoring volunteer leaders and donors. Many but not all of PPI's clients are based in New York City.

An event managed by PPI will generally raise $400,000 to $600,000, but the proceeds may be much higher. The firm's client list includes: Phoenix House, the New York Botanical Garden, the Metropolitan Opera, Cancer Care, Boys Clubs of America, Girl Scouts New York Council, the International Center for the Disabled. PPI's largest single event is the Sloan Kettering Frank Sinatra Concert, which they have run since 1980 and which raised $3.5 million in 1983 alone.

For the last several years PPI has limited its business to managing 22 events a year, which raise a combined total of $11 million. Stoil and Liner each oversee half of the business so that they know exactly what is happening on every account and can maintain supervisory control. Essentially, what PPI does is to take over the management of an event from the beginning to the end. Stoil says, "We work with our client to get the idea, the chairman, the guest of honor. We shape the event so that it has the right personality and fundraising appeal."

PPI then takes the event in-house, that is, the PPI office becomes the campaign committee's headquarters. The firm handles planning, forming committees, scheduling, the writing and printing of literature, preparing direct mail, working with subcontractors, publicity, telephoning, selling tickets, and whatever else is required. Everything is done with the approval of the client and PPI assumes responsibility for the financial success of the event.

PPI has a staff of over 20 people, including nine dinner coordinators, three researchers who prepare a unique mailing list for every event, and support staff. Stoil says, "We have no secretaries. Our office functions with a nonauthoritarian work style. We believe that by encouragement we get the best performance out of people. It works. The majority of our people have been with us for five to ten years." She points out that this is unusual in the fundraising industry where job turnover is very high.

Stoil says that 90 percent of the money raised from the special events she manages comes from corporate philanthropy, and therefore she has to know, "what is going on, who knows whom, and what the corporate environment is like." The chairperson, the honoree, and the honorary and associate chairpersons for the event are likely to be prominent in the business, social, and philanthropic world. Therefore, the special event that honors them or uses their names has to reflect their style, taste, and preferences and attract the interest and support of their peers. Every detail has to be carefully planned and executed to reflect well on the sponsoring organization, its corporate and individual donors, and on the honorees. "Not only do we look after everyone's interests, but we also serve as a liaison to all of those people."

How She Got There

Penny Stoil grew up in Brooklyn during the post-Depression years. She was surrounded by poverty. Both through her family and the surrounding community she developed an interest in social programs and social justice. She attended Brooklyn College and majored in English. Her first job after graduation was in the public relations business and her second job was with Frank Berend Associates, the first special events management firm in the nation. During her 15 years with Frank Berend, Stoil learned the special events business from the ground up. She became a vice-president of the firm, as did Fran Liner.

When it became apparent to both women that they would never achieve any ownership in the firm, they left to form their own business, Projects Plus, Inc., the second special events firm in America. They had five clients during their first year, eight clients the second year, and thirteen their third. Their experience and contacts have paid off and now they limit their clients to large organizations that sponsor major events on an annual basis.

Stoil has been an active longtime member of the board of the New York Chapter of the National Society of Fund Raising Executives, and she is now an Honorary Member of the Board, a distinction accorded to only one other person. She is an active panelist and lecturer on special events.

Advice to Others

From the vantage point of some 30 years in the special events business, Stoil sees growth in the field. Currently, there are several special events firms in New York City, and companies like hers are starting to be formed in major cities across the country. She summarizes what she believes a special events manager needs:

- "You have to be a cause person, to have a genuine understanding and feeling for what each client is trying to do."
- Sensitivity to people, the ability to talk to them, to gain their confidence, to understand their style.
- A sense of organization and the ability to handle a tremendous amount of small detail. Stoil says, "A special event is a lot of small details put together in a way that embarrasses nobody." She adds, "This is a business of sweat and a lot of logistics."
- The ability to write well.

Stoil believes smart, nontraditional, self-directed people do best in this business, people who respond positively to problems and who learn from experience. It is a good field for people who can keep track of details. She advises those who want to break into special events fundraising to start with a fundraising job that will provide a broad framework for understanding the industry as a whole, and then to move into the more narrowly focused special events business.

James P. Clark

Director
ACCESS—Networking in the Public Interest

"Find out what makes your blood boil. Find out what you are about
. . . . What do you see in the world that interests you, where you can
make a difference? What draws you to it? Young people need an ob-
jective to draw them into participation and involvement. . . . Get in-
volved and you will make a difference."

What He Does

Jim Clark is probably the most successful young entrepreneur in the nonprofit sector. With
a clear purpose, bold determination, and high energy, Clark organized ACCESS in 1985 while
he was still a student at Wesleyan University. ACCESS is an information broker, providing
job listings, personnel recruiting services, and a database of nonprofit organization networking
opportunities. Clark has developed ACCESS into a viable nonprofit organization with growing
national impact. The organization is now based in Cambridge in space made available by
Harvard's John F. Kennedy School of Government.

As director of ACCESS, Clark has worked to develop services to respond to two interactive
needs. On the one hand, information about public interest employment opportunities is not
available to college graduates and others seeking employment in a nonprofit organization.
On the other hand, nonprofits with low or nonexistent personnel budgets need a way to reach
college seniors and others to let them know about their current personnel needs.

Clark thought of a way to address both sets of concerns. Working with a mailing list of
450,000 nonprofit organizations, ACCESS regularly surveys a segment of these organizations
to obtain information on their background and personnel needs. This information is entered
into the ACCESS database.

ACCESS publishes *Opportunities in Non-Profit Organizations,* a directory of position listings
in looseleaf format that is updated monthly. The directory is sold to college and university
career guidance offices, libraries, and other counseling and referral organizations. Clark believes that "career offices are the most underrated power centers in the country." Acknowledging the influence of this new resource, the College Placement Council designated ACCESS
its "liaison to the nonprofit sector." Individuals who do not have access to the directory can
use it through the ACCESS Job Search Service. For a modest fee ACCESS will search its

database for suitable leads, after receiving a résumé and letter specifying an individual's goals and interests.

Clark works with ACCESS's prestigious national board as well as seven full-time managers and a support staff. Clark's natural inclination is "not to look at the tiny pieces, but to look at the big picture." Consequently, most of his time is devoted to the tasks necessary to building a young organization—planning, and developing new projects and seeking new contacts and support. Last fall, ACCESS introduced a new publication for law school career offices, *Opportunities in Public Interest Law*. In its first year, the response was enthusiastic, with 96 of the 171 U.S. law schools subscribing. Other new initiatives in various stages of development are:

- *Regional Offices*. A Western Regional Office has been open since September, 1987, at the University of California at Berkeley. The Southern Regional Office opened in 1988 at Duke University, and a Midwestern office is planned for early 1989, probably in Chicago.

- *Working Dinners*. A series of monthly get-togethers, which each regional office will host, to create provocative interdisciplinary discussion forums on public service issues. Summarized versions of the discussions will be published.

- *Student Working Forums*. College campus speeches by noted public or community service leaders, followed by open discussions. Videotapes will be available as well.

- *Public Service/Public Library*. This project will gather information from third parties on public and community service issues, on public service careers and specific job opportunities in the nation's nonprofit organizations. The information will be computerized and accessible through terminals at public libraries nationwide. Research and development for this project is already quite far along.

How He Got There

Clark comes from New York City. He attended the academically select Horace Mann High School where his early interests focused on marine biology. Then an influential history teacher sparked Clark's curiosity about why human beings act as they do. A strong interest in current events led to his becoming active in the Horace Mann Political Affairs Society. He also worked for the school's current events magazine. He recalls writing an article about Anwar Sadat because he was impressed by "Sadat's detachment from short-term politics, which allowed him to see the big picture."

At Wesleyan University in Connecticut, Clark was drawn to political science and became active in Amnesty International, running one of the most productive groups in the organization's history. During the summers he sought varied kinds of work experiences. He worked as an intern for an environmental group, for a Parisian law firm, and for the Comptroller of the City of New York.

He spent his junior year in England studying economics at Cambridge University's Corpus Christi College. At the end of that year he had "a flash," an idea on how to get people interested and willing to try a career in public service. Clark realized the government was taking less and less responsibility for meeting public needs and that these needs were not disappearing. He thought that if people were exposed to information about a range of causes and organizations in the nonprofit sector, they would find what interested them and be more likely to choose a career in public service. This was the genesis of ACCESS. Clark says ACCESS works with information (raw material), communication (dissemination of that raw material), and education (what happens when that raw material runs into a human being).

During the start-up phases of the project, Clark obtained support from his peers, encouragement from leaders in the sector, and concrete help from the then-president of Wesleyan University, who offered to be the organization's fiscal agent in Clark's senior year. Clark started with one computer, helpful friends, and a lot of library research. He put up some of his own money and received a few small donations. The first task was to compile a mailing list of 4,000 nonprofit organizations. A simple mail survey of this group surprisingly yielded a 6 percent return. The project moved from Wesleyan to NYU and then to Harvard. The first edition of the directory was produced in January 1987, and was tested at six universities. Clark found that the referral service worked! An article in the *Washington Post* stimulated considerable interest in ACCESS, and the organization was on its way.

A measure of the organization's program is the change in the organization's budget. ACCESS's first-year budget was $7,000; its second-year budget was $60,000; and its third-year budget was $160,000. The budget for the next year is expected to top $500,000. Fees for service as well as corporate, foundation, and academic support have all contributed to the organization's growth. Clark envisions considerable expansion in the coming years as ACCESS develops additional services and becomes better known. His long-term goal is for ACCESS to be a place where anyone asking J. F. Kennedy's question—what can I do for my country?—will find answers. In his view, "ACCESS exists to provide a mechanism for harnessing Americans' civic energy." Clark wants to encourage active citizenship and believes that the "clearest way to do that in the long-term is to begin with job referral in the nonprofit sector."

Advice to Others

Reflecting on his experience and achievement in three short years, Clark says, "If you see something that is being done in a way that you wouldn't do it, talk to people and figure out how else it might be done. . . . Do it yourself. No one is stopping you. A lot of people in society will help you do it. It doesn't require an immense amount of money. It doesn't require a huge amount of institutional support. These things make it easier. A lot of people who want to make a difference themselves, and who don't want to make a full commitment to do it, will help you. Their best instincts will express themselves vicariously through you."

(See Section 11 for further information on ACCESS and *Opportunities in Non-Profit Organizations*.)

Sally Ashbery Baines

President
GSB Associates, Inc.

"We look at direct marketing as an integral part of a nonprofit organization's overall financial development picture. . . . We examine each organization's unique needs and goals. . . . Our role is to bring in new members or donors to organizations through the mail; then cultivate and resolicit those donors using mail and telemarketing strategies."

What She Does

Sally Ashbery Baines is a founding partner and president of a fundraising consulting firm in Falls Church, Virginia, that specializes in direct mail and telemarketing. GSB clients include national and local public interest groups, health, welfare, and service organizations, and political candidates and committees. Many of the firm's clients represent liberal causes including groups like Americans United for Separation of Church and State, the National Coalition to Ban Handguns, the Native American Rights Fund, the Religious Coalition for Abortion Rights, Jobs with Peace Campaign, and the Overseas Education Fund. Baines says, "We have to believe in what we are doing—and, politically, we are to the left of center." She emphasizes that there are other firms like hers that work with groups across the political spectrum. They are all in the business of helping to identify and build a national constituency for particular issues or causes.

GSB is a small firm by design. A cohesive staff of five women includes a creative director, a fundraising director, and a production director. Although direct marketing is their major business, the firm also offers planning and implementation services in all aspects of fundraising.

Direct mail is an inexpensive means of reaching a wide audience to build and maintain a membership base. It is part art, part craft, part science. Baines says, "Very simply, direct mail is writing a letter describing an organization's programs and asking for support. We try to be as personal as we can in this approach, but we are dealing with large volumes." She adds:

> The initial and most difficult goal is donor acquisition, in which we are asking people to support an organization for the first time. We try to develop that into a direct mail package. At the heart of the direct mail package is the message—one that embodies the essence of the organization's purpose and goals—and one that captures the readers' attention.

Arriving at the concept for a direct mail package, for both donor acquisition and donor development, requires a series of creative meetings with client staff, copywriters, and graphic designers. GSB actively participates in and manages this process including research, fundraising plan development, mailing list selection, and all phases of production. This involves working directly with writers, artists, list brokers, printers, data-processing firms, telemarketing firms, and mailing houses.

Technical expertise in list identification for donor acquisition is essential for direct mail marketing. Developing a profile of the audience that an organization wants to reach and assessing available lists to find these people is a complex process. As with the direct mail package itself, mailing lists are continually tested and retested to determine the optimum combination of message and audience. Good lists will on average yield a 1 percent return. Baines notes that organizations embarking on a donor acquisition campaign should just expect to break even with the first donation, and there are times when subsidizing donor acquisition is justified.

When an issue is hot in the media, nonprofits should be prepared to take advantage of the public's interest to capture their attention. With the donor development programs that follow, the investment in donor acquisition quickly begins to pay off. Baines cites the 1987 Bork nomination to the Supreme Court as an example, when many organizations on both sides of the issue conducted heavy direct mail campaigns.

After a donor has given the first gifts, the next step is to begin to bond the new donor to the organization. This begins with the acknowledgment process, wherein the donor is thanked for their first gift. Then the cultivation and fundraising efforts are continued with information mailings (i.e., newsletters) and a series of fundraising efforts that include membership renewals, special appeals, pledge programs, and reinstatement programs using both direct mail and telemarketing.

As prospect lists are critical to the donor acquisition process, so is house file segmentation to the donor development process. The three basic segmentation criteria are: recency, frequency, and giving level. For example, high-dollar and multiple-gift donors are given special attention to maximize their involvement and giving potential. Lapsed donors are given special attention as well, often with a telemarketing reinstatement effort, in an attempt to keep active as many donors as possible.

The overall goal of donor development programs is to achieve maximum net income for an organization's programs through carefully planned campaigns designed to continually maintain an active donor base.

How She Got There

After completing her studies in liberal arts and nursing at the University of Michigan and Cornell, Baines spent 15 years working with Project HOPE. Project HOPE is an international organization involved in medical teaching and training—on-site in developing countries throughout the world, where self-help programs are designed to meet the unique needs of each area.

At Project HOPE, Baines learned and practiced for fundraising skills—under the tutelage of Richard Crohn, who was then direct mail consultant to Project HOPE. Her evolving responsibilities included development of national direct mail efforts, management of major gift funding from foundations, corporations, and individuals, deferred giving, special events, and affiliate and volunteer fundraising.

In 1980, Baines left Project HOPE to work with Craver, Mathews, Smith & Company, one of the largest direct mailing consulting firms in the country serving liberal clientele. Her responsibilities there were to plan and analyze donor development fundraising programs for more than 30 public interest and political organizations.

By 1983, Baines was ready to strike out on her own. She and a partner set up GSB Associates. They went to work in a small office, with two rented typewriters, some card tables, a telephone, and two projects in hand. GSB's business grew rapidly through referral but remains, by design, a modest-size firm. Baines is pleased with the personal service reputation of GSB. She says, "I'm sitting in the best of both worlds. I'm making a difference for causes I truly believe in, have the independence of my own business, and opportunity to pass on my fundraising knowledge to younger people on my staff."

Advice to Others

Baines says that people generally come into the fundraising business in one of two ways: through their interest in a cause, which leads them to acquire the technical expertise, or through learning the business from the bottom up, beginning in clerical positions. College courses in fundraising are becoming more common, as are seminars and workshops.

For people who write well, or may have journalism or advertising experience, she thinks freelance copywriting is a good and lucrative opportunity. Baines says that experienced copywriters are generally willing to help newcomers to the field. Small firms like GSB prefer to work with a group of freelance copywriters because it helps assure the uniqueness and originality of each package they produce.

For people who have an affinity for detail and management, direct marketing production provides a career opportunity. Also, for people who have an aptitude for numbers, direct marketing analysis and planning is a natural career path. Working as an assistant for either a nonprofit organization or direct marketing agency is one of the best ways to learn and practice these skills.

PART THREE

Practical Information for the Job Hunt

Lilly Cohen

10

The Sector's Best-Kept Secret: Associations as Employers and Professional Development Resources

Although associations are everywhere and affect all aspects of our lives, job seekers and career planners in this country are largely unaware of their existence. Associations contribute to all sectors of the economy—public, private, and nonprofit. They are especially important to individuals interested in management positions in nonprofit organizations, for they are potential employers as well as significant resources for career advancement. R. William Taylor, President of the American Society of Association Executives (ASAE), noted:

> The United States is a nation of associations. . . . Americans have the propensity to band together for a common cause. . . . Thousands of associations are formed every year. They call themselves by many names: institute, council, alliance, federation, club, network, and center. By some counts there are upwards of a half a million associations in this country.

What Are Associations?

Associations are nonprofit tax-exempt organizations whose purpose is to work for the benefit of their members, satisfying their needs and concerns. They are formed to share and communicate information and ideas. They set standards for the industries, professions, or interest groups they represent, and they lobby on issues that affect member interests. They create opportunities for networking and provide member services. There are various types of associations including advocacy and public interest groups like Common Cause that promote their own positions and self-help groups like Alcoholics Anonymous. The two major categories of associations are as follows.

Professional Associations. These groups, also known as professional societies, are voluntary membership organizations of individuals with a common background in a subject or a profession. Their focus is the expansion of knowledge and professionalism. According to ASAE (the association of association executives), members of professional societies join to increase their expertise or to achieve recognition or monetary gain. Membership may be based on credentials, experience, certification in a profession, or may simply be based on interest. Examples of well-known professional associations are the American Bar Association and the American Medical Association. Examples in the nonprofit sector are the National Society of Fund Raising Executives, the National Association of Social Workers, and the American College of Health Care Administration.

Trade Associations. Also known as industry associations, these are voluntary membership organizations, comprised of firms who are primarily business competitors. They are formed to help members with mutual problems and to promote financial success. Examples of well-known trade and industry associations are the National Association of Manufacturers and the American Bankers Association. Examples in the nonprofit sector are the American Association of Fund-Raising Counsel, the American Association of Museums, the Council on Foundations, and the Council for Advancement and Support of Education.

Associations Play a Unique Role in American Life

The French writer Alexis de Tocqueville described associations in 1835 in *Democracy in America:*

> Americans of all ages, all conditions and all dispositions constantly form associations. They have not only commercial and manufacturing companies, in which all take part, but associations of a thousand other kinds, religious, moral, serious, futile, general or restricted, enormous or diminutive. The Americans make associations to give entertainment, to found seminaries, to build inns, to construct churches, to diffuse books, to send missionaries to the antipodes; in this manner they found hospitals, prisons and schools. If it is proposed to inculcate some truth or to foster some feeling by the encouragement of a great example, they form a society. Wherever at the head of some new undertaking you see the government in France, or a man of rank in England, in the United States you will be sure to find an association.

More recently, *The 1986 Association Factbook*, published by the American Society of Association Executives, summarized the contribution of associations to American life in the following way:

> One of the primary strengths of the American people lies in their ability to join together in associations to achieve what no person could achieve alone. Associations have flourished in this country because the principles that make them possible—freedom to meet, freedom to speak, and freedom to organize—are rooted in the founding traditions of America.

Associations as Resources for Career Advancement

Most associations provide significant professional support to their members, meeting the needs of entry-, middle-, and top-level professionals. They are also eager to provide help to students and potential entrants into the trade or profession they represent. Services offered vary from one association to another, but in general they include:

- conventions

- professional certification programs leading to association credentials
- continuing education programs—conferences, institutes, courses, seminars, workshops
- publications and audio-visual materials
- employment referral and mentor systems
- reduced membership fees for students

We have identified many associations that support the work of nonprofit managers, agencies, institutions, and related businesses. Our listings are organized by subsector of "mini-industry." These listings describe association services specifically related to career advancement and professional development. (See listings on the concluding pages of this section.)

Careers in Association Management

Associations are major employers in the nonprofit sector, accounting for more than 1 million jobs. Many of these jobs are in Washington, D.C., New York, and Chicago, where the national associations are located. *The Encyclopedia of Associations* listed 20,000 national associations in 1987, and the universe is known to include several hundred thousand regional, state, and local associations.

There are several indicators that association management is a growth occupational field. National associations have grown from 5,000 in 1956 to 20,000 in 1987. Six universities offer degree or certificate programs in association management and a number of others offer individual courses. The American Society of Association Executives (ASAE) now has 16,000 members, representing 7,000 state and national associations and serving more than 80 million people and organizations. In 1985, the association industry spent $24 billion on 227,000 meetings and conventions attended by 31.6 million people.

The staff size of associations varies from those employing one or two people to those with a staff of 7,200 people, as reported by the YMCA in 1986. According to ASAE, the average staff size of a national association is 27, and their average budget is $2.3 million.

Since association work is a people business, good oral, written, and interpersonal skills are important. Association personnel typically consist of top- and middle-level managers, as well as support and clerical staff. There are association jobs for both generalists and specialists. The smaller associations, in particular, need generalists who can take on a variety of assignments such as fundraising, membership, and publishing. Fifty percent of all association jobs are at the executive level, and, since promotion from within is common, you can start at the bottom and work your way up. *The Association Factbook* promotes the advantages of association work as follows:

> Associations offer diversity, security, professional growth, and salaries competitive with private industry. They represent all fields of interest throughout the country. If you enjoy working with people, are well organized, and have specific interests and professional experience, employment with associations is worth investigating.

Figure 10.1 shows the classification of association jobs developed by the ASAE.

FIGURE 10.1 ASSOCIATION JOBS

Chief Paid Executive. The top spot in an association. Requires excellent administrative, leadership, financial control, government/legislative expertise, and oral and written communication skills.

No. 2 Executive. Second highest spot on staff. Requires experience in most of the above-named skill areas and often special knowledge of other skills, such as publishing, conventions/expositions, fundraising.

Department Head. Examples: Administration, Communications, Government Relations, Meetings, Education, Membership Services.

Legislative. Job might require federal, state, or local legislative experience.

Meeting Planner. Ability to plan and execute many meetings per year, negotiate with hotels, plan food and beverage functions, promote attendance, receive and deposit fees.

Financial Control. Solid accounting and bookkeeping skills required. Having a CPA is helpful for multimillion-dollar budget associations.

Convention/Expositions. Ability to plan and execute conventions from all aspects, including negotiating for exhibit space, selling booth space, working out floor plans, dealing with several local unions, announcement of conventions, collecting and handling large sums of money.

Legal. Most associations have legal counsel. Many have several lawyers working in specific areas dealing with federal or state governments, agencies, courts.

Communications. These positions usually refer to getting out magazines, house organs, newsletters. They require good writing, editing, printing, and production skills.

Public Relations. May mean dealing with the media, writing press releases, holding press conferences, speech writing, testimony preparation.

Membership Services. Jobs might require skills in handling insurance programs, research, statistical programs, maintenance of an information center, setting up "hotlines" to answer emergency questions from members or the public, or a host of other services.

Membership Promotion/Retention. Marketing ability to plan strategies and campaigns to build membership and to retain those you already have.

Fundraising. Knowledge of the intricacies and details of effective fundraising. Often needs to know how to write proposals for grants.

Source: American Society of Association Executives

Education and Training Programs for Association Management

Academics and practitioners, recognizing that association managers need association management as well as basic management skills, have created several programs in association management.

Executive Development Program. This one-year certificate program is a joint project of the ASAE and the University of Maryland College of Business and Management. It consists of 37 three-hour seminars plus one day of orientation. This intensive course of study is designed for the working part-time student. Its stated goal is, "To broaden perspectives and provide intellectual challenges to emerging executives in association management."

Classes meet at the ASAE Conference Center in downtown Washington, D.C. Seminars are taught by a mix of MBA faculty from the University of Maryland and top-level association practitioners. The curriculum focuses on the Practice of Management, Finance and Administration, Marketing, Communication, Human Resources, Law, Government Relations and Education, and Convention and Meeting Management. Participants who complete the program also earn credits towards the Certified Association Executive (CAE) Credential awarded by ASAE.

For information contact: ASAE Executive Development Program, 1575 Eye Street, N.W., Washington, DC 20005. Tel: (202) 606-2754.

Master's Degree in Association Management. This is a 42-credit interdisciplinary degree program offered by the School of Government and Business Administration of the George Washington University. It is offered in cooperation with four academic departments: Business Administration, Public Administration, Management Science, and Accounting. The program is designed for, "Practitioners who work with associations and seek to expand their knowledge, capabilities and skills as managers, analysts and policymakers."

Courses are taught by full-time faculty and adjunct faculty with experience in associations. The program may be taken on a full-time or part-time basis. Seventy percent of the students are employed. The curriculum covers: Comparative Institutions, Marketing, Communication, Media and Information Systems, Association Management, Finance and Accounting, and Analytical and Research Methods.

For information contact: Office of Enrollment Development and Admission, School of Government and Business Administration, George Washington University, Washington, DC 20052. Tel: (202) 676-6584 or (202) 676-6295.

Concentration in Association Management. This concentration is offered within a Master of Science in Management Program or a Master of Business Administration Program at the Graduate School of Business, La Salle University. This is a program of La Salle University and the Delaware Valley Society of Association Executives.

The Concentration in Association Management is a new option, and it is a part-time evening program for working professionals. The number of credit hours required depends upon the degree toward which the student is working. Courses are taught by a mix of full-time faculty and adjunct faculty who are practitioners in the field. The curriculum includes a management core plus specialized courses in association management.

For information contact: Association Management Program, Graduate School of Business, La Salle University, 20th and Olney Avenue, Philadelphia, PA 19141. Tel: (215) 951-1059.

MBA with Association Management Concentration. This is a program of DePaul University's Graduate School of Business and the Chicago Society of Association Executives. This is a part-time evening program for association professionals. "It was designed by and for association executives working with DePaul's faculty to provide a valuable background of knowledge for executives in the field and for those who have recently entered or decided to make association management their career."

The program includes 22 courses. Students with a business undergraduate degree may on a case-by-case basis obtain waivers for certain requirements previously satisfied. The program takes two to four years to complete and may be taken on a full-time basis. The curriculum is broken down into courses in: Concepts and Methods, Functional Areas of Business, Environmental Perspectives, Decisions in Business Areas, Association Management, plus electives.

For information contact: DePaul University, Graduate School of Business, 25 East Jackson Boulevard, Chicago, IL 60604. Tel: (312) 341-8810.

Administrative Specialty in Association Management. North Carolina State University offers an administrative specialization in Association/Nonprofit Management as part of the Master of Public Affairs (MPA) curriculum. Courses include: Association Management, Problems in Public Relations, and Organizational Communication. The concentration in Association/Nonprofit Management satisfies a 9-credit-hour minimum requirement in a minor field.

For information contact: North Carolina State University, Master of Public Affairs Program, Raleigh, NC 27695. Tel: (919) 737-2481.

Certificate Program in Association Management. This new certificate program is offered by the School of Continuing Education, Management Institute, New York University. It consists of six noncredit courses, three courses in association management topics, and three courses in nonprofit management topics.

For information contact: School of Continuing Education, Management Institute, NYU, 48 Cooper Square, New York, NY 10003.

To Learn More About Association Management Careers

The authors recommend reading in this book the career profiles of Ann Bryant, of John Bailey, and of Albert Sunseri. Their personal experience may offer useful insights. The authors also recommend that you write for *The Association Factbook* and other current ASAE information; the address is: Public Relations Division, American Society of Association Executives, 1575 Eye Street, N.W., Washington, DC 20005.

The following recommended readings should also be helpful and informative:

Bailey, John N. "The Unique World of Associations," *Public Relations Careers Directory*, New York: Career Publishing Corp., 1986, pp. 87-93.

Beckson, Alyse. "Nonprofit Organizations Offer Profitable Work," *New York Times* (October 16, 1983).

Coek, Karin E., and Susan Boyles Martin. *The Encyclopedia of Associations.* Detroit, Michigan: Gale Research Center, 1985.

Leighton, Joel B. "If Benjamin Franklin Were Alive Today, He'd Probably be an Association Executive," *Association Management* (Washington, DC), 1985.

Schwinn, Beth. "Survey Shows Rising Demand for Managers of Nonprofits," *Washington Business,* (March 9, 1987), p. 6.

"Top Executives at Nonprofit Agencies Receive Big Salaries Survey Shows," *Washington Business,* (September 16, 1986), pp. 5–6.

Wickwire, Pat Nellor. "Career Education and the Professional Association," *Journal of Career Development,* Vol. 13, No. 3, (Spring, 1987), pp. 63–70.

For current news about association activities you should read:

- *Association Management* (monthly) ASAE magazine
- *Association and Society Manager* (monthly)
  Barrington Publications, Inc.
  825 South Barrington Avenue
  Los Angeles, CA 90049
- *Association Trends* (weekly newspaper)
  4948 St. Elmo Avenue
  Bethesda, MD 20814
- *U.S. Association Executive* (weekly newspaper)
  4341 Montgomery Avenue
  Bethesda, MD 20814

Associations that Serve the Nonprofit Sector

The following association listing includes information that would be of interest to a job seeker, job changer, or counselor. Other significant functions performed by these associations, but unrelated to the purposes of this book, have been excluded. Associations are listed in six categories:

- Arts and Culture
- Education
- Health
- Religion
- Social Services
- General Services and Management

Arts and Culture Associations

American Association of Museums
American Symphony Orchestra League
National Assembly of Local Arts Agencies

American Association of Museums (AAM)
1225 Eye Street, N.W., Suite 200
Washington, DC 20005
(202) 289-1818

Purpose: To strengthen the museum profession and promote standards of excellence for museum administration.

Founded in 1906, 5,600 members comprised of museum professionals and volunteers. Sponsors regional workshops and seminars; annual national meeting; committees for professional networking. Job listings in monthly *Adviso* newsletter. Placement office at annual meeting. Publisher of *Museum-News*. Membership fees based on annual income. Student rate $25 yearly. Career information available on request.

American Symphony Orchestra League (ASOL)
633 E Street, N.W.
Washington, DC 20004
(203) 628-0099

Purpose: To provide leadership and service to over 1,500 American orchestras to ensure their artistic, organizational, and financial strength.

Founded in 1942. Offers week-long orchestra management seminars in various parts of the country for arts administrators, volunteers, managers, students, and professionals seeking new career opportunities. Competitive orchestra management fellowship program selects eight trainees. National conference. Publishes *Symphony Magazine*. Circulates position announcements. Individual membership open to all, $25.

National Assembly of Local Arts Agencies (NALAA)
1420 K Street, N.W., Suite 204
Washington, DC 20005
(202) 371-2830

Purpose: To promote local arts agencies and strengthen the effectiveness of executive staff and volunteer leaders through professional development and other services.

Founded in 1978, 55 members. Workshops and training seminars on local arts agency management. Annual convention and regional conferences. Employment opportunities published in *Connections Monthly*. *Connections Quarterly* covers arts agency management. Individual membership, $75. Student membership, $25. Publication: *The Arts Administrator: Job Characteristics 1985 Survey*.

Education Associations

Association for Institutional Research
Council for Advancement and Support of Education
National Association of Independent Schools
National Association of Student Personnel Administrators

National Council for Community Relations
National Council for Resource Development
National Council of University Research Administrators

Association for Institutional Research (AIR)

314 Stone Building
Florida State University
Tallahassee, FL 32306
(904) 644-4470

Purpose: Professional organization of institutional research administrators in higher education.

Founded in 1965, 2,090 members. Sponsors annual forum. Focus is on information systems, research, and analytic studies and their utilization to improve planning management and resource allocation. Regional workshops and seminars. Publishes quarterly monograph series and *AIR Newsletter*. Conducts placement service. Member fees: $55 individual.

Council for Advancement and Support of Education (CASE)

11 Dupont Circle, Suite 400
Washington, DC 20036
(202) 328-5900

Purpose: To represent the professional interests of institutional advancement officers in colleges, universities, and independent schools.

Founded in 1974, represents 2,600 colleges and universities and 12,000 individuals. Sponsors national and regional conferences, seminars, and summer institutes for entry-level, middle management, and senior officers. Programs cover alumni administration, education fundraising, information seminars and publications, student recruitment, marketing, executive management, computer systems. Annual Assembly. Certification program. Publishes *Currents* monthly magazine and *Placement Letter* with job listings both available by subscription to nonmembers. Publications program. Institutional memberships only.

National Association of Independent Schools (NAIS)

18 Tremont Street
Boston, MA 02108
(617) 723-6900

Purpose: To assist and strengthen independent elementary and secondary schools by providing professional development and support services.

Founded in 1962, nearly 1,000 member schools in the U.S. and abroad. Serves trustees, school heads, teachers, admission directors, development officers, public relations personnel, alumni affairs directors, business officers, administrators, and other associations of independent schools. Annual national education conference. Leadership workshops and seminars. Publications program, *Quarterly* magazine, resource library, Administrative Clearinghouse Service—a résumé and information exchange for administrators, admission officers, business managers, and development officers.

National Association of Student Personnel Administrators (NASPA)
1700 18th Street, N.W., Suite 301
Washington, DC 20009-2508
(202) 265-7500

Purpose: To develop leadership and improve practices in student affairs administration.

Founded in 1919, 3,100 members with three divisions and seven regions. Sponsors regional and national seminars, meetings, conferences, and institutes for top-level administrators. Job placement service held at annual conference. Publishes *NASPA Journal* and *NASPA Forum,* a periodic newsletter. Professional membership $45, Student Affiliate $20.

National Council for Community Relations (NCCR), an affiliate of
   the American Association of Community and Junior Colleges
Aims Community College
5401 West 20th Street
Greeley, CO 80634
(303) 330-8008

Purpose: To support community, junior, and technical college professionals in public relations, community relations, public affairs marketing, and coordination of special events.

Founded in 1974. Sponsors national and regional conferences and workshops. Publishes quarterly newsletter *Counsel.* Membership fees: Individual $35; Organizational $75.

National Council for Resource Development (NCRD), an affiliate of the
   American Association of Community and Junior Colleges
One Dupont Circle, N.W., Suite 410
Washington, DC 20036-1176
(202) 293-7050

Purpose: To promote professionalism in the field of resource development in community and junior colleges.

Founded in 1973, 1,000 members. Sponsors a two-week Resource Development Specialist Training Program. Hosts annual national conference for beginner and veteran development professionals. Offers regional conferences. Publishes quarterly newsletter *Dispatch.* Maintains a strong network of members for job referrals. Membership fees: $60.

National Council of University Research Administrators (NCURA)
One Dupont Circle, N.W., Suite 618
Washington, DC 20036
(202) 466-3894

Purpose: To foster the development of sponsored program administration research, education, and training as a professional field, primarily at colleges and universities.

Founded in 1959, 1,740 members, seven regional organizations. Training sessions for new and experienced administrators are offered through "Workshop" (in-depth series of training sessions for new and experienced research administrators) which precedes the annual meeting. Regional meetings. Publishes bimonthly *NCURA Newsletter* with job listings; *NCURA Journal*. Membership fees: $75.

Health Associations

American College of Health Care Administrators
American College of Health Care Executives
American Health Care Association
American Hospital Association
American Organization of Nurse Executives
American Society of Directors of Volunteer Services
American Society for Healthcare Education and Training
American Society for Healthcare Environmental Services
American Society for Healthcare Human Resources Administration
American Society for Healthcare Risk Management
American Society for Hospital Food Service Administration of the American Hospital Association
American Society for Hospital Marketing and Public Relations
American Society for Hospital Materials Management
Association of Mental Health Administrators
The Association of University Programs in Health Administration
Healthcare Financial Management Association
Healthcare Information and Management Systems Society
National Association for Hospital Development
National Health Council, Inc.
National Society of Patient Representatives
Society for Ambulatory Care Professionals
Society for Hospital Planning and Marketing
Society for Hospital Social Work Directors
The National Assembly of National Voluntary Health and Social Welfare Organizations, Inc.

American College of Health Care Administrators (ACHCA)
8120 Woodmont Avenue, Suite 200
Bethesda, MD 20814
(301) 652-8384

Purpose: To advance the skills, abilities, and competencies of professional administrators of long-term health care organizations.

Founded in 1962, 6,500 members, 52 chapters. Sponsors educational and training programs; self-study continuing education courses; professional certification and national and regional conferences. Job opportunities are listed in Professional Referral Service section of *Long-Term Care Administrator Newsletter*. Career information available. Also publishes journal. Membership fees: Active $185 and Student $40.

American College of Health Care Executives (ACHE)
840 North Lake Shore Drive
Chicago, IL 60611
(312) 943-0544

Purpose: Bringing excellence to health care management. To keep health care management on the fast track to cost-effective quality care. To expand management expertise with state-of-the art techniques and approaches.

Founded in 1933, over 20,000 members. Catalog of professional development seminars; Career Decisions, Inc., a subsidiary of ACHE, offers career counseling services; Career Mark provides national career listings. Publications: bimonthly journal *Hospital and Health Services Administration, Healthcare Executive, Executive News,* monthly newsletter, *Learning Resources Director.* Membership: Eight categories of membership include Student Associate, $20.

American Health Care Association (AHCA)
1200 15th Street, N.W.
Washington, DC 20005
(202) 833-2050

Purpose: To promote standards for professionals in long-term health care facilities.

Founded in 1949, its 9,000 individual facility members provide nursing care and related services to some 900,000 elderly, convalescent, and chronically ill residents (twenty percent of facilities are nonprofits). Fifty state affiliates offer educational programs for administrator license and for other professional staff. Produces publications and audiovisual materials. Monthly magazine *Provider.* Membership fees: associate professionals $100 per year.

American Hospital Association (AHA)
840 North Lake Shore Drive
Chicago, IL 60611
(312) 280-6000

Purpose: To help members fulfill their commitment to maintain and improve the nation's health care system.

Founded 1906, 43,000 members. Sponsors educational programs and leadership seminars. Annual national convention and regional programs. Publishes periodicals, books, manuals, newsletter. Maintains AHA Resource Center, a library and information and data retrieval service.

There are 17 personal membership groups under the AHA umbrella, classified by job responsibility. Size of membership in these separately organized professional societies ranges from 600 to 4,000. Depending upon the group, membership may be open to students and nonmember employees. All groups sponsor meetings, educational programs, and publications. AHA publishes a directory describing these groups. The groups include:

- American Organization of Nurse Executives
- American Society of Directors of Volunteer Services

- American Society for Healthcare Education and Training
- American Society for Healthcare Environmental Services
- American Society for Healthcare Human Resources Administration
- American Society for Healthcare Risk Management
- American Society for Hospital Food Service Administrators
- American Society for Hospital Marketing and Public Relations
- American Society for Hospital Materials Management

American Organization of Nurse Executives (AONE)
(A Personal Membership Group of the AHA)
840 North Lake Shore Drive
Chicago, IL 60611
(312) 280-5213

Purpose: To promote safe and effective patient care through the advancement of its members and leaders of a clinical discipline and executives in health care management.

Founded in 1968, nearly 4,000 members in 57 chapters. Annual meeting with educational seminars and workshops. Periodic continuing education programs across the country. Member fees: $100.

American Society of Directors of Volunteer Service (ASDVS)
(A Personal Membership Group of the AHA)
840 North Lake Shore Drive
Chicago, IL 60611
(312) 280-6110

Purpose: Professional organization for directors of volunteer services in health care institutions.

Founded in 1968, 1,700 members. Sponsors educational programs and institutes for new and experienced managers. Annual meeting and educational conference. Publishes quarterly newsletter *Volunteer Services Administration* and biweekly journal *Hospitals*. Member dues: $60 if affiliated with a member institution of the American Hospital Association; $90 if not member institution.

American Society for Healthcare Education and Training (ASHET)
(A Personal Membership Group of the AHA)
840 North Lake Shore Drive
Chicago, IL 60611
(312) 280-6113

Purpose: To develop the leadership skills of those responsible for education and training in health care institutions.

Founded in 1970, 1,800 members. Career development through educational programs at annual meeting and periodic workshops, seminars, and teleconferences. *Journal of Healthcare Education and Training, Dateline* newsletter published quarterly, and *Hospitals*. The magazine *Healthcare Executives* published biweekly. Member fees: regular $75, associate $105, students $37.50.

American Society for Healthcare Environmental Services (ASHES)
(A Personal Membership Group of the AHA)
840 North Lake Shore Drive
Chicago, IL 60611
(312) 280-6245

Purpose: To represent the needs of environmental service, housekeeping, and laundry professionals who are under pressure to increase operating efficiency and to meet compliance requirements of federal agencies.

Founded in 1986, 600 members. Annual conference. Educational programs. Bimonthly newsletter. Members fees: $75 to AHA members; $105 to nonmembers.

American Society for Healthcare Human Resources Administration (ASHHRA)
(A Personal Membership Group of the AHA)
840 North Lake Shore Drive
Chicago, IL 60611
(312) 280-6111

Purpose: To serve the professional needs of human resources managers in health care.

Founded in 1964, 2,500 members. Educational opportunities include annual meeting and educational conference; regional workshops and seminars; and satellite teleconferences. Health Care Employment Network. Publishes newsletter, *Newsletter Resources Administration,* and *Labor Relations Report.* Member fees: Regular $70 and Student $35.

American Society for Healthcare Risk Management (ASHRM)
(A Personal Membership Group of the AHA)
840 North Lake Shore Drive
Chicago, IL 60611
(312) 280-6425

Purpose: To implement activities that help promote professional development of those working in health care risk management and to encourage the application of effective risk management techniques in hospitals and other health care settings.

Founded in 1980, 1,940 members. Annual meeting and educational conference. National Education Program of seminars, workshops, symposia in various locations. Publications include *Perspectives in Healthcare Risk Management,* a quarterly. Job clearinghouse. Member fees: range from $60 to $100 depending on category; student member fees: $35/year.

American Society for Hospital Food Service Administration
(A Personal Membership Group of the AHA)
840 North Lake Shore Drive
Chicago, IL 60611
(312) 280-6416

Purpose: To provide continual improvement of the administrative functions of food and nutrition services departments of health care institutions.

Founded in 1967, represents more than 2,000 members. Regional and national education programs. Annual conference. Professional recognition program. Scholarships for undergraduate and graduate students. Summer Field Experience Program for students of food service management. Member fees: depending on employment status; students: $30.

American Society for Hospital Marketing and Public Relations (ASHMPR)
(A Personal Membership Group of the AHA)
840 North Lake Shore Drive
Chicago, IL 60611
(312) 280-6359

Purpose: To provide leadership to food and nutrition services administration professionals in a rapidly changing environment.

Founded in 1899, approximately 2,000 members. Annual conference and educational workshops. Quarterly newsletter. Scholarships and Summer Field Experience Program. Member fees: from $60 to $200 depending on category; $30 for students.

American Society for Hospital Materials Management (ASHMM)
(A Personal Membership Group of the AHA)
840 North Lake Shore Drive
Chicago, IL 60611
(312) 280-6137

Purpose: To provide leadership and advance effective practices in the health care materials management field.

Founded in 1962, over 1,800 members. Annual conference. Educational seminars held across the U.S. Credentialling mechanism for materials managers. *Hospital Materials Management News,* bimonthly; *Perspectives,* quarterly case study and research newsletter; and *Sample Job Descriptions for Hospital Materials Management Functions.* Member fees: $60 to $130 depending on category.

Association of Mental Health Administrators (AMHA)
840 North Lake Shore Drive, Suite 1103W
Chicago, IL 60611
(312) 943-2751

Purpose: To promote professional growth in the field of behavioral health/disability administration.

Founded in 1959, 1,950 members, state chapters. Holds seminars and workshops at the annual national meeting or locally. Offers Certified Mental Health Administrator credentials. Monthly newsletter carries job listings; resume exchange and on-site interviews at annual meeting. Publishes biannual *Journal of Mental Health Administration.* Member fees: Active, $100; Student, $20.

The Association of University Programs in Health Administration (AUPHA)
1911 North Fort Myer Drive
Arlington, VA 22209
(703) 524-5500

Purpose: To improve health services through education for health management.

Founded in 1948, 1,200 members. A consortium of universities and supporting institutions and individuals, interested in attracting high-potential students, financial assistance, supporting management development for practitioners. Publications program includes: *The Journal of Health Care Administration,* monthly; annual guide to *Health Services Administration Education; The Challenge of Administering Health Services, Career Pathways; Health Administration Employment, A Survey of Early Career Opportunities.* Maintains placement files, provides career information. Membership fees: $45 for an individual.

Healthcare Financial Management Association (HFMA)
1900 Spring Road, Suite 500
Oak Brook, IL 60521
(312) 571-4700

Purpose: To bring together health care financial management professionals for networking, career advancement, and problem solving.

Founded in 1946; 26,000 members and 75 chapters. Learning opportunities include regional educational programs and seminars at the Annual National Institute and the Institute of Current Financial Issues. Offers certification. Job listings in journal, *Healthcare Financial Management.* Membership fees: $135.

Healthcare Information and Management Systems Society (HIMSS)
(A Personal Membership Group of the AHA)
840 North Lake Shore Drive
Chicago, IL 60611
(312) 280-6023

Purpose: To meet the professional needs of management engineers, information systems, and telecommunications professionals devoted to systems analysis in health care and to the information system that ties this organization together.

Founded in 1961, 2,929 members. Annual conference. Educational programs and teleconferences. Publishes *Health Care Systems,* quarterly newsletter. Provides guidance to members in career planning, development, and placement. Member fees: $65 to $115 depending on category; student membership available to qualified applicants, $30.

National Association for Hospital Development (NAHD)
112-B East Broad Street
Falls Church, VA 22046
(703) 532-NAHD

Purpose: To strengthen the performance of development officers in health care and encourage excellence in the profession.

Founded in 1964, 2,200 members. Education programs of conferences and institutes. Over 100 courses at primary, intermediate, advanced, and executive management levels. Annual conferences in 13 regions. Five-day annual NAHD Institute for Hospital Philanthropy at University of Wisconsin. Executive Management Institute at Duke University awards continuing education units. Resource Information Center provides materials for independent study and career enhancement. Accreditation Program. Executive Search Service offers professional career planning services. Membership fees: $250 for active Membership; $150 Associate Membership open to students and others ineligible for Active Membership.

National Health Council, Inc. (NHC)
622 Third Avenue
New York, NY 10017-6768
(212) 972-2700

Purpose: To serve as a clearinghouse and cooperative effort for voluntary health agencies and others; to stimulate greater public awareness of health and related concerns, etc.

Founded in 1920, 74 member organizations. Since 1973 has published and distributed *200 Ways to Put Your Talent to Work in the Health Field,* an updated booklet that explains health and allied health careers and information sources.

National Society of Patient Representatives (NSPR)
(A Personal Membership Group of the AHA)
840 North Lake Shore Drive
Chicago, IL 60611
(312) 280-6424

Purpose: To increase the awareness of the vital role of patient representatives as customer relation specialists, to ensure that health care consumers have access to a strong health advocacy system.

Founded in 1972, 1,050 members and 31 chapters. Annual meeting and conference. Educational programs. Member fees: $75.

Society for Ambulatory Care Professionals (SACP)
(A Personal Membership Group of the AHA)
840 North Lake Shore Drive
Chicago, IL 60611
(312) 280-6456

Purpose: To meet the needs of ambulatory care professionals through the development, dissemination, and sharing of expertise in an area experiencing growth and prominence.

Founded in 1986, 2,500 members. Publications include: *Outreach,* bimonthly newsletter; *Ambulatory Care Alert, Ambulatory Care Management Information Briefings.* Member fees: range from $65 to $200 depending on category; student membership, $35.

Society for Hospital Planning and Marketing (SHPM)
(A Personal Membership Group of the AHA)
840 North Lake Shore Drive
Chicago, IL 60611
(312) 280-6788

Purpose: To integrate strategic planning and marketing concepts and techniques as key components of the health care management process.

Founded in 1978, 3,200 members. Educational programs include: annual meeting, National Forum on Medical Staff Marketing, and one-day seminars. Monthly *Career Opportunities Bulletin;* bimonthly *Hospital Planning and Marketing Newsletter.* Member fees: $75 to $120, depending on category; students, $30.

Society for Hospital Social Work Directors (SHSWD)
(A Personal Membership Group of the AHA)
840 North Lake Shore Drive
Chicago, IL 60611
(312) 280-6415

Purpose: To promote the universal availability, accessibility, coordination, and effectiveness of health care that address the psychosocial components of health and illness.

Founded in 1966, 2,500 members. Annual meeting and conference offers intensive skills workshops. Annual Discharge Planning Symposium. Thirteen-month course in social work management. Periodic seminars offered at sites across the country. Publications: *Social Work Administration,* bimonthly newsletter; *Discharge Planning Update,* bimonthly. Member fees: $79 to $109 depending on category.

The National Assembly of National Voluntary Health and Social Welfare Organizations, Inc.
1319 F Street, N.W.
Suite 601
Washington, DC 20004
(202) 347-2080

Purpose: An association of national voluntary human service organizations, established to facilitate communication and cooperation among member agencies.

Founded in 1923, Assembly's membership is open to national, voluntary human service organizations. The Assembly provides specialized assistance for volunteer leaders, chief executive officers, and agency staff. Publishes *Assembly Line,* a monthly newsletter of issues affecting human service organizations. Sponsors educational forums, task forces, and compiles a management compensation report. Membership fees are based on a sliding scale.

Religion Associations

Christian Ministries Management Association

National Association of Church Business Administration
National Association for Church Personnel Administrators
National Association of Temple Administrators
National Catholic Development Conference
The Religious Public Relations Council

Christian Ministries Management Association (CMMA)
P.O. Box 4638
Diamond Bar, CA 91765
(714) 861-8861

Purpose: To provide services to managers and fundraisers of Christian organizations that will help them to do a better job in all areas of management.

Founded in 1976, 2,400 members. Annual Christian Management Institute offers professional development. CMMA sponsors training, seminars, national and regional conferences. Job referral service and job listings in bimonthly *Christian Management Report.* Produces books and tapes on management. Annual membership fee: $70.

National Association of Church Business Administration (NACBA)
7001 Grapevine Highway, Suite 324
Fort Worth, TX 76118
(817) 284-1732

Purpose: To provide an interdenominational organization for church business administrators that fosters professional growth and provides support to members working in congregations, military chapels, or religious institutions.

Founded in 1956, 1,000 members, 35 chapters. Sponsors seminars and consulting services. Offers certifications as Fellow in Church Business Administration (CFCBA) through continuing education program. National conference and regional meetings. Placement service to members and non-members. Publishes *NACBA Gram,* monthly, with career opportunities section. Member fees: Active $100; Associate $70.

National Association for Church Personnel Administrators (NAPCA)
100 East Eighth Street
Cincinnati, OH 45202
(513) 421-3131

Purpose: To promote professional and effective human resource management within the Catholic Church.

Founded in 1971, 725 members. Sponsors regional training workshops and consultations for personnel administrators in performance evaluation, planning, and career development. Holds annual national convocation with seminars for new and experienced personnel directors. Membership fees: $125 for individual.

National Association of Temple Administrators (NATA)
838 Fifth Avenue
New York, NY 10021
(212) 249-0100

Purpose: To provide preparation and training to synagogue administrators of Reform Congregations.

Founded in 1941, 219 members. Provides workshops and in-service training; professional certification, Fellow in Temple Administration. Annual national and regional conference and Professional Development Institutes. Conducts a placement service. Publishes *NATA Journal.* Maintains library of publications on temple administration.

National Catholic Development Conference (NCDC)
86 Front Street
Hempstead, NY 11550
(516) 481-6000

Purpose: Membership association for religious fundraising organizations.

Founded in 1968, with 400 members. Conducts a four-day training program at annual conference. Regional workshops and seminars. *Dimensions,* a monthly periodical, has job listings. Resource library of books and tapes at national office. Associate membership: $150.

The Religious Public Relations Council (RPRC)
359 Righters Mill Road
P.O. Box 315
Gladwyne, PA 19035
(215) 642-8895

Purpose: To establish, raise, and maintain high standards of public relations and communications in organizations of all religious faiths.

Founded 1929, 500 members, 13 chapters. Sponsors annual national convention with program of courses for continuing education credit (through local universities), week-long Summer Academy. Regional workshops, quarterly newsletter, *The Counselor Media Kit.* Membership fees: $70 national dues, plus chapter dues.

Social Services Associations

American Public Welfare Association
National Association of Community Action Agencies
National Association of Social Workers
Society for Hospital Social Work Directors

American Public Welfare Association (APWA)
1125 Fifteenth Street, N.W.
Washington, DC 20005
(202) 293-7550

Purpose: To represent state human service departments, local welfare agencies, nonprofit agencies, and individuals with interest in publicly funded human services.

Founded in 1930, 7,000 members. Provides technical assistance, in-house research. Publishes quarterly journal *Public Welfare* and *APWA News*. Sponsors regional and national conferences and workshops; executive, mid-management, and specialized training courses. Regular membership $35; student $15.

National Association of Community Action Agencies (NACAA)
1411 K Street, N.W., Suite 1010
Washington, DC 20005
(202) 737-9895

Purpose: To improve leadership and effectiveness of nonprofit Community Action Agencies.

Founded in 1971, 600 members. Conducts management seminars and educational programs for staff and executive directors. Holds national annual conference and periodic regional training workshops in management strategies. Job listings appear in *NACAA Network*, a monthly publication. Organizational membership fees are based on funding levels; no individual membership rate.

National Association of Social Workers (NASW)
7981 Eastern Avenue
Silver Springs, MD 20910
(301) 565-0333

Purpose: To promote the professional development of social workers and to create and maintain professional standards for social work practice; and to propose and promote public policies and programs aimed at meeting human need and improving the quality of life.

Founded in 1955, 121,000 members and 55 chapters. Sponsors national and state conferences, conducts job bank at annual conference. Offers credentials through the Academy of Certified Social Workers. Publishes *NASW News* with career opportunities listed by state, *Social Work* journal, and specialty publications. Students attending annual conference as on-site volunteers may receive complimentary registration. National and state chapter regular membership, $125; student rate, $31.

Society for Hospital Social Work Directors is listed under Health Associations.

Other Associations that Serve Nonprofit Managers

American Association of Fund-Raising Counsel, Inc.
American Management Association
American Prospect Research Association
American Society of Association Executives
Association of Labor-Management Administrators
Association of Voluntary Action Scholars
Association for Volunteer Administration

Council on Foundations
Direct Marketing Association
Independent Sector
National Society of Fund Raising Executives
Nonprofit Management Association
The Public Affairs Council
Public Relations Society of America (PRSA)
Society for Nonprofit Organizations
Women and Foundations/Corporate Philanthropy

American Association of Fund-Raising Counsel, Inc. (AAFRC)

AAFRC Trust for Philanthropy
25 West 43rd Street
New York, NY 10036
(212) 354-5799

Purpose: To maintain high standards of ethics in fundraising counseling, to study trends in American philanthropy and disseminate this information to encourage professional training in fundraising techniques.

Founded in 1937, 30 members are professional fundraising firms. Participates in decisions that shape the role of philanthropy and fundraising in the U.S. Fair Practice Code sets standard for industry. AAFRC Trust for Philanthropy annually publishes *Giving USA*, the authoritive annual report on charitable giving; bimonthly, *Fund Raising Review*. In cooperation with Association of American Colleges sponsors awards to colleges and universities to develop undergraduate courses in philanthropy.

American Management Association (AMA)

135 West 50th Street
New York, NY 10020
(212) 586-8100

Purpose: Membership organization of managers (at all levels) in the private, public, and nonprofit sector.

Founded in 1927, 78,000 members. Sponsors multifaceted program of management training seminars, courses, and seminars. Extension Institute offers guided home study. Produces publications, films, and videos. Publishes: *Management Review*, *AMA Survey Reports*, and *Management Briefings*. Designs training seminars for public service organizations. Encourages organizational membership. Associate membership available to individuals for $40 a year.

American Prospect Research Association (APRA)

P.O. Box 10179
Minneapolis, MN 55458-3179
(612) 332-5545

Purpose: To promote the field of prospect research and to provide networking support on a national and local basis.

Founded in 1981, 90 members. Sponsors a national conference and regional meetings. Publishes a quarterly *APRA Newsletter* and annual membership directory. Membership dues: $25.

American Society of Association Executives (ASAE)
The ASAE Building
1575 Eye Street, N.W.
Washington, DC 20005
(202) 626-2728

Purpose: To enhance the professionalism of association executives and to improve the performance of membership organizations.

Founded in 1920, 14,000 members. Conducts training seminars and workshops. Professional certification through the Certified Association Executive (CAE) Program. Holds annual meeting and spring convention; Management Conference and regional conferences. Executive search and referral services. Publishes monthly *Association Management* and *Vanguard* newsletter. Library at headquarters. Membership fees: $140.

Association of Labor-Management Administrators and Consultants on Alcoholism, Inc. (ALMACA)
1800 N. Kent Street
Suite 907
Arlington, VA 22209
(703) 522-6272

Purpose: International association of professionals in employee assistance programs.

Founded in 1971, 5,100 members in 60 chapters. Sponsors annual meeting and monthly chapter meetings. Offers credentials through the Employee Assistance Certification Commission. Publishes monthly news magazine, *The ALMACAN Info-Line*, a monthly newsletter and membership directory, and other books and periodicals. Membership fees: individuals $110, students $35.

Association of Voluntary Action Scholars (AVAS)
Lincoln Filene Center
Tufts University
Medford, MA 02155
(617) 381-3452

Purpose: Association of scholars and professionals interested in dissemination of voluntary action research and management materials to fellow professionals and leaders in voluntary agencies.

Founded in 1971, with 500 members. Calls for papers and publishes *Journal of Voluntary Action Research* and the *AVAS Newsletter,* sponsors annual conferences. Membership $30 for individuals; $20 students.

Association for Volunteer Administration (AVA)
P.O. Box 4584
Boulder, CO 80306
(303) 497-0238

Purpose: To promote and strengthen the profession of volunteer services management and administration.

Founded in 1961, 1,500 members, 13 regional chapters. Training workshops; performance-based professional certification (C.V.A.); annual national and regional conventions on skill development and career advancement. Publications: *Update,* a bimonthly newsletter, and the quarterly *Journal of Volunteer Administration.* Membership fees: active $75; student $40.

Council on Foundations (CF)
1828 L Street, N.W., Suite 1200
Washington, DC 20036
(202) 466-6512

Purpose: Membership organization of independent, community, and public foundations and grant-makers working to develop and maintain a supportive environment for philanthropy.

Founded in 1949, 1,031 members, 23 Regional Associations of Grantmakers. Sponsors educational workshops, seminars, and conferences; annual conference; Institute for New Staff; Professional Development Program. Publishes *Foundation News,* a bimonthly journal; *Foundation Management Report* on staff compensation, benefits, and personnel policies; plus books and reprints helpful to professionals and newcomers to foundation work.

Direct Marketing Association, Inc. (DMA)
6 East 43 Street
New York, NY 10017
(212) 689-4977

Purpose: Trade association for firms that use direct response marketing and advertising, or suppliers of services and products to these firms. DMA Nonprofit Council addresses concerns of nonprofit direct mail. The Direct Marketing Educational Foundation, a separate entity under the DMA umbrella, is dedicated to improving the quality and increasing the scope of direct marketing education at the college and university level.

Founded in 1917, 5,295 members, no chapters. DMA, NPC, and the Educational Foundation sponsor institutes, conferences, annual meetings for staff of member organizations. The Direct Marketing Educational Foundation offers Direct Marketing Institute for Professors, fellowships to DMA seminars for educators, Educational Membership for professors, Visiting Executive Program to campuses. Sponsors five-day Collegiate Institute for college seniors, summer internship program, publishes career literature. Although not a placement service, accepts résumés of top students for referral to employers. Students may use DMA Library. Publishes *Direct Mail Marketing Manual, Direct* Line (monthly), *Directions* (bimonthly), *DMA Matters* (quarterly). Membership fees apply to organizations only.

INDEPENDENT SECTOR (IS)
1828 L Street, N.W.
Washington, DC 20036
(202) 223-8100

Purpose: To preserve and enhance the national tradition of giving, volunteering, and nonprofit initiative.

Founded in 1980, nonprofit coalition of 650 corporate, foundation, and voluntary organization members. IS conducts and fosters basic research on critical issues and concerns of the sector, holds conferences, and has an extensive publication program. *An Independent Sector Resource Directory of Education and Training Opportunities and Other Services* is published annually. Member fees: individuals can be nonvoting Associates for $50 and receive monthly *Update* and other publications.

National Society of Fund Raising Executives (NSFRE)
1101 King Street, Suite 3000
Alexandria, VA 22314
(703) 684-0410

Purpose: To serve and promote the fund-raising profession.

Founded in 1961, 10,000 members and 85 chapters. Sponsors training and continuing education courses, conferences, and institutes at all professional levels. Provides credentials (CFRE) for senior fundraising executives through professional certification program. Sponsors Executive Search and Resume Referral Services, internship programs, and (MAP) Mentoring Assistance Program. Holds international conference annually. Local chapters meet regularly. Publishes *NSFRE Journal* and *NSFRE News*. Maintains national Fund Raising Library to provide resource information by phone, mail, or personal visit. National membership fees: regular $125, student $40. Average chapter fees: regular $150, student $80.

Nonprofit Management Association (NMA)
1309 L Street, N.W.
Washington, DC 20005
(202) 638-3503

Purpose: Membership association for individuals and organizations seeking to improve the effectiveness of nonprofit management.

Founded in 1982, 200 members. Sponsors educational services through annual conference, preconference workshops. Information and referrals by phone and through directories. *Help for Nonprofits*, a monthly newsletter. Member fees: organizational $250 and individual $125. Associate $70.

The Public Affairs Council (PAC)
Suite 750
1255 Twenty-Third Street, N.W.
Washington, DC 20037
(202) 872-1790

Purpose: To strengthen the role of public affairs executives, stimulating corporate citizenship and social responsibility.

Founded in 1954, PAC sponsors technique-oriented conferences, seminars, and workshops. Annual Public Affairs Institute offers career enhancement program. Job referral services. Monthly newsletter. Catalog of information resources.

Public Relations Society of America (PRSA)
33 Irving Place
New York, NY 10003
(212) 995-2230

Purpose: Professional development of public relations practitioners. Encourages high standards of conduct and public practice. Strengthens the relationship of public relations professionals with employers, clients, government, educators, media, and the public.

Founded in 1947, 14,265 members, 90 chapters. Fifteen professional interest sections with their own educational programs include: Association, Education and Cultural Organizations, Health, Hospital Academy, Public Affairs, Social Services. Other educational programs include national conference, regional and local seminars and workshops, cooperation with university programs, self-study cassettes, and publications accreditation program. Research Information Center. Monthly *Public Relations Journal* and *PRSA Newsletter*.

Public Relations Student Society (PRSSA) has 5,000 members and PRIDE Internship program. Foundation for Public Research and Education (an independent nonprofit) provides research grants, educational awards, scholarships, and sponsors student competitions and publications. The Professional Connection, a career referral service, offers telephone recordings of current openings. For a fee PRSA will forward resumes of members and nonmembers.

Two membership categories: regular or associate.

Society for Nonprofit Organizations (SNPO)
6314 Odana Road, Suite 1
Madison, WI 53719
(608) 274-9777

Purpose: To link and advance all nonprofit organizations.

Founded in 1983, with 3,000 members. A membership organization that works with leaders and professional staff. Sponsors national conference, Nonprofit World Assembly, and regional education programs. Conducts a National Referral Service of job candidates. Publishes *The Nonprofit World*, a bimonthly leadership and management magazine. Membership fees: individual $75, organizational $125.

Women and Foundations/Corporate Philanthropy (WAF/CP)
141 Fifth Avenue 7-S
New York, NY 10010
(212) 460-9253

Purpose: An affinity association to increase the support for programs that benefit women and girls and increase opportunities for women as staff or trustees within philanthropy.

Professional networking in New York, Denver, Chicago, Philadelphia, Minneapolis/St. Paul, and other parts of the country. Publications and workshops. Fees: $50 per year.

11

Getting a Job in the Sector

There's an old saying that "finding a job is a job." A job search is a sequential process consisting of a number of related initiatives such as doing research, developing contacts, going to meetings, having interviews, making phone calls, writing letters, and following up on leads. Carried out in a persistent and thoughtful manner, these transactions will ultimately lead you to the opportunity you want. After you have found a job, you can look back at the chain of events that led you to the achievement of your goal, but while you are in the midst of the search the prize may seem elusive.

Knowledge of self, one's interests, values, skills and abilities, is a precondition for the job search. *What Color Is Your Parachute: A Practical Manual for Job Hunters and Career Changers*, a popular reference that is revised annually, can be extremely helpful in the self-assessment process; also in later stages of the job search.

The elements of a job search are: (1) setting goals, (2) identifying information resources, (3) talking to people, (4) preparing a résumé, (5) developing a job search strategy, and (6) having job interviews.

Libraries are filled with how-to books on all aspects of the job search. Browsing through some of these references, you will find a wide variety of advice, sometimes conflicting. The best approach is to glean from these guides whatever hints and ideas seem comfortable to you and then to let your own common sense be your guide. Too much advice from too many sources can be distracting. It is easier to proceed confidently with the management of your job search if you trust your own preferences, style, and pace.

Step 1. Setting Goals

Before embarking on your campaign, you should define what kind of job opportunity you are looking for, the type of organization you would like to work for, the geographic area to which your search is limited, and the minimum amount of money you need to earn. This is particularly important in a sector where compensation tends to be modest. You will be well advised to set up a tentative timetable for each stage of the job search, as this will enable you to give yourself some measure of progress. In the beginning your overall goals may be a bit fuzzy. As you gather information about the job market and gain experience through interviews, your focus will sharpen.

Step 2. Identifying Resources

We are surrounded by resources, but unless we are aware of their existence and know how to use them, we cannot mobilize them for our own benefit. Start a list of the resources that can help you in your campaign. Your list should include:

- Helpful individuals. These may be family members, friends, acquaintances, colleagues, former employers or teachers, board members of voluntary organizations you are involved with, ministers, and doctors—anyone who knows a lot of people. Most people are willing to assist or advise you, providing you can explain what you want from them, e.g., contacts, ideas, or references. Be specific about steps you would like them to take on your behalf. Using the people you know can be productive. Be sure the person you are asking is a good source for the help you are expecting. Once secure about that, go ahead and ask.

- Organizations and professional or social networks can give you visibility and the chance to interact with lots of people, particularly new people. This is your opportunity to be bold, to make contacts, and to let it be known that you are in the market for a job. Invest your time in attending conferences and meetings. They may turn out to be your ticket to the future.

- Printed materials. Be on the alert for information about the field you want to work in, key people and activities, trends, or anything that can provide clues to where you should go and what you should do. Read newspapers, journals, books, promotional literature, association materials, annual reports, catalogs, and directories. An amazing amount of information is available at your local public library, at university libraries, and at special purpose libraries.

- Employment agencies and executive search firms have discovered the nonprofit market. A number of them specialize in recruiting for this market and are active in major cities.

Step 3. Talking to People

It is not enough to identify the people who can help you. You must talk to them. Tell everyone you know what kind of job opportunity you are seeking. Solicit their advice and contacts. Use both formal meetings and chance encounters as an occasion to publicize your search and to gather information. If possible, try to set up short information interviews with individuals in a position to give you useful career information about a field or type of organization that interests you. If someone wants or needs to know more about you after a conversation, send them a short follow-up letter together with a copy of your résumé. This is not the time to be shy. Most people respect assertive and entrepreneurial initiatives carried out with grace and style.

Step 4. Preparing a Résumé

Although you may read advice against having a résumé, you need to write one, for résumés are a standard business convention used by employers to save time. Preparing a résumé may be a difficult task, but the process of doing it has unanticipated benefits. When you are forced to be clear about who you are and what you have done, you are in fact putting together a case, a marketable package, which you can sell. That package is you. When you have internalized the central messages about what you have to offer a prospective employer, you are ready for interviews.

Writing a well organized, easy-to-read résumé that sells, takes time. Writing several drafts will give you the opportunity to define and refine the message. Remember that you want to give the reader a brief profile of what you have done. Clear language and good organization are essential, and these qualities reflect on you. Be selective about what you include. If the information sells you, include it; if not, leave it out. Excessive detail is distracting to the reader, who will skim your résumé rather than read it word for word. Therefore, concentrate on major ideas that you want to convey. Dates and facts count, but use them with discretion. Let your best draft copy cool for a day or two before you do the final editing. Then read the résumé again, this time as if you were an employer. Is it convincing? If so, get it into final shape. If not, try to get some help in rethinking and rewording it.

Your general-purpose résumé may not seem appropriate for every situation. The résumé can always be adapted for a particular situation. Also, there are other opportunities to add information or highlight certain experiences you have had. You may do so at the interview, in the cover letter that is attached to your résumé, or in the follow-up letter of thanks that you send after your interview.

Nonprofit organizations do look for certain personality traits in job applicants that are of less interest to public and private organizations. Nonprofits are interested in your volunteer experience, your commitment to causes, and any other characteristics that will fit in with a value-driven organization that works closely with volunteers. Because of their dependence on fundraising and membership, nonprofit organizations are also interested in any marketing, communications, and development experience you may have had. Some of us have backgrounds or skills that we do not relate to the work setting but that can add to our chances for being employed. Extensive travel, fluency in languages, and writing ability can be great assets, particularly to an international development agency or a hospital with a multi-ethnic population.

Step 5. Developing a Job Search Strategy

With resources, résumés, and supportive material in hand, you are ready to proceed with specific initiatives. Your plan must be fluid and open-ended. As you begin to make contacts, explore possibilities, and have interviews, you will be reassessing your next steps continuously.

At this stage, initiative and persistent activity are essential. Nothing will happen unless you make it happen. Make direct contact with prospective employers. Read the classified ads, visit employment agencies or your college placement office, meet people for lunch. Try to set up interviews and, in general, maintain a high profile. ·

Step 6. Preparing for Interviews

It is wise to obtain information about the organization and perhaps the person you are going to see before you go for an interview. This will put you more at ease and cannot help but impress the prospective employer. Be organized. Dress in a businesslike fashion. Arrive on time for your appointment and try to stay relaxed. Every interview is a learning experience whether anything comes of it or not. The positive impression you leave behind you may not work for you in the situation at hand but may lead to another opportunity later. If the interview does not go well, you will learn from your mistakes. Remember there has to be a fit between what you have to offer and what the organization needs. And, after everything else, there has to be a certain compatibility between you and the person for whom you will be working.

As you prepare for your interviews, it may help you to have some insight into common characteristics of nonprofit managers. From the interviews we conducted for this book, we have put together a composite profile of common motives, talents, and ways of work in the nonprofit field, included as Figure 11.1. We observed that, regardless of their original interests or education, these men and women have been highly adaptive, able to transfer their talents to new settings, and willing to acquire new professional skills.

FIGURE 11.1. COMMON CHARACTERISTICS OF NONPROFIT MANAGERS.

Motives

- Interest in the betterment of society
- Commitment to causes
- Public service orientation

Talents

- Ability to work with different kinds of people: volunteer leaders, superiors, subordinates, fellow professionals, special populations
- Strong communications skills
- Entrepreneurship
- Creativity and vision
- Ambition, energy, and competitive spirit

Ways of work

- Respect for state-of-the-art management practice and technology
- Understanding the role of process in the organization, vis-à-vis boards and committees, fundraising, program development, and staff development

- Belief in and support for professional education and training
- Giving volunteer service to other organizations

Internships

Internships offer a way for individuals to learn new job skills, test existing job skills, and make contacts. Once the exclusive province of college and graduate students, they are increasingly being used by career re-entry women and career changers. An internship is an arrangement between an organization and an individual in which the organization offers work experience, supervision, and on-the-job training, and the intern works for no salary or a small salary.

Internships are available, but finding them may require a little research. Technical assistance centers, like the Support Centers of America, use interns, as do all sorts of agencies and foundations. Some organizations have formal programs, others set up an internship if they have a special project or find a person with special qualifications. Internship listings are included in the resource section that follows.

Resources for Further Information

The following resource section covers fellowships, internships, financial support, management training, career references, and relevant periodicals.

Fellowships

Boys Clubs of America
National Training Service
771 First Avenue
New York, NY 10017
(212) 351-5900

The Robert W. Woodruff Fellowship Program. The purpose of this program is to develop professional leadership for boys clubs. The Master's Internship Program combines a three- to six-week internship at various Boys Clubs, with relevant field of study, such as public administration, business administration, nonprofit management, or social work. Participants must be accepted at an accredited college or university and receive a masters degree within two years of the date of acceptance with the fellowship program. Stipends of up to $15,000 are available.

The Specialized Internship Program develops and enhances leadership skills and competencies of Boys Club professionals who already have a master's degree and have two years' experience working at a Boys Club of America affiliated club. The length of the internship will vary according to the professional growth needs of each individual fellow within an 18-month period. Fellows will spend 3-6 months in internship experiences. A maximum of $7,000 is available for each participant.

The John Hopkins University
Institute for Policy Studies
Shriver Hall
Baltimore, MD 21218
(301) 338-7174

International Fellowships in Philanthropy. This program will support advanced study, research, or training at the Institute for Policy Studies for five or six persons each year who are involved in studying or managing private, nonprofit, or philanthropic organizations abroad. There are no restrictions as to nationality, *except that U.S. citizens are excluded from eligibility.*

Junior Fellowships are available to graduate students and young professionals below the age of 35 who are involved in voluntary or philanthropic organizations or in any academic discipline. Junior Fellowships cover a nine-month period.

Senior Fellowships are open to individuals age 30 and over who hold positions in academic institutions, voluntary organizations, or foundations. Senior Fellowships cover a fourmonth period.

Internships

Center for Consumer Services
National Consumer Affairs Internship Program
017-HEW-Oklahoma State University
Stillwater, OK 74078-0337

National Consumer Affairs Internship Program. This program offers graduate students, undergraduate students, and faculty the opportunity to supplement academic study by working in a consumer affairs office (public, private, or nonprofit). Interns work full-time in the summer, fall, or spring during an 11-week period. They receive a $200 relocation allowance and $200 a week. Eligible applicants must be nominated by a faculty member. Applications are ranked. Participating organizations receive up to three files and make the final decision.

The CEIP Fund, Inc.
(formerly the Center for Environmental Interns Program)
68 Harrison Avenue
Boston, MA 02100-1907
(617) 426-4375

This nonprofit organization is committed to the management and decision-making process in environmental protection, resource management, and community development. The CEIP Fund connects individuals and employers by recruiting short-term assignments (associate positions) in the public, private, and nonprofit sector. They publish a guide, *Becoming an Environmental Professional: Strategies for Career Planning.*

Institute for Community Economics, Inc. (I.C.E.)
151 Montague City Road
Greenfield, MA 01301
(413) 774-7956

ICE is a nonprofit organization that works for economic justice by providing technical and financial assistance and public education to housing and economic development projects in low-income communities. They hire interns for nonprofessional staff roles for a one-year period.

Opera America
777 14th Street, N.W., Suite 520
Washington, DC 20005

Fellowship and Internship Program. Opera America, a membership association of 111 opera companies in the U.S. and Canada, sponsors four Administrative Internships a year, for anyone interested in entering the field of opera administration. Two of the internships last six months and involve placement with one opera company. The other two internships last a year and involve a rotation in three opera companies. Stipends and expenses are paid. Opera America also sponsors Executive Fellowships, a program in which an employee of a member company seeks out a mentor at another company in order to improve his/her skills in a chosen area, for example, marketing, public relations, development, or membership. These individually designed programs may last from two weeks to three months. Fellows receive a stipend; mentors receive an honorarium.

The Washington Center
514 Tenth Street, N.W., Suite 600
Washington, DC 28804
(202) 289-8680

Internship Initiative in the Independent Sector. This program is designed to prepare students to meet the need for leadership in the independent sector. Each term 25 college students, representing every academic discipline, will have access to senior executives in nonprofit organizations, foundations, public agencies, and congressional offices, through semester-long internships. To apply, students must have at least 3.0 grade point average and be second-semester sophomores or above. Participating students will receive a job placement, a $1,000 stipend, low-cost housing, a weekly academic seminar, and academic credit.

Financial Support

Every academic program and center has financial aid and fellowship funds for graduate students. Applicants should explore the options. The following examples are both unusual and illustrative.

Nonprofit Management Fellowship Fund
Non-Profit Management Club
Harvard Business School
Gallatin 3-B
Soldiers Field
Boston, MA 02163

The Nonprofit Management Fellowship Fund was started in 1981 to enable Harvard MBA students to take summer and post-graduate jobs with nonprofit organizations that could not otherwise afford the services of business students. Fellowships supplement the salary paid by the nonprofit organization, allowing the student to earn a total salary that is comparable to private sector opportunities.

Public Source Loan Assistance Program
Yale School of Management Admissions Office
Box 1A
New Haven, CT 06520

Because of the disparity in income potential in the public and nonprofit sectors compared to the private sector, Yale has instituted an assistance program. First, eligible graduates receive school loans on an annual basis to cover the amount by which their educational loan obligations exceed a certain percentage of their income. Second, the school will then gradually forgive these shortfall loans over a 20-year period if a graduate's income remains below the ceiling set by the program. The program is designed so that only graduates who face a severe educational debt burden, relative to their income level, would qualify to participate.

Management Training

United Way
Personnel Development Division
701 North Fairfax Street
Alexandria, VA 22314-204

The United Way Management Training Program is a one-year training program for individuals interested in pursuing a professional position with a United Way organization. The program serves as an employment resource for some 2,300 United Ways throughout the country. United Way of America will assist participants (who must be able to relocate) in the job search. Applicants must have a bachelor's degree or equivalent and must show evidence of high academic standing, leadership ability, effective oral and written communications skills, and an orientation toward the field of community service. Salaries and benefits during the training year depend on background and experience and start at $18,000. Training and supervision is in the area of fundraising, community planning and problem solving, fund distribution, agency relations, communications, and administration. Interns make a two-year commitment to United Way after the training.

Career References

Employment Opportunities in Nonprofit and Voluntary Organizations. This 43-page publication describes post-baccalaureate employment opportunities in 40 nonprofit organizations. Each listing specifies the purpose of the organization, the programs, career opportunities, requirements, salary range, and contact person. The guide was written by Kathiravelu K. Navaratorden, Oscar M. Williams, and Ernest E. Andrews; Virginia Cooperative Extension Service, Virginia Polytechnic Institute and State University, Blacksburg, VA 24061.

Good Works: A Guide to Careers in Social Change. A 288-page compilation with listings of over 600 social change groups and 12 career profiles. Edited by Joan Anzalone. Foreword by Ralph Nader. New York: Dembner Books, 1985.

Internships: On-the-Job Training Opportunities for All Types of Careers. Lists many nonprofit institution internships and includes a chapter on volunteering. Lisa S. Hulse, ed. Cincinnati, OH: Writers Digest Book, 1986.

Jobs in Arts and Media Management; What They Are and How to Get One. An excellent comprehensive resource, by Stephen Langley and James Abruzzo. New York: Drama Book Publishers, 1986.

Careers in the Nonprofit Sector: Doing Well by Doing Good. A ground-breaking book, the first one to describe the nonprofit sector as a good place to work. A personal account by an experienced manager. Carefully researched and documented, by Terry W. McAdam. Washington, DC: The Taft Group, 1986.

The National Directory of Internships. Edited by Sally A. Migliore. Descriptions of 26,000 student internship opportunities in over 2,000 organizations across the country. Raleigh, NC: National Society for Internships and Experiential Education, 1987.

Opportunities in Non-Profit Organizations: A National Listing of Career Opportunities in the Non-profit Sector. A looseleaf directory, *Opportunities,* can be found in many placement offices and libraries and is updated monthly. ACCESS sends out thousands of survey/questionnaires each month asking nonprofits to describe their organization and any current job opportunities they have. ACCESS also operates a Job Search Service for mid-careerists looking for middle- and upper-level positions. For a small processing fee, they will search their database, providing they receive a résumé cover letter describing geographical location, desired area of interest, skills, and other pertinent data. ACCESS: Networking in the Public Interest, 96 Mt. Auburn Street, Cambridge, MA 02138. (617) 495-2178. (You may also be interested in reading in this book the career profile of James P. Clark, the founder and director of ACCESS.)

Public Interest Profiles. A highly organized information resource about 250 public policy/public interest groups. Job seekers interested in advocacy organizations will find all sorts of useful facts, including staff size, budget, profile of the director, scope, purpose, method of operation, current concerns, and recent publications. Foundation for Public Affairs, 1255 Twenty-Third Street, N.W., Suite 750, Washington, DC 20037. (202) 872-1750.

Taft Directory of Nonprofit Organizations: Profiles of America's Major Charitable Institutions. The first edition of this directory provides in-depth data and analyses on 1,125 major nonprofits. It profiles their programs, personnel, and finances. The addresses, phone numbers, and names of executive officers are particularly helpful to job seekers. Edited by Susan E. Elnicki. Washington, DC: The Taft Group.

Relevant Periodicals

Classified ads and clues about new or expanding projects can be found in periodicals. Among the general nonprofit periodicals, those with the broadest coverage are: *Foundation News, Fund Raising Management, Nonprofit Executive, Nonprofit Times, Nonprofit World, The Chronicle of Higher Education,* and *The Chronicle of Philanthropy.*

Community Jobs. This monthly subscription newsletter lists hundreds of current job openings and internships in socially concerned organizations across the country. Some of the opportunities listed are in community organizing, law, women's issues, consumer rights, food coops, and the environment. Jobs range from internships and entry-level jobs to top management positions. Community Careers Resource Center, 1516 P Street, N.W., Washington, DC 20005. (202) 667-0661.

Appendix A

United Way of America 1987 Summary of Position Classifications

The following job titles and descriptions are designed to allow categorization of United Way jobs based on *similarity of function*. The information is not meant to represent any actual or ideal structure. The assignment of any position code infers that a staff function is basically similar to the generic job description provided.

Administration

010 — **President and Chief Professional Officer (CPO):** Reporting to the Board, directs the overall operation of a *fundraising* organization as its chief operating executive.

011 — **Vice President:** Reporting to the CPO, serves as deputy in the overall operation of a *fundraising* organization. May have responsibility in the administration of line programs, i.e., campaign, planning, allocations, etc., and/or staff functions.

012 — **Area Director:** Reporting to the CPO, directs the overall operation of a *fundraising* organization within a specific geographic area.

020 — **Executive Director:** Reporting to the Board, directs the overall operation of a *planning* or *planning and allocation organization* as its chief operating officer.

021 — **Associate Executive Director:** Reporting to the Executive Director, serves as deputy in the overall operation of a *planning or planning and allocating organization.* May have responsibility in the administration of line programs, i.e., planning or allocations, and/or staff functions.

022 — **Area Director:** Reporting to the CPO, directs the overall operation of a *planning or planning and allocating organization* within a specified geographic area.

040 — **Executive Director:** Reporting to the board, directs the overall operation of an allocating organization as its chief operating officer.

041 — **Associate Executive Director:** Reporting to the Executive Director, serves as deputy in the overall operation or an allocating organization. May have responsibility in the administration of line programs and/or staff functions.

042 — **Area Director:** Reporting to the Executive Director, directs the overall operation of an *allocating organization* within a specified geographic area.

100 — **Director, Finance and Administration:** Reporting to the CPO or designee, directs the administration of internal organizational functions and directs the development and operations of the financial system, including budgeting, auditing, accounting, and financial reporting. Assumes responsibility for the treasurer functions of investment and cash flow control and for governmental reporting and insurance matters. Note: If a position is reported under this code, do not report a position under code 102.

101 — **Finance and Administration Staff:** Professional staff primarily engaged in the financial and administrative operations of the organization.

102 — **Director, Finance:** Reporting to the CPO, directs the development and operation of the financial system, including budgeting, auditing, accounting, and financial reporting. Also responsible for treasurer functions of investment and cash flow control and for governmental reporting and insurance matters. May provide a centralized bookkeeping service for agencies.

103 — **Finance Staff:** Professional staff engaged primarily in the operations of the financial system.

104 — **Director, Administration:** Reporting to the CPO or designee, directs the administration of internal organizational functions (MIS, personnel, office services, property management, etc.).

105 — **Administration Staff:** Professional staff engaged primarily in the operation of internal organizational functions.

106 — **Controller:** Reporting to the Director, Finance, operates the budgeting, auditing, accounting, and financial reporting system. Where there is no separate Director, Finance, reports to the CPO and additionally may assume the treasurer function. May manage a centralized bookkeeping service for agencies.

107 — **Accountant:** Reporting to the Controller, performs professional budget or accounting work in planning or recording financial transactions, accounts receivable, accounts payable, general ledger, and payroll.

108 — **Auditor:** Reporting to the senior financial officer, carries out the internal audit program applicable to campaign accounting and reporting, and other internal systems and procedures. Provides support to the Allocations Director when responsibilities include audit of member agencies or an analysis of member agencies, budgets, financial reports and/or audits.

109 — **Director/Staff, Special Accounting Systems:** Performs special accounting services such as Agency Accounting Programs, Auditing Services, etc.

110 — **Administration Assistant:** Assists the CPO and senior staff by performing administrative duties at a professional level.

120 — **Director, Management Information Systems (MIS):** Plans and directs all MIS operations, including systems analysis and design, programming, and computer operations.

121 — **Assistant Director, MIS:** Reporting to the Director, MIS, serves as deputy in the overall MIS operation and may have specific functional responsibilities in such areas as systems analysis and design, programming, and computer operations.

123 — **MIS Staff:** Professional staff engaged primarily in MIS operations.

130 — **Director, Personnel:** Manages the organization's human resource development activities, including employment, staff training, affirmative action, benefits administration, etc.

133 — **Personnel Staff:** Professional staff engaged primarily in personnel activities.

140 — **Office Services Manager:** Manages support services for the organization or for a large division, including general clerical work, production, liaison with MIS, etc. May screen and recommend hiring of support staff and assist in evaluation.

150 — **Word Processing Manager:** Directs the work of staff engaged in word processing activities. Prioritizes and assigns work, acts as liaison with operating departments.

Campaign

200 — **Director, Resource Development:** Reporting to the CPO or designee, directs the organization and conduct of fund-and/or goods- generating programs.

210 — **Director, Campaign:** Reporting to the CPO or designee, or the Director, Resource Development, directs the organization and conduct of the campaign.

211 — **Assistant Director, Campaign:** Reporting to the Director, Campaign, assists in the organization and conduct of the overall campaign, *or* organizes and conducts several divisions of the total campaign. May also have personal responsibility for one or more campaign divisions. Supervises other professional staff.

212 — **Division Director Campaign:** Reporting to the Director, Campaign, or Assistant Director, Campaign, organizes one or more specific divisions of the campaign. May supervise other professional staff.

213 — **Campaign Staff:** Professional staff primarily engaged in the organization and conduct of the campaign.

220 — **Director, Endowment/Deferred Giving/Gifts in Kind:** Reporting to the CPO or designee, or the Director, Resource Development, directs the organization and conduct of endowment, deferred giving, or gifts in kind programs.

223 — **Endowment/Deferred Giving/Gifts in Kind Staff:** Professional staff primarily engaged in endowment, deferred giving, or gifts in kind programs.

Planning and Allocations

300 — **Director, Planning and Allocations:** Reporting to the CPO or designee, directs the operation of the planning and allocating functions. Directs the community and volunteer efforts and maintains working relationships with member agencies.

301 — Assistant Director, Planning and Allocations: Reporting to the Director, Planning and Allocations, assists in the overall direction of planning and allocations activities and supervises other professional staff engaged in these activities.

302 — Senior Planning and Allocations Staff: Performs complex planning and allocations activities requiring advanced level of related expertise.

303 — Planning and Allocations Staff: Professional staff engaged in planning and allocations activities.

310 — Director, Planning: Reporting to the CPO or designee, organizes and directs efforts to assess the community's human services system and to improve the capabilities of the system in meeting human needs.

311 — Assistant Director, Planning: Reporting to the Director, Planning, assists directing the overall community planning effort. Supervises professional staff engaged in staffing community planning projects.

312 — Senior Planning Staff: Performs complex planning activities requiring an advanced level of related expertise.

313 — Planning Staff: Professional staff primarily engaged in community planning projects.

320 — Director, Allocations: Reporting to the CPO or designee, organizes and directs the fund distribution process to member agencies. Staffs allocations committees and establishes and maintains effective working relations with member agencies.

321 — Assistant Director, Allocations: Reporting to the Director, Allocations, assists in the direction of overall allocations functions and supervises professional staff engaged in allocations activities.

322 — Senior Allocations Staff: Performs complex allocations activities requiring an advanced level of related expertise.

323 — Allocations Staff: Professional staff primarily engaged in allocations activities.

Communications

400 — Director, Communications: Reporting to the CPO or designee, designs, plans, and executes the public relations, educational, and promotional programs of the organization.

401 — Assistant Director, Communications: Reporting to the Director, Communications, assists in the overall direction of communications activities. May assume responsibility for directing one or more specific parts of the communications program.

402 — Senior Communications Staff: Performs complex communications activities requiring an advanced level of related expertise.

403 — Communications Staff: Professional staff primarily engaged in communications activities.

Service Programs

500 — **Director, Service Programs:** Reporting to the CPO or designee, plans and directs service programs for agencies and the community; i.e., Information and Referral, Volunteer Bureau, Management Assistance, etc.

503 — **Service Program Staff:** Professional staff primarily engaged in service program activities.

510 — **Director, Information and Referral (I&R):** Reporting to CPO or designee, or Director, Service Programs, plans and directs the operation of an information and referral service to the community.

511 — **Assistant Director, Information and Referral:** Reporting to the Director, I&R, assists in the overall operation of the I&R program and may have specific functional responsibilities.

513 — **Information and Referral Staff:** Professional staff primarily engaged in the operation of an I&R program.

520 — **Director, Volunteer Bureau:** Reporting to the CPO or designee, or Director, Service Programs, plans and directs programs that develop and utilize volunteer resources in the community.

521 — **Assistant Director, Volunteer Bureau:** Reporting to the Director, Volunteer Bureau, assists in the overall operation of the Volunteer Bureau and may have specific functional responsibilities.

523 — **Volunteer Bureau Staff:** Professional staff primarily engaged in the operation of a Volunteer Bureau.

530 — **Director, Training:** Reporting to the CPO or designee, or Director, Service Programs, plans and directs training programs for volunteers of the organization and/or its agencies.

533 — **Training Staff:** Professional staff primarily engaged in training programs for volunteers and/or agencies.

540 — **Director, Management Assistance Program (MAP):** Reporting to the CPO or designee, or Director, Service Programs, plans and directs programs that enhance the effectiveness of agencies' operations.

543 — **Management Assistance Program Staff:** Professional staff primarily engaged in programs designed to enhance the effectiveness of agencies' operations.

Research

600 — **Director, Research:** Reporting to the CPO or designee, plans and directs the research activities of the organization.

603 — **Research Staff:** Professional staff primarily engaged in research activities.

Labor

700 — **Director, Labor:** Reporting to the CPO of designee, plans and directs the development of support and participation of labor in the planning and financing of human services.

703 — **Labor Staff:** Professional staff primarily engaged in labor activities.

Government Relations

710 — **Director, Government Relations:** Plans and directs the preparation and administration of proposals, grants, and contracts with government agencies; advocates human service needs as they relate to the government.

713 — **Government Relations Staff:** Professional staff primarily engaged in government relations activities.

Marketing

800 — **Director, Marketing:** Reporting to the CPO or designee, plans and directs the organization's marketing effort.

803 — **Marketing Staff:** Professional staff primarily engaged in marketing activities.

Workplace Year-Round Education

810 — **Director, Workplace Year-Round Education:** Reporting to the CPO or designee, plans and directs the administration of a workplace year-round education program.

813 — **Workplace Year-Round Education Staff:** Professional staff primarily engaged in workplace year-round education programs.

Special Projects

820 — **Director, Special Projects:** Reporting to the CPO or designee, plans and directs special projects that may be funded, at least in part, by outside sources.

821 — **Assistant Director, Special Projects:** Reporting to the Director, Special Projects, assists in the overall operation of special projects activities and may have specific functional areas of responsibility.

823 — **Special Projects Staff:** Professional staff primarily engaged in special projects activities.

Appendix B

Foundation Position Definitions

(1) CHIEF EXECUTIVE OFFICER: Responsible for directing the overall program and administrative activities of the foundation. Responsible for the effective use of financial and human resources of the foundation.

(2) ASSOCIATE DIRECTOR or
(3) VICE PRESIDENT (General): Number two person. Responsible for directing more than one major program or administrative activity of the foundation. Exercises discretionary power in significant matters, and is designated the officer in charge of the foundation's daily activities in the absence of the CEO.

(4) VICE PRESIDENT (Program): Responsible for directing the program activities of the foundation, including the grantmaking program, special projects, or programs operated by the foundation. Responsible for establishing policies and procedures to manage programs.

(5) VICE PRESIDENT (Administration): Responsible for directing the internal administrative activities of the foundation, personnel, and office administration. May also oversee financial activities in some organizations. Responsible for establishing policies and procedures to manage support activities.

(6) SECRETARY OF THE CORPORATION: Responsible for corporate records. May also be responsible for handling legal matters if there is not a general counsel.

(7) TREASURER (Chief Financial Officer): Responsible for directing the financial/accounting activities, including investments management or monitoring outside investment management.

(8) SECRETARY/TREASURER: Responsible for the duties of both positions as outlined above.

(9) CONTROLLER: Responsible for operation of financial and bookkeeping services, including preparation of financial analyses, income and expense reports, budgets, and governmental reports. May also be responsible for directing purchasing, payroll, and other financial operations.

(10) INVESTMENT OFFICER: Manages investment assets. May oversee outside investment managers.

(11) GENERAL COUNSEL: Responsible for directing the legal activities of the foundation. Responsible for coordinating legal matters with outside counsel and for advising staff on legal matters pertaining to the foundation.

(12) ASSISTANT VICE-PRESIDENT/ ASSISTANT DIRECTOR: Provides professional level assistance to vice president or associate director for duties outlined in (2)–(5) above.

(13) ASSISTANT SECRETARY: Provides professional assistance to corporate secretary for duties outlined in (6) above.

(14) ASSISTANT TREASURER: Provides professional assistance to treasurer for duties outlined in (7) above.

(15) ASSISTANT CONTROLLER: Provides professional assistance to controller for duties outlined in (9) above.

(16) PROGRAM DIRECTOR: Responsible for managing the grantmaking program of a particular subject area (education, arts/humanities, health, etc.) or geographic region. In larger-staffed foundations, a senior level program officer who supervises other program staff in carrying out grantmaking or in-house programs. Recommends (or has authority to approve in some cases) distribution of grant dollars within budget for the program area.

(17) PROGRAM OFFICER: Responsible for investigating and evaluating grant proposals and/or carrying out in-house projects. In larger-staffed foundations, this may involve one subject area or geographic region. In smaller foundation programs, officers are usually responsible for most aspects of the grantmaking process (including program research, proposal evaluation, grant tracking, post-grant evaluation, etc.).

(18) PROGRAM ASSOCIATE: Evaluates grant proposals, does background research, and prepares for funding. Is often an entry level program officer position in larger-staffed foundations.

(19) COMMUNICATIONS OFFICER: Responsible for directing the communications activities of the foundation, including publications, public/press relations, production of annual report. Establishes policies and practices to develop and maintain the desired image of the foundation.

(20) FUNDRAISING OFFICER: In *community foundations only*—responsible for establishing and maintaining fundraising efforts of the foundation. May have responsibility for other donee relations activities.

(21) RESEARCH PROFESSIONAL: Responsible for directing the foundation's research activities or for carrying out foundation-funded research projects. Often part of a fellowship or in-house operating research program.

(22) COMPUTER PROFESSIONAL: Responsible for programming, data processing, or database management activities. May assist other staff (financial grants managers, others) in using the foundation's computer equipment.

(23) OFFICE MANAGER: Responsible for operation and maintenance of all facilities. Develops, recommends, and implements policies and procedures for office operation and often for personnel policies.

(24) LIBRARIAN: Manages in-house library and may assist program staff by doing background research.

(25) ACCOUNTANT: Maintains financial record systems, provides auditing services and financial statements to the foundation managers.

(26) PROGRAM ASSISTANT: Assists the program officers with proposals evaluation and provides some administrative support. May also keep track of grants if there is no grants manager.

(27) RESEARCH ASSISTANT: Assists research professional with duties outlined in (21) above, and provides some administrative support.

(28) FINANCIAL ASSISTANT/BOOK-KEEPER: Provides a variety of recordkeeping services to accountant, controller, or others managing the foundation's finances.

(29) GRANTS MANAGER: Keeps track of grants made by the foundation, obtaining and maintaining reports required from grantees.

(30) ADMINISTRATIVE ASSISTANT: Performs a variety of responsible clerical duties requiring independent analysis, judgment, and knowledge of foundation or departmental functions. Maintains records, processes complex documents, compiles regular and special reports.

(31) SECRETARY: Performs standard secretarial functions. Includes executive, administrative, other secretarial positions.

(32) WORD PROCESSING OPERATOR: Produces typed copy on automated office equipment.

(33) CLERK: Includes file, mail clerks, clerk-typists, and other clerical positions.

(34) RECEPTIONIST: Greets visitors, handles switchboard. May also do typing and related clerical tasks.

Source: 1984 Foundation Management Report Council on Foundations.

Appendix C

Finding Work with Grant-makers and other Nonprofit Organizations

Foundations

Familiarize yourself with basic staffing patterns in foundations by consulting THE FOUN-DATION MANAGEMENT REPORT, published by the Council on Foundations. This survey gives staffing information for over 500 foundations.

The 990-PF RETURNS filed annually with the IRS by all private foundations in the United States contain information about executive staff and their compensation, if any, and sometimes about other employees. The size of a foundation in terms of assets, grants made, and fields of interest can also be determined by studying these returns.

Other excellent sources of information about a foundation's fields of interest are ANNUAL REPORTS, when published, and THE FOUNDATION DIRECTORY, with its subject index. There are also STATE DIRECTORIES of foundations available for most states, some with subject indices.

Also, The Foundation Center publishes WORKING IN FOUNDATIONS, which surveys the staffing patterns of approximately 438 foundations.

Corporate Contributions Programs

Company-sponsored foundations are private foundations and information concerning their interests and staff will appear in the sources described above. If you are seeking information about corporate contributions programs, the following may be useful:

National Directory of Corporate Giving. Suzanne W. Haile, Editor. Profiles 1,551 companies making contributions to nonprofit organizations.

Taft Corporate Giving Directory. Taft Corporate Information System. Annual Publication. Profiles of over 570 companies.

Corporate 500: The Directory of Corporate Philanthropy. Public Management Institute. Annual Publication. Profiles large and small companies giving over $500,000 annually.

The Corporate Fundraising Directory. Public Service Materials Center. Information about over 500 of the largest corporations representing approx. 90% of all business grants.

Guide to Corporate Living in the Arts. American Council for the Arts. Information on over 700 of the country's largest corporations.

Standard & Poors. Three volumes: Corporations, Directors and Executives, Index.

Nonprofit Organizations

Periodicals listing employment opportunities in non-profit organizations:

ACA Updates. Monthly publication of the American Council for the Arts.

Arts Reporting Service. Bimonthly publication of the Arts Resource Corp.

Artsearch. The National Employment Service Bulletin for the Performing Arts. Published twice monthly by Theatre Communications Group, Inc.

ASTC Newsletter. Bimonthly publication of the Association of Science-Technology Centers.

Chronicle of Higher Education. Weekly.

Community Jobs. Monthly publication of the Comm. Careers Resource Center.

The Executive Administrator. Monthly Publication of the Center for Management Systems.

Foundation News. Bimonthly publication of the Council on Foundations.

Nonprofit Executive. Monthly publication of the Taft Corporation.

Appendix D

The Foundation Center's Network of Cooperating Collections

THE FOUNDATION CENTER COOPERATING COLLECTIONS NETWORK
Free Funding Information Centers

The Foundation Center is an independent national service organization established by foundations to provide an authoritative source of information on private philanthropic giving. The New York, Washington, DC, Cleveland and San Francisco reference collections operated by the Foundation Center offer a wide variety of services and comprehensive collections of information on foundations and grants. Cooperating Collections are libraries, community foundations and other nonprofit agencies that provide a core collection of Foundation Center publications and a variety of supplementary materials and services in areas useful to grantseekers. The core collection consists of:

Foundation Directory	Foundation Fundamentals	Foundation Grants Index Bimonthly
Foundation Directory Supplement	Corporate Giving Directory	National Data Book of Foundations
Source Book Profiles	Foundation Grants Index	Foundation Grants to Individuals

Many of the network members have sets of private foundation information returns (IRS 990-PF) for their state or region which are available for public use. A complete set of U.S. foundation returns can be found at the New York and Washington, DC offices of the Foundation Center. The Cleveland and San Francisco offices contain IRS 990-PF returns for the midwestern and western states, respectively. Those Cooperating Collections marked with a bullet (●) have sets of private foundation information returns for their state or region.

Because the collections vary in their hours, materials and services, IT IS RECOMMENDED THAT YOU CALL EACH COLLECTION IN ADVANCE. To check on new locations or more current information, call 1-800-424-9836.

Reference Collections Operated by the Foundation Center

The Foundation Center
8th Floor
79 Fifth Avenue
New York, NY 10003
212-620-4230

The Foundation Center
Room 312
312 Sutter Street
San Francisco, CA 94108
415-397-0902

The Foundation Center
1001 Connecticut Avenue, NW
Washington, DC 20036
202-331-1400

The Foundation Center
Kent H. Smith Library
1442 Hanna Building
Cleveland, OH 44115
216-861-1933

ALABAMA

● Birmingham Public Library
2100 Park Place
Birmingham 35203
205-226-3600

Huntsville Public Library
915 Monroe St.
Huntsville 35801
205-532-5940

University of South Alabama
Library Reference Dept.
Mobile 36688
205-460-7025

● Auburn University at
Montgomery Library
I-85 @ Taylor Rd.
Montgomery 36193-0401
205-271-9649

ALASKA

Juneau Public Library
292 Marine Way
Juneau 99801
907-586-5249

● University of Alaska
Anchorage Library
3211 Providence Drive
Anchorage 99508
907-786-1848

ARIZONA

● Phoenix Public Library
Business & Sciences Dept.
12 East McDowell Road
Phoenix 85257
602-262-4636

● Tucson Public Library
200 South Sixth Avenue
Tucson 85726-7470
602-791-4393

ARKANSAS

● Westark Community College
Library
5210 Grand Avenue
Fort Smith 72913
501-785-7000

● Central Arkansas Library System
Reference Services
700 Louisiana Street
Little Rock 72201
501-370-5950

CALIFORNIA

● California Community Foundation
Funding Information Center
3580 Wilshire Blvd., Suite 1660
Los Angeles 90010
213-413-4042

● Community Foundation for
Monterey County
420 Pacific Street
Monterey 93940
408-375-9712

California Community
Foundation
13252 Garden Grove Blvd.
Garden Grove 92643
714-750-7794

Riverside Public Library
3581 7th Street
Riverside 92501
714-782-5201

California State Library
Reference Services, Rm. 301
914 Capitol Mall
Sacramento 95814
916-322-4570

● San Diego Community
Foundation
525 "B" Street, Suite 410
San Diego 92101
619-239-8815

● Grantsmanship Resource Center
1762 Technology Dr., Suite 225
San Jose 95110
408-452-8181

● Orange County Community
Developmental Council
1695 W. MacArthur Blvd.
Costa Mesa 92626
714-540-9293

● Peninsula Community
Foundation
1204 Burlingame Avenue
Burlingame 94011-0627
415-342-2505

● Santa Barbara Public Library
40 East Anapamu
Santa Barbara 93102
805-962-7653

Santa Monica Public Library
1343 Sixth Street
Santa Monica 90401-1603
213-451-8859

Tuolumne County Free Library
480 Greenley Rd.
Sonora 95370
209-533-5507

COLORADO

Pikes Peak Library District
20 North Cascade Avenue
Colorado Springs 80901
719-473-2080

● Denver Public Library
Sociology Division
1357 Broadway
Denver 80203
303-571-2190

CONNECTICUT

Danbury Public Library
170 Main Street
Danbury 06810
203-797-4527

● Hartford Public Library
Reference Department
500 Main Street
Hartford 06103
203-293-6000

D.A.T.A.
25 Science Park
Suite 502
New Haven 06511
203-786-5225

DELAWARE

● University of Delaware
Hugh Morris Library
Newark 19717-5267
302-451-2965

FLORIDA

Volusia County Library Center
City Island
Daytona Beach 32014-4484
904-255-3765

● Jacksonville Public Libraries
Business, Science & Documents
122 North Ocean Street
Jacksonville 32206
904-630-2665

● Miami–Dade Public Library
Humanities Department
101 W. Flagler St.
Miami 33130
305-375-2665

● Orange County Library System
101 E. Central Blvd.
Orlando 32801
407-425-4694

Selby Public Library
1001 Boulevard of the Arts
Sarasota 33577
813-951-5501

Leon County Public Library
Funding Resource Center
1940 North Monroe Street
Tallahassee 32303
904-487-2665

Palm Beach County Community
Foundation
324 Datura Street, Suite 340
West Palm Beach 33401
407-659-6800

GEORGIA

Atlanta–Fulton Public Library
Ivan Allen Department
1 Margaret Mitchell Square
Atlanta 30303-1089
404-730-1700

HAWAII

University of Hawaii
Thomas Hale Hamilton Library
2550 The Mall
Honolulu 96822
808-948-7214

Hawaiia Community Foundation
Hawaii Resource Room
212 Merchant Street
Suite 330
Honolulu 96813
808-599-5767

IDAHO

Boise Public Library
715 S. Capitol Blvd.
Boise 83702
208-384-4466

Caldwell Public Library
1010 Dearborn Street
Caldwell 83605
208-459-3242

ILLINOIS

Belleville Public Library
121 East Washington Street
Belleville 62220
618-234-0441

DuPage Township
241 Canterbury Lane
Bolingbrook 60439
312-759-1317

Donors Forum of Chicago
53 W. Jackson Blvd., Rm. 430
Chicago 60604
312-431-0265

Evanston Public Library
1703 Orrington Avenue
Evanston 60201
312-866-0305

Sangamon State University
Library
Shepherd Road
Springfield 62794-9243
217-786-6633

INDIANA

Allen County Public Library
900 Webster Street
Fort Wayne 46802
219-424-7241

Indiana University Northwest
Library
3400 Broadway
Gary 46408
219-980-6580

Indianapolis–Marion County
Public Library
40 East St. Clair Street
Indianapolis 46206
317-269-1733

IOWA

Public Library of Des Moines
100 Locust Street
Des Moines 50308
515-283-4259

KANSAS

Topeka Public Library
1515 West Tenth Street
Topeka 66604
913-233-2040

Wichita Public Library
223 South Main
Wichita 67202
316-262-0611

KENTUCKY

Western Kentucky University
Helm-Cravens Library
Bowling Green 42101
502-745-6125

Louisville Free Public Library
Fourth and York Streets
Louisville 40203
502-561-8600

LOUISIANA

East Baton Rouge Parish Library
Centroplex Branch
120 St. Louis Street
Baton Rouge 70802
504-389-4960

New Orleans Public Library
Business and Science Division
219 Loyola Avenue
New Orleans 70140
504-596-2580

Shreve Memorial Library
424 Texas Street
Shreveport 71120-1523
318-226-5894

MAINE

University of Southern Maine
Office of Sponsored Research
246 Deering Ave., Rm. 628
Portland 04103
207-780-4871

MARYLAND

Enoch Pratt Free Library
Social Science and History
Department
400 Cathedral Street
Baltimore 21201
301-396-5320

MASSACHUSETTS

Associated Grantmakers of
Massachusetts
294 Washington Street
Suite 840
Boston 02108
617-426-2608

Boston Public Library
666 Boylston St.
Boston 02117
617-536-5400

Western Massachusetts Funding
Resource Center
Campaign for Human
Development
73 Chestnut Street
Springfield 01103
413-732-3175

Grants Resource Center
Worcester Public Library
Salem Square
Worcester 01608
508-799-1655

MICHIGAN

Alpena County Library
211 North First Avenue
Alpena 49707
517-356-6188

University of Michigan–Ann
Arbor
209 Hatcher Graduate Library
Ann Arbor 48109-1205
313-764-1149

Henry Ford Centennial Library
16301 Michigan Avenue
Dearborn 48126
313-943-2337

Wayne State University
Purdy-Kresge Library
Detroit 48202
313-577-4040

Michigan State University
Libraries
Reference Library
East Lansing 48824-1048
517-353-8818

Farmington Community Library
32737 West 12 Mile Road
Farmington Hills 48018
313-553-0300

University of Michigan–Flint
Library
Reference Department
Flint 48502-2186
313-762-3408

Grand Rapids Public Library
Business Dept.
60 Library Plaza NE
Grand Rapids 49503-3093
616-456-3600

Michigan Technological
University Library
Highway U.S. 41
Houghton 49931
906-487-2507

Sault Ste. Marie Area
Public Schools
Office of Compensatory
Education
460 W. Spruce St.
Sault Ste. Marie 49783-1874
906-635-6619

MINNESOTA

Duluth Public Library
520 W. Superior Street
Duluth 55802
218-723-3802

Southwest State University
Library
Marshall 56258
507-537-7278

Minneapolis Public Library
Sociology Department
300 Nicollet Mall
Minneapolis 55401
612-372-6555

Rochester Public Library
11 First Street, SE
Rochester 55902-3743
507-285-8002

St. Paul Public Library
90 West Fourth Street
Saint Paul 55102
612-292-6307

MISSISSIPPI

Jackson Metropolitan Library
301 North State Street
Jackson 39212
601-968-5803

MISSOURI

Clearinghouse for Midcontinent
Foundations
Univ. of Missouri
Law School, Suite 1-300
52nd Street and Oak
Kansas City 64113-0680
816-276-1176

Kansas City Public Library
311 East 12th Street
Kansas City 64106
816-221-9650

Metropolitan Association for
Philanthropy, Inc.
5585 Pershing Avenue
Suite 150
St. Louis 63112
314-361-3900

Springfield–Greene County
Library
397 East Central Street
Springfield 65801
417-866-4636

MONTANA

Eastern Montana College Library
1500 N. 30th Street
Billings 59101-0298
406-657-1662

- Montana State Library
Reference Department
1515 E. 6th Avenue
Helena 59620
406-444-3004

NEBRASKA

- University of Nebraska
106 Love Library
14th & R Streets
Lincoln 68588-0410
402-472-2848

- W. Dale Clark Library
Social Sciences Department
215 South 15th Street
Omaha 68102
402-444-4826

NEVADA

- Las Vegas–Clark County Library
District
1401 East Flamingo Road
Las Vegas 89119-6160
702-733-7810

- Washoe County Library
301 South Center Street
Reno 89501
702-785-4012

NEW HAMPSHIRE

- New Hampshire Charitable Fund
One South Street
Concord 03301
603-225-6641

Littleton Public Library
109 Main Street
Littleton 03561
603-444-5741

NEW JERSEY

Cumberland County Library
800 E. Commerce Street
Bridgeton 08302-2295
609-453-2210

The Support Center
17 Academy Street, Suite 1101
Newark 07102
201-643-5774

County College of Morris
Masten Learning Resource
Center
Route 10 and Center Grove Rd.
Randolph 07869
201-361-5000 ext. 470

- New Jersey State Library
Governmental Reference
185 West State Street
Trenton 08625
609-292-6220

NEW MEXICO

Albuquerque Community
Foundation
6400 Uptown Boulevard N.E.
Suite 500-W
Albuquerque 87105
505-883-6240

- New Mexico State Library
325 Don Gaspar Street
Santa Fe 87505
505-827-3824

NEW YORK

- New York State Library
Cultural Education Center
Humanities Section
Empire State Plaza
Albany 12230
518-474-5161

New York Public Library
Bronx Reference Center
2556 Bainbridge Avenue
Bronx 10458
212-220-6575

Brooklyn in Touch
One Hanson Place
Room 2504
Brooklyn 11243
718-230-3200

- Buffalo and Erie County Public
Library
Lafayette Square
Buffalo 14202
716-858-7103

Huntington Public Library
338 Main Street
Huntington 11743
516-427-5165

- Levittown Public Library
One Bluegrass Lane
Levittown 11756
516-731-5720

SUNY/College at Old Westbury
Library
223 Store Hill Road
Old Westbury 11568
516-876-3156

- Plattsburgh Public Library
15 Oak Street
Plattsburgh 12901
518-563-0921

Adriance Memorial Library
93 Market Street
Poughkeepsie 12601
914-485-3445

Queens Borough Public Library
89-11 Merrick Boulevard
Jamaica 11432
718-990-0700

- Rochester Public Library
Business Division
115 South Avenue
Rochester 14604
716-428-7328

Staten Island Council on the Arts
One Edgewater Plaza, Rm. 311
Staten Island 10305
718-447-4485

- Onondaga County Public Library
at the Galleries
447 S. Salina Street
Syracuse 13202-2494
315-448-4636

- White Plains Public Library
100 Martine Avenue
White Plains 10601
914-682-4480

- Suffolk Cooperative Library
System
627 North Sunrise Service Road
Bellport 11713
516-286-1600

NORTH CAROLINA

- Asheville-Buncomb Technical
Community College
Learning Resource Center
340 Victoria Rd.
Asheville 28801
704-254-1921 x300

- The Duke Endowment
200 S. Tryon Street, Ste. 1100
Charlotte 28202
704-376-0291

Durham County Library
300 N. Roxboro Street
Durham 27702
919-683-2626

- North Carolina State Library
109 East Jones Street
Raleigh 27611
919-733-3270

- The Winston-Salem Foundation
229 First Union Bank Building
Winston-Salem 27101
919-725-2382

NORTH DAKOTA

Western Dakota Grants Resource
Center
Bismarck State Community
College
Bismarck 58501
701-224-5400

- The Library
North Dakota State University
Fargo 58105
701-237-8886

OHIO

- Public Library of Cincinnati and
Hamilton County
Education Department
800 Vine Street
Cincinnati 45202-2071
513-369-6940

The Public Library of Columbus
and Franklin County
96 S. Grant Avenue
Columbus 43215
614-645-2275

- Dayton and Montgomery County
Public Library
Grants Information Center
215 E. Third Street
Dayton 45402-2103
513-227-9500 ext. 211

- Toledo–Lucas County Public
Library
Social Science Department
325 Michigan Street
Toledo 43623
419-259-5245

Ohio University-Zanesville
Community Education and
Development
1425 Newark Road
Zanesville 43701
614-453-0762

Stark County District Library
715 Market Avenue North
Canton 44702-1080
216-452-0665

OKLAHOMA

- Oklahoma City University Library
2501 North Blackwelder
Oklahoma City 73106
405-521-5072

- Tulsa City–County Library System
400 Civic Center
Tulsa 74103
918-596-7944

OREGON

- Multnomah County Library
Government Documents Room
801 S.W. Tenth Avenue
Portland 97205-2597
503-223-7201

Oregon State Library
State Library Building
Salem 97310
503-378-4274

- Pacific Non-Profit Network
Grantsmanship Resource Library
33 N. Central, Ste. 211
Medford 97501
503-779-6044

PENNSYLVANIA

Northampton Community College
Learning Resources Center
3835 Green Pond Road
Bethlehem 18017
215-861-5360

- Erie County Public Library
3 South Perry Square
Erie 16501
814-451-6927

- Dauphin County Library System
101 Walnut Street
Harrisburg 17101
717-234-4961

Lancaster County Public Library
125 North Duke Street
Lancaster 17602
717-394-2651

- The Free Library of Philadelphia
Logan Square
Philadelphia 19103
215-686-5423

- University of Pittsburgh
Hillman Library
Pittsburgh 15260
412-648-7722

Economic Development Council
of Northeastern Pennsylvania
1151 Oak Street
Pittston 18640
717-655-5581

RHODE ISLAND

• Providence Public Library
  Reference Department
  150 Empire Street
  Providence 02903
  401-521-7722

SOUTH CAROLINA

• Charleston County Library
  404 King Street
  Charleston 29403
  803-723-1645

• South Carolina State Library
  Reference Department
  1500 Senate Street
  Columbia 29211
  803-734-8666

SOUTH DAKOTA

• South Dakota State Library
  800 Governors Drive
  Pierre 57501-2294
  605-773-3131
  800-592-1841 (SD residents)

  Sioux Falls Area Foundation
  321 S. Phillips Avenue, Rm. 404
  Sioux Falls 57102-0781
  605-336-7055

TENNESSEE

• Knoxville-Knox County Public
  Library
  500 West Church Avenue
  Knoxville 37902
  615-544-5750

• Memphis & Shelby County
  Public Library
  1850 Peabody Avenue
  Memphis 38104
  901-725-8876

• Public Library of Nashville and
  Davidson County
  8th Ave. N. and Union St.
  Nashville 37211
  615-259-6256

TEXAS

  Amarillo Area Foundation
  70 1st National Place I
  800 S. Fillmore
  Amarillo 79101
  806-376-4521

• Hogg Foundation for Mental Health
  University of Texas
  Austin 78713
  512-471-5041

  Community Foundation of Abilene
  Funding Information Library
  708 NCNB Bldg.
  402 Cypress
  Abilene 79601
  915-676-3883

• Corpus Christi State University
  Library
  6300 Ocean Drive
  Corpus Christi 78412
  512-994-2608

• El Paso Community Foundation
  201 E. Main
  El Paso 79901
  915-533-4020

• Texas Christian University Library
  Funding Information Center
  Ft. Worth 76129
  817-921-7664

• Houston Public Library
  Bibliographic Information Center
  500 McKinney Avenue
  Houston 77002
  713-236-1313

• Lubbock Area Foundation
  502 Commerce Bank Building
  Lubbock 79401
  806-762-8061

• Funding Information Library
  507 Brooklyn
  San Antonio 78215
  512-227-4333

• Dallas Public Library
  Grants Information Service
  1515 Young Street
  Dallas 75201
  214-670-1487

• Pan American University
  Learning Resource Center
  1201 W. University Drive
  Edinburg 78539
  512-381-3304

UTAH

• Salt Lake City Public Library
  Business and Science Dept.
  209 East Fifth South
  Salt Lake City 84111
  801-363-5733

VERMONT

• Vermont Dept. of Libraries
  Reference Services
  109 State Street
  Montpelier 05602
  802-828-3268

VIRGINIA

• Hampton Public Library
  Grants Resources Collection
  4207 Victoria Blvd.
  Hampton 23669
  804-727-1154

• Richmond Public Library
  Business, Science, & Technology
  101 East Franklin Street
  Richmond 23219
  804-780-8223

  Roanoke City Public Library
  System
  Central Library
  706 S. Jefferson Street
  Roanoke 24014
  703-981-2477

WASHINGTON

• Seattle Public Library
  1000 Fourth Avenue
  Seattle 98104
  206-386-4620

• Spokane Public Library
  Funding Information Center
  West 906 Main Avenue
  Spokane 99201-0976
  509-838-3364

WEST VIRGINIA

• Kanawha County Public Library
  123 Capital Street
  Charleston 25304
  304-343-4646

WISCONSIN

• Marquette University
  Memorial Library
  1415 West Wisconsin Avenue
  Milwaukee 53233
  414-288-1515

• University of Wisconsin-Madison
  Memorial Library
  728 State Street
  Madison 53706
  608-262-3242

WYOMING

• Laramie County Community
  College Library
  1400 East College Drive
  Cheyenne 82007-3299
  307-778-1205

AUSTRALIA

  ANZ Executors & Trustees Co.
  Ltd.
  91 William St., 7th floor
  Melbourne VIC 3000
  648-5768

CANADA

  Canadian Centre for Philanthropy
  74 Victoria Street, Suite 920
  Toronto, Ontario M5C 2A5
  416-368-1138

ENGLAND

  Charities Aid Foundation
  18 Doughty Street
  London WC1N 2PL
  01-831-7798

JAPAN

  Foundation Center Library
  of Japan
  Elements Shinjuku Bldg. 3F
  2-1-14 Shinjuku, Shinjuku-ku
  Tokyo 160
  03-350-1857

MEXICO

  Biblioteca Benjamin Franklin
  American Embassy, USICA
  Londres 16
  Mexico City 6, D.F. 06600
  905-211-0042

PUERTO RICO

  University of Puerto Rico
  Ponce Technological College
  Library
  Box 7186
  Ponce 00732
  809-844-4150

  Universidad Del Sagrado
  Corazon
  M.M.T. Guevarra Library
  Correo Calle Loiza
  Santurce 00914
  809-728-1515 ext. 357

U.S. VIRGIN ISLANDS

  University of the Virgin Islands
  Paiewonsky Library
  Charlotte Amalie
  St. Thomas 00802
  809-776-9200 ext. 1487

THE FOUNDATION CENTER AFFILIATES PROGRAM

As participants in the cooperating collection network, affiliates are libraries or nonprofit agencies that provide fundraising information or other funding-related technical assistance in their communities. Affiliates agree to provide free public access to a basic collection of Foundation Center publications during a regular schedule of hours, offering free funding research guidance to all visitors. Many also provide a variety of special services for local nonprofit organizations using staff or volunteers to prepare special materials, organize workshops, or conduct library orientations.

The Foundation Center welcomes inquiries from agencies interested in providing this type of public information service. If you are interested in establishing a funding information library for the use of nonprofit agencies in your area or in learning more about the program, we would like to hear from you. For more information, please write to: Anne J. Borland, The Foundation Center, 79 Fifth Avenue, New York, NY 10003.

References

American Association of Fund-Raising Counsel Trust for Philanthropy
  1988   *Giving U.S.A.* New York: AAFRC Trust for Philanthropy. Annual.

American Society of Association Executives
  1987   *1987 Association Executive Compensation Study.* Washington, DC.

American Society of Association Executives
  n.d.   *The Association Factbook.* Washington, DC

Association of Art Museum Directors
  1987   *1987 Salary Survey.* Montreal: Association of Art Museum Directors.

Bolles, Richard W.
  1987   *The 1987 What Color Is Your Parachute? A Practical Manual for Job Hunters and Career Changers.* Berkeley: Ten Speed Press.

Borjas, George J., H.E. Frech, III, and Paul Ginsberg
  1983   "Property Rights and Wages: The Case of Nursing Homes." *Journal of Human Resources,* 18, 2 (spring), pp. 231–246.

Callahan, Jacqueline A.
  1987   *Overview of Survey on Higher Education for Volunteer Managers.* Boulder, CO: Association for Volunteer Administration.

Center for Non-Profit Corporations
  1987   Salary Study of 196 Nonprofit Organizations. Trenton, NJ: Center for Non-Profit Corporations.

Cohen, Lilly
  1984   "The Case for Graduate Education in Fund Raising: Report on a Successful Pilot Program." In *Grants Magazine,* Vol. 7, no. 7, June. New York.

Commission on Private Philanthropy and Public Needs
  1977   *Giving in America.* Washington, DC: U.S. Department of the Treasury, 1975.

Corporation for Public Broadcasting
  1987   *Salary Report for Public Television Licensees.* Washington, DC: Corporation for Public Broadcasting.

Council on Foundations
  1982   *1982 Compensation and Benefits Survey.* Washington, DC: Council on Foundations.

Cutlip, Scott M.
  1965   *Fund Raising in the United States: Its Role in America's Philanthropy.* New Brunswick, NJ: Rutgers University.

Daniels, Arlene K.
  1988   "Career Scenarios in Foundation Work," In *Educating Managers for Nonprofit Organizations.* New York: Praeger.

de Tocqueville, Alexis
   1840   *Democracy in America.* Thomas Bender, ed. New York: Random House, 1981.

Foundation Center, The
   1989   *The Foundation Directory,* 12th edition. New York: The Foundation Center.

Fowler, Elizabeth M.
   1984   "A Business Theology Curriculum." *New York Times,* Nov. 21, p. 104.

Gray, Sandra T.
   1987   *An Independent Sector Resource Directory of Education and Training Opportunities and Other Services.* Washington, DC: Independent Sector.

Gurin, Maurice G.
   1987   "Courses in Philanthropy: A First in U.S. Colleges." *Fund Raising Management.* August.

Hall, Peter Dobkin
   1987   "A Historical Overview of the Private Nonprofit Sector." In Walter W. Powell, ed., *The Nonprofit Sector: A Research Handbook.* New Haven, CT: Yale University Press.

Hansmann, Henry.
   1987   "Economic Theories of Nonprofit Organization." In Walter W. Powell, ed., *The Nonprofit Sector: A Research Handbook.* New Haven, CT: Yale University Press.

Haronian, Rita, and Barbara Shilling
   1986   *1986 Wage and Benefit Survey of and for San Francisco Bay Area Tax-Exempt Nonprofit Organizations.* San Francisco, CA: The Management Center.

Hillman, Howard
   1980   *The Art of Winning Corporate Grants.* New York: The Vanguard Press.

Hodgkinson, Virginia A., and Murray S. Weitzman
   1988   *Dimensions of the Independent Sector: A Statistical Profile,* Interim Update, Fall. Washington, DC: Independent Sector.

Hodgkinson, Virginia A., and Murray S. Weitzman
   1986   *Dimensions of the Independent Sector: A Statistical Profile.* Washington, DC: Independent Sector.

Hoewing, Raymond L.
   1982   "Dynamics and Role of Public Affairs." In *Public Affairs Handbook.* New York: American Management Association.

Independent Sector
   1986   *The Charitable Behavior of Americans: Findings from a National Survey.* Conducted by Yankelovich, Skelly, and White, Inc., and commissioned by the Rockefeller Brothers Fund. Washington, DC.

Johnston, David
   1988   "Alternative Funds Band Together Under Shared Name." In *Nonprofit Times.* April.

Joseph, James A., Elizabeth T. Boris, and Carol A. Hooper
 1984 *Foundation Management Report.* Washington, DC: Council on Foundations

Lusterman, Seymour
 1987 *The Organization and Staffing of Corporate Public Affairs.* New York: The Conference Board.

Middleton, Melissa
 1986 *Nonprofit Management: A Report on Current Research and Areas for Development.* PONPO Working Paper No. 108 and ISPS Working Paper No. 2108. New Haven, CT: Yale University.

Ministers Financial Service Association
 1986 *1986 National Church Staff Salary Survey.* Compiled by Michael J. Springer and Martin Meyers. Co-written with National Association of Church Business Administrators, Texas.

Mirvis, Philip H., and Edward J. Hackett
 1983 "Work and Workforce Characteristics in the Nonprofit Sector." *Monthly Labor Review,* April.

Mongon, George J., Sr.
 1988 "Profile 1988 NSFRE Membership Career Survey." In *Contemporary Issues in Fund Raising,* Winter. Alexandria, VA: National Society of Fund Raising Executives.

National Association of Independent Schools
 1986 *National Association of Independent Schools Member School Tuition, Fees, Teacher Salaries, Administrator and Staff Salaries, 1986-87.* Boston, MA: National Association of Independent Schools.

National Association of Temple Administrators
 1986 *Survey of Salary and Other Remuneration, Employment and Working Conditions of Temple Administrators, 1986-1987.* Prepared by Doris P. Markoff. New York: National Association of Temple Administrators.

National Center for Charitable Statistics
 1987 "National Taxonomy of Exempt Organizations." Washington, DC: National Center for Charitable Statistics, a program of the Independent Sector.

National Council, Inc.
 1987 *1987 Compensation Report: Voluntary Health and Human Service Organizations.* Co-written with National Assembly of Voluntary Health and Social Welfare Organizations. Washington, DC.

National Society of Fundraising Executives
 1985 *National Society of Fundraising Executives Profile.* Compiled by George J. Morgon. Alexandria, VA: National Society of Fundraising Executives.

Nielsen, Waldemar A.
 1983 "The Third Sector: Keystone of a Caring Society." In Brian O'Connell, ed., *America's Voluntary Spirit.* New York: The Foundation Center.

Nonprofit Times
     Princeton, NJ: Davis Information Group. Monthly.

O'Connell, Brian
     1987   "Corporate Philanthropy: Getting Bigger, Broader, and Tougher to Manage." In
            Corporate Philanthropy: An Information Service. Washington, DC: Independent Sector.

O'Neill, Michael, and Dennis R. Young, eds.
     1988   *Educating Managers of Nonprofit Organizations.* New York: Praeger.

Odendahl, Teresa J., Elizabeth T. Boris, and Arlene K. Daniels
     1985   *Working in Foundations: Career Patterns of Women and Men.* New York: The Foundation
            Center.

Olson, Paul M.
     1988   "Straight Talk ABout Our Future." In *Foundation News,* September/October. Wash-
            ington, DC: Council on Foundations.

Plinio, Alex J., and Joanne B. Scanlon
     1984   *Resource Raising: The Role of Non-Cash Assistance in Corporate Philanthropy.* Washington,
            DC: Independent Sector.

Powell, Walter W., ed.
     1987   *The Nonprofit Sector: A Research Handbook.* New Haven, CT: Yale University Press.

Preston, Anne
     1989a "The Non-Profit Worker in a For-Profit World." *Journal of Labor Economics,*
            forthcoming.

Preston, Anne
     1989b "Women in the White Collar Nonprofit Sector: The Best Option or the Only Op-
            tion." SUNY at Stony Brook: Harriman School working paper.

Preston, Anne
     1988a "Wage Differentials between Nonprofit and Public Sector Employees." Unpublished
            manuscript.

Preston, Anne
     1988b "The Effects of Property Rights on Labor Costs of Non-Profit Firms: An Application
            to the Day Care Industry." In *Journal of Industrial Economics,* forthcoming.

Preston, Anne
     1987   "Compensation Patterns in the Nonprofit Sector: A Case Study of Long Island."
            SUNY at Stony Brook: Harriman School working paper.

Public Affairs Research Group
     1984   "Public Affairs Offices and their Functions: Highlights of a National Survey." In
            Public Affairs Review/Public Affairs Survey. Washington, DC: The Public Affairs Council.

Rudney, Gabriel
     1987   "The Scope and Dimensions of Nonprofit Activity." In Walter W. Powell, ed., *The
            Nonprofit Sector: A Research Handbook.* New Haven, CT: Yale University Press.

Rudney, Gabriel, and M. Weitzman
    1983   "Significance of Employment and Earnings in the Philanthropic Sector, 1972-73." PONPO Working Paper No. 77. Institution for Social and Policy Studies. New Haven, CT: Yale University.

Salamon, Lester
    1983   *The Nonprofit Sector and the Rise of Third Party Government.* Washington, DC: Urban Institute Press.

Schubert, Richard F.
    1985   Talk presented to National Health Care Council. In minutes of October, 1985. Committee of Voluntary Health Agencies, National Health Council.

Simon, John
    1987   "The Tax Treatment of Nonprofit Organizations: A Review of Federal and State Policies." In Walter W. Powell, ed., *The Nonprofit Sector: A Research Handbook.* New Haven, CT: Yale University Press.

Technical Assistance Center
    1987   *1987 Colorado Wage and Benefits Survey.* Denver, CO: Technical Assistance Center.

Truschke, Edward F.
    1985   "Marketing Corporate Social Policy Programs." In *Foundation News,* March/April. Washington, DC: Council on Foundations.

United Way of America
    1985   *Rethinking Tomorrow and Beyond: Some Thoughts on the Continuing Evolution of United Way as a Responsive and Inclusive Community Caring System.* Alexandria, VA: United Way of America.

U.S. Department of Labor, Bureau of Labor Statistics
    1986–87   *Occupational Outlook Handbook.* Washington, DC: U.S. Department of Labor, Bureau of Labor Statistics. April 1986, pp. 208–210.

Weisbrod, Burton A.
    1988   *The Nonprofit Economy.* Cambridge, MA: Harvard University Press.

Weisbrod, Burton, A.
    1983   "Non-Profit and Proprietary Sector Behavior: Wage Differentials among Lawyers." *Journal of Labor Economics,* 1, 3 (July), pp. 246–263.

Ylvisaker, Paul N.
    1987   "Foundations and Nonprofit Organizations." In Walter W. Powell, ed., *The Nonprofit Sector: A Research Handbook.* New Haven, CT: Yale University Press.

Young, Dennis, et al.
    1987   *The Nonprofit Sector and NASPAA's Redefinition of Public Service.* Report of the National Association of Schools of Public Affairs and Administration Ad Hoc Committee for Nonprofit Management. October.

INDEX